Practical Guide to Auditing SAP® Systems

Sebastian Mayer
Martin Metz

Thank you for purchasing this book from Espresso Tutorials!

Like a cup of espresso coffee, Espresso Tutorials SAP books are concise and effective. We know that your time is valuable and we deliver information in a succinct and straightforward manner. It only takes our readers a short amount of time to consume SAP concepts. Our books are well recognized in the industry for leveraging tutorial-style instruction and videos to show you step by step how to successfully work with SAP.

Check out our YouTube channel to watch our videos at https://www.youtube.com/user/EspressoTutorials.

If you are interested in SAP Finance and Controlling, join us at http://www.fico-forum.com/forum2/ to get your SAP questions answered and contribute to discussions.

Related titles from Espresso Tutorials:

► Tracy Juran:
  Beginner's Guide to SAP® Security and Authorizations
  http://5013.espresso-tutorials.com

► Maxim Chuprunov:
  Leveraging SAP® GRC in the Fight Against Corruption and Fraud
  http://5216.espresso-tutorials.com

► Bert Vanstechelman, Chris Walravens, Christophe Decamps:
  Securing SAP® S/4HANA
  http://5258.espresso-tutorials.com

Sebastian Mayer, Martin Metz
Practical Guide to Auditing SAP® Systems

ISBN: 978-3-96012-640-9

Editor: Tracey Duffy

Cover Design: Philip Esch

Cover Photo: istockphoto # 15939021 (c) Yuri

Interior Book Design: Johann-Christian Hanke

All rights reserved.

1st Edition 2019, Gleichen

© 2019 by Espresso Tutorials GmbH

URL: *www.espresso-tutorials.com*

Feedback
We greatly appreciate any feedback you may have concerning this book. Please send your feedback via email to: *info@espresso-tutorials.com*.

Table of Contents

Preface

To call a spade a spade, SAP is unique. Even with a lot of experience in auditing non-SAP IT systems, you might still find it tough to ask the right questions, to meet SAP administrators on equal terms, or to find your way through the opaque correlations of hundreds of SAP tables, the configuration settings, the authorization concept, or application controls in SAP systems.

Have you been lucky enough to have been tasked with auditing a tricky SAP system? Are you preparing the audit plan for the next fiscal year and thinking that an SAP system should be one of the targets? Are you aware of the growing SAP system landscape in your company and the mission-critical importance of SAP? Are you wondering how to control these systems efficiently? If you are a security officer, an auditor, a compliance officer, an SAP administrator, a consultant, or a developer and have asked yourself one of the questions above, this book is for you. The book addresses those who are responsible for SAP security and controls and who are eager to learn how to cope with the security challenges an SAP system poses, how to detect misconfiguration quickly, and how to evaluate the security status of an SAP system.

This book focuses on the tasks of an auditor and the techniques needed to determine the high-level security status of an SAP system quickly. Aside from the fact that this book examines SAP from the audit perspective, SAP administrators and security consultants among the readers are encouraged to reverse the control content and ask themselves: "What do I need to do to successfully complete such an audit? Which settings and processual changes are necessary to meet these requirements?" By doing this, you can use the standard control procedure presented in this book as a guideline to improve the security posture of your SAP system.

Chapter 1 explains the basic principles of a company's audit function, including the role of the audit function within the three lines of defense model, as well as recent studies covering the tasks and the current priorities of the internal audit function. This chapter also provides further valuable information such as regulatory requirements behind audits, leading practices, and a primary methodology for conducting information system (IS) audits in general.

Chapter 2 looks at SAP and specific audit issues relating to SAP systems more closely, including the business relevance and market share of SAP within and beyond the ERP market. The chapter also discusses the components and general technical architecture of an SAP system, thereby deriving a general approach to an SAP-focused IS audit.

SAP provides some valuable system-internal tools and functionalities that we introduce in Chapter 3. Auditors can use these tools as they offer extensive query capabilities and pre-defined reports, along with a variety of controls. You will learn how to apply these tools as they are a primary means in the daily business of an SAP auditor. Understanding them is vital for an efficient audit and will save you a lot of time.

Chapter 4 is the centerpiece of this book. It guides you through the top 12 controls that should be included in your audit activities. These controls cover areas such as accounts and authorizations, the changeability settings, clients, and entire systems, change logs, and security configuration settings. For each control, we introduce the background to the control as well as the risks associated with the control. You will also learn how to assess the efficiency of the controls. Understanding the risks that the controls are intended to counteract is key to a discussion on equal terms with auditees. You will want to be able to answer their questions, such as: "Why should I change the password of this technical user? What could someone do with this account?" Explanations about how various vulnerabilities can be exploited will help you to respond to such questions. This chapter will be useful as a manual during your audit.

Chapter 5 rounds the book up and provides an overview of upcoming challenges posed by SAP systems and the implications for future audit priorities. The driving topics here are HANA, mobile, and cloud.

This book provides an overview of the reasons why internal audit exists, special aspects relating to SAP systems, and detailed controls and practical instructions to help you through your next audit, regardless of whether you are the auditing or the audited party.

We have added a few icons to highlight important information. These include:

Tips
Tips highlight information that provides more details about the subject being described and/or additional background information.

Examples
Examples help illustrate a topic better by relating it to real world scenarios.

Attention
Attention notices highlight information that you should be aware of when you go through the examples in this book on your own.

Finally, a note concerning the copyright: All screenshots printed in this book are the copyright of SAP SE. All rights are reserved by SAP SE. Copyright pertains to all SAP images in this publication. For simplification, we will not mention this specifically underneath every screenshot.

1 The principles of auditing IT systems

This chapter provides a general introduction to the internal audit function. Topics include the reason for the internal audit function as well as the underlying regulatory requirements and standards of this internal audit function. The chapter also presents a general procedure for an information systems (IS) audit and the most common steps of every IS audit.

1.1 Legal basis for internal audit

Why does a company need an *internal audit function*? Well, do you ask the owner of a restaurant how good his dishes are? Or do you put more trust in Google reviews or comments by disappointed or impressed visitors on TripAdvisor? Independence is the key word. From the perspective of experienced auditors, after years of auditing information systems and hundreds of serious findings, internal audit must be considered a centerpiece of a company's governance structure, providing the board of directors, audit committee, and executives with an independent view of the risk management and control environment within the company. But do lawmakers share this opinion?

At the beginning of the 2000s, Enron was a much-hyped company, comparable perhaps to today's Internet giants. Furthermore, investing in Enron was highly recommended. However, the accounting practices at Enron were illegal, and revenues and profits were made up on a large scale. One of the biggest bankruptcies according to the US Chapter 11 bankruptcy code was that of Enron in 2001. The revelations about the accounting practices also led to the dissolution of Enron's accounting firm. This event triggered a new law, which has widely influenced internal audit: the *Sarbanes-Oxley Act (SOX)*. Every publicly traded company in the US must comply with this law. Section 404 of SOX is very important, as it states that companies are obliged to include an internal control report within their annual report. This control report should explicitly state the responsibility of the management to establish an *internal control system (ICS)* for financial reporting and to assess the effectiveness of this ICS every year. Furthermore, the management's assessment of the effectiveness of its internal control system must be certified. This is where audit companies and audit departments come into play. Within the context of section 404 of SOX and the certification requirement, the role of internal audit is to:

- ▶ Act as a consultant and assist in the setting up of an ICS
- ▶ Test internal controls within the ICS
- ▶ Review the results of a SOX audit that has been performed by another unit
- ▶ Advise the team that is performing a SOX audit
- ▶ Audit the ICS together with an external auditor

SOX has been widely adopted by countries around the world, culminating in a China SOX, Japanese J-SOX, Canadian C-SOX, or the German Corporate Governance Code. The Principles of Corporate Governance of The Organisation for Economic Co-operation and Development (OECD) also recommend establishing procedures to ensure the effectiveness of the ICS ("G20/OECD Principles of Corporate Governance", p. 52).

However, the internal audit function is also explicitly required by other laws. One example is the Israeli Companies law 5759 from 1999, which states in Part IV, Chapter four, Paragraph 146–153, amongst other things, that:

- ▶ The board of directors must appoint an internal auditor whose superior must be the chairman of the board of directors or the general manager
- ▶ The internal auditor must submit their findings to the chairman of the board of directors
- ▶ The annual work program of the internal auditor must be approved either by the audit committee (which is required by the same law) or the board of directors

Another example is the German Banking Act (Kreditwesengesetz, KWG), which requires financial institutions to install internal control mechanisms, including an internal control system and an internal audit function. Publicly traded companies are required by the German Stock Corporation Act (Aktiengesetz, AktG) §91 to implement a company-wide monitoring system to identify risks that could jeopardize the business.

Stock exchanges also have specific rules. The Asian Confederation of Institutes of Internal Auditors surveyed Asian stock exchanges in 2015 and found mandatory requirements for internal audit functions in companies listed on the stock exchange in China, India, and Indonesia, and other Asian nations (*https://iaonline.theiia.org/blogs/chambers/2015/no-internal-audit-function-investors-beware*).

However, many countries today do not have explicit requirements for an internal audit function. More often, internal audit is indirectly part of the laws and rules on internal control systems (ICS). But what exactly is the ICS and why do people assume that internal audit is part of it?

The most common standard for internal control systems is the *Committee of Sponsoring Organizations of the Treadway Commission (COSO)* and its famous *cube*, which portrays the elements of an ICS (see Figure 1.1).

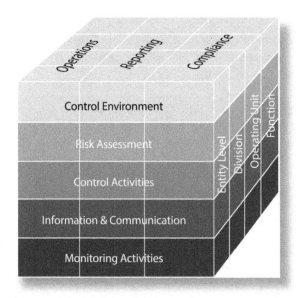

Figure 1.1: COSO cube (https://www.coso.org/Documents/COSO-ICIF-11x17-Cube-Graphic.pdf)

The top of this cube represents the objectives of an organization in the fields of operations, reporting, and compliance. The columns at the side represent the areas of application for these objectives. From single functions to entire entities, all areas can use these fields to set objectives.

The face of the cube is comprised of five elements of internal control.

The first of these elements is the control environment. It is the framework in which the internal controls of a company are embedded. Through policies, standards, guidelines, standard operating procedures (SoPs), and control descriptions, the framework provides the basis for conducting control activities. The control environment provides structure through organizational charts, reporting lines, and processes. It also entails the company culture, which is as essential for the will to comply with and conduct controls as the ethical setup of the company.

The risk assessment element represents the risk management processes through which a company identifies risks that could hamper its objectives and defines ways to mitigate them. These risks include potential events with a negative impact on the ICS.

Control activities include all actions that help to continuously mitigate risks and to support the achievement of business objectives. The information and communication element represents the aspect of ensuring that all parties involved know their role within the ICS.

With regard to the scope of this book, the monitoring activities are vital. They include the means necessary for assessing how the components of the ICS are working. The COSO framework states two principles for this ICS component:

1. The organization selects, develops, and performs ongoing and/or separate evaluations to ascertain whether the components of internal control are present and functioning.

2. The organization evaluates and communicates internal control deficiencies promptly to those parties responsible for taking corrective action, including senior management and the board of directors, as appropriate.

Companies have a variety of means at hand to perform these monitoring activities. These means range from automated technical control procedures, through self-assessments, to audits performed either by internal or external auditors. Among the means stated in the COSO guidance on monitoring, the periodic evaluation and testing of controls by internal audits is the first procedure mentioned. ("COSO_Guidance_On_Monitor-ing_Intro_online1_002", p. 7).

Thus, internal audit is indeed a paramount component of an ICS. As laws, rules, etc. require the implementation of an ICS, they indirectly urge the incorporation of an internal audit function.

1.2 Importance and background of the audit function

"Dear colleagues, today I received confirmation that we are going to be audited starting next week. Please make sure you put the current date on our documents!" To begin in the middle with the importance of audits: an audit is far more than the above sentence suggests.

The importance of the audit function can, for instance, be captured by concentrating on its role within the *three lines of defense model*, where it is essential and plays an extraordinary role.

The three lines of defense model describes the roles and tasks related to risk management across the company's departments and external functions. The first line of defense is made up of business functions and owners, with an employee who is responsible for identifying and managing risks related to the activities performed. The second line of defense is responsible for risk management, setting rules, and issuing policies and standards. The third line of defense conducts the assurance work by evaluating the effectiveness and efficiency of the risk management, the control processes, and the governance. The assurance work falls under the role of internal auditors, which is where this book comes into play.

The three lines of defense—SAP Basis

 The SAP Basis team is always eager to install new security patches as they plug security holes to recover the security posture of a company. Thereby, the Basis team is the first line of defense. It not only tries to preserve the integrity of its systems—it also follows the policy of *vulnerability management*, which requires close monitoring of security updates and quick installation of related patches.

The risk and compliance departments, which created this policy and defined a binding standard, are the second line of defense. Once the Basis team has established its risk report and described how to manage vulnerabilities in the SAP system, the risk department evaluates and assesses this report. The audit department comes into play as the third line of defense. It is responsible for objectively assessing the effectiveness and efficiency of the risk management processes and controls. When the audit department chooses the vulnerability management process for an audit, it reviews the relevance of related policies and how the business complies with them. The testing of controls concerned with vulnerability management is part of this audit. Furthermore, the auditors advise the business on how to optimize the entire process and they track the completion of the measures agreed. In this case, the three-layered security structure mitigates the risk of adversaries exploiting vulnerabilities and jeopardizing the business achieving its objectives.

Figure 1.2 depicts the three lines of defense, their typical representatives, and their reporting lines.

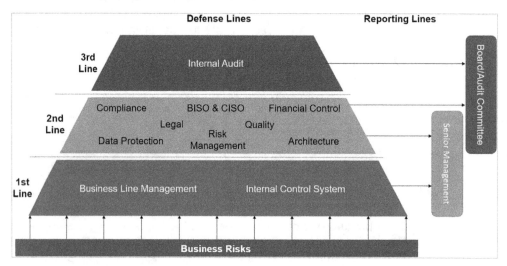

Figure 1.2: Adapted model of the three lines of defense (Institute of Internal Auditors, IIA)

As shown in the example, the work of internal audit extends from monitoring risk management processes and compliance through control testing to internal consultancy and process optimization. Another objective of internal audit is to detect and thus prevent fraudulent activities.

KPMG's Global Audit Committee Pulse survey confirms the actuality of these tasks and lists the most significant challenges and areas of concern to audit departments across the globe in 2017: in first place is the effectiveness of the risk management program, followed by legal/regulatory compliance and cybersecurity risks (*https://bit.ly/2PLoX47*, slide 15).

The latter is one of the top priorities for internal audit in 2017, alongside technology risks due to the increasing use of mobile and cloud technologies (*https://bit.ly/2PLoX47*, slide 18), which are also relevant to the use of SAP systems.

Contractual obligations might also be a reason for internal audits. In the case of a second-party audit, there is a contractual work relationship between an auditee (usually a vendor) and an auditor (the client). The client performs audits to evaluate the situation at the vendor, to identify risks, and to derive potential contractual adjustments.

Clients might even request audits without a contractual obligation by the vendor. A prominent example is the case of the shareholders of Volkswagen, who asked a special auditor to assess the details of the recent emissions scandal.

This situation is comparable to incident-based audits. A company might suffer from an incident and wants to conduct an internal audit to identify any evidence for the rationale of the incident, what led to the issues, and how to prevent it in the future. As the incident might be to the result of criminal acts, it is necessary to establish a chain of custody and make sure that the evidence collected can be submitted before the court.

Furthermore, you might want to audit an aspect of interest for none of the reasons above simply to improve organization, processes, or current projects.

Regardless of whether you are considering internal control systems, the three lines of defense model, or further reasons for an audit function, overall, organizations need an independent, objective party to ensure risk management, control processes, and governance. While external auditors focus on financial reporting, the internal audit department takes a broader look paired with internal knowledge. Internal audit is therefore vital to ensure that an organization works. IS audits are one of the most necessary means of performing assurance work. As today's business processes depend heavily on the use of information systems, IS audits look at these applications and systems, their technology, settings, underlying infrastructure, network, and other aspects. Thus, IS audits are one component of internal audits with a focus on the information systems layer (see Figure 1.3).

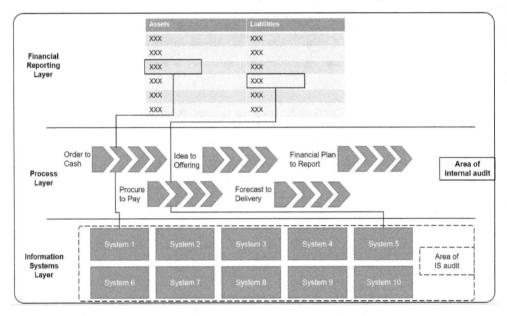

Figure 1.3: The layers of an IS audit

To use an analogy, internal audits assess the processes and controls on a ship's bridge, whereas IS audits take a more in-depth look at the ship's engine room. Just as the processes on the deck require standards, so do the processes in the engine room.

1.3 Standards for auditing information systems

Internal audit organizations or other professional associations have created a variety of standards for IS audits. These standards have become a discipline for both external and internal auditors around the world. The section below highlights the standards of the *Institute of Internal Auditors (IIA)* and the *Information Systems Audit and Control Association (ISACA)*.

Both ISACA and IIA provide and propagate codes of ethics for the practice of internal audit. As hundreds of thousands of auditors around the world are members of these associations and are well informed about their ethical requirements, these organizations play an essential role in the entire practice and credibility of auditing. The IIA's code of ethics contains the following principles:

▶ Integrity

▶ Objectivity

▶ Confidentiality

▶ Competency

Competency is, of course, crucial to the success of an audit and as IS audits are something special, associations like ISACA have developed certification programs for training, assessing, and proving the qualification of IS auditors in particular. ISACA's *Certified Information Systems Auditor (CISA)* certificate is very often a requirement for becoming an IS auditor.

The IIA has developed the *International Professional Practices Framework (IPPF)*, and further technology-specific guides that help IS auditors.

ISACA has published the *Information Technology Assurance Framework (ITAF)* for IS audits. This framework comprises standards and guidelines for IS audit and assurance. These standards and guidelines give detailed and precise instructions on the following aspects of audits:

▶ Audit charter

▶ Organizational independence

▶ Professional independence

- ▶ Reasonable expectation
- ▶ Due professional care
- ▶ Proficiency
- ▶ Assertions
- ▶ Criteria
- ▶ Engagement planning
- ▶ Risk assessment in planning
- ▶ Performance and supervision
- ▶ Materiality
- ▶ Evidence
- ▶ Using the work of other experts
- ▶ Irregularity and illegal acts
- ▶ Reporting
- ▶ Follow-up activities

Auditors complying with these standards should always scrutinize the source, nature, and authenticity of all information gathered during audits. ISACA's standard 1205, for example, covers the collection and handling of evidence. The associated guidelines support the clarification of these standards.

Hundreds of further standards and guidelines exist around internal audit and IS audit in general. Furthermore, security standards are a good source for concrete audit plans. Some of these even list specific requirements for SAP systems, such as those of the *German Federal Office for Information Security (BSI)*.

As explained above, there is a myriad of laws, standards, and reasons for conducting IS audits. We will now take you through the process of performing such an audit.

1.4   General approach for auditing information systems

All IS audits start with an initiation process and end in follow-up activities to make sure that the audit was not performed in vain. This means that IS audits share common process steps, which are portrayed in Figure 1.4.

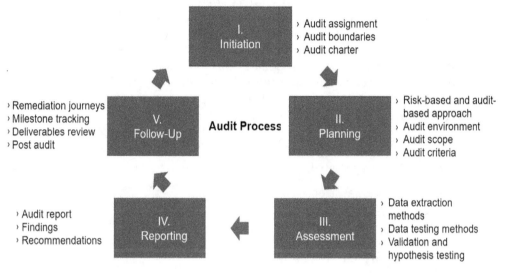

Figure 1.4: Audit process

1.4.1   Audit initiation

The centerpiece of the initiation process is the audit assignment. A company requests an auditor and agrees the type of audit as well as its rough boundaries. Other aspects relevant to the audit assignment include: financial matters (e.g., fees payable), non-disclosure agreements, a legal disclaimer of liability, responsibilities, a timeline, and obligations of the auditee, etc. For an internal audit, an audit charter usually defines most of the above aspects that are valid for all internal audits.

Once the project has been initiated, the planning process commences.

1.4.2 Audit planning

There are two major audit approaches: the *risk-based* approach and the *control-based* approach.

Risk-based approaches look at the risk capacity, risk appetite, risk register, risk assessments, and risk treatments of a company. Thus, this type of audit is based on the risk management processes of a company. An auditor identifies the most significant risks, evaluates the measures taken, and compares them to the risk appetite. The audit thus thrives on assuring the board of directors that the risk management processes are working correctly and that risks are being managed according to the company's risk appetite. In risk-based audits, auditors want to assess how:

▶ Risks are identified, evaluated, and managed

▶ Risk management is performed according to the risk appetite

▶ Risks are classified

▶ Risks and responses are reported

▶ The effectiveness and efficiency of the risk management framework are monitored

The auditors must ensure that:

▶ The risk management processes are effective

▶ The management of the essential risks and controls is effective

▶ The risk classification and reporting are appropriate

Another main audit approach is the control-based approach. This focuses on the company's internal control system (ICS), current control deficiencies, and non-compliance with policies and procedures. Using this approach, auditors want to assess:

▶ How controls are designed

▶ Whether controls are effective and efficient

This way, the auditors can ensure that:

▶ Controls have been adequately designed to prevent, detect, or correct financial misstatements and other events that impact the availability, confidentiality, and integrity of data

▶ The controls implemented are operated effectively, efficiently, and consistently

Both approaches require a deep understanding of either the risk management framework of a company or the internal control system. In the planning process for an audit, both approaches require the definition of the *audit environment* and *audit criteria*.

The audit environment comprises all items that are relevant for achieving the objectives of the audit assignment. It includes crucial places, personnel, information systems, data, and documents. Typically, budgets suffer from restraints. For this reason, an auditor defines the boundaries of an audit within a broader environment. Focusing on, for example, specific systems, reports, documents, etc., makes an audit more efficient. If the audit team tries to consider too many aspects, results will tend to be superficial. While the audit scope defines where, when, and with whom the audit takes place, the audit criteria set the basis for the specific audit plan and define the requirements and controls that fall within the scope of the audit. These include, among other things:

▶ Regulatory requirements

▶ Standards such as NIST, ISO, COSO, etc.

▶ Policies, guidelines, standard operating procedures, process definitions

▶ Customer requirements

Environment of a PAM audit

 A company started an IS audit assignment to assess its *privileged account management (PAM)* environment. PAM systems manage the most privileged accounts of a company, lock in passwords, and monitor all activities performed on these accounts. The overall environment includes the

PAM solution with a password safe, a jump host for monitoring administrative sessions, and an analytics engine for analyzing administrative sessions. Furthermore, it covers lots of interfaces—for example, to an identity management system or IT service management, target systems such as infrastructure components and applications, a reporting engine, as well as archives and backups. Because of the risk focus, an auditor may want to reduce this vast scope and instead, focus on the password safe, as this is the centerpiece of a PAM solution. An adequate monitoring of sessions would probably be of interest as well. Of all the target systems connected/monitored, the focus should be on the databases and servers within the infrastructure cluster. This is because unauthorized access to the databases and servers has more impact than access to a single application. Without a backup procedure, this critical PAM solution could fail without having any chance to recover. A proper and operationally efficient process design and governance are required to make the solution sustainable.

Therefore, the audit environment contains the safe, jump hosts, selected target systems, the backup, as well as processes and governance (see Figure 1.5).

Based on the audit criteria, the auditor assembles the audit plan, which includes all detailed audit activities. Regardless of the form, all audit plans usually include:

- ▶ The field of work/process cluster
- ▶ The underlying risk
- ▶ The associated control targets
- ▶ The precise audit activities
- ▶ The related controls of leading practices like COSO, ISO, etc.

More often than not, to prepare for an audit, audit databases with predefined sets of controls and control activities are used and simply adjusted to the customer specifics. Another popular format is the Excel-based risk control matrix, which contains the information in the bulleted list above. The information collected is put into the matrices or databases and provides an overview of the status of each risk or control respectively.

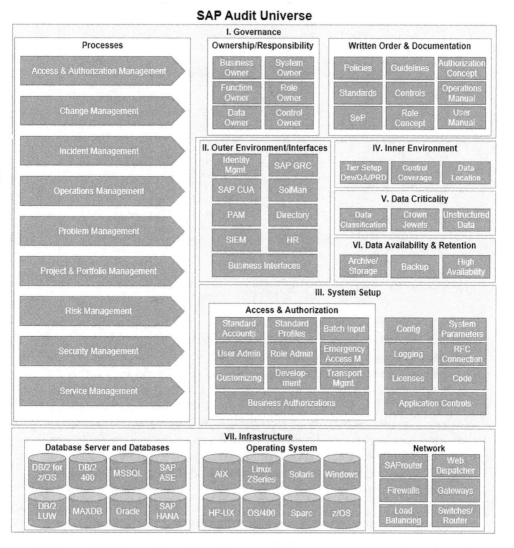

Figure 1.5: Example audit environment for PAM

*The following example (*Figure 1.6) depicts the usual minimum setup of such a risk control matrix.

Cluster	Control ID	Risk	Control Description	Test Procedure	Observations	Results
Business Operations	BOP-01	Data availability: After a system failure, critical business data cannot be restored.	According to the backup policy BOP_ESPRESSO_01, critical data is to be backed up and retained. A monitoring process is established to identify potential errors and resolve them in a timely manner according to criticality	- Take sample dates and test the successful completion of the backups. Check whether they are complete and available. - Check whether identified errors were remediated in follow-up actions. - Check whether backup and restore tests are conducted in a regular manner.	Internal audit took ten sample dates of the last three months and found that two out of ten samples showed errors that were not remediated (see reference #01). Furthermore, internal audit found that on two additional sample dates, no backups were created at all (see reference #02). Internal audit found that no backup and restore tests were performed in 2018 (see reference #03).	Exceptions noted

Figure 1.6: Example risk control matrix

Once the precise audit plan has been set up, the data and information required is defined and requested. The necessary information and data include not only documents and reports, but also system access and authorizations needed to perform specific activities in the systems within the audit environment. Regulations regarding the handling of data (especially personal data) are also considered as part of this planning process (e.g., General Data Protection Regulation (GDPR) requirements). The result of this step is usually a request document that lists all the requirements identified above. The auditor hands this list over to the auditees or assigned dispatcher to obtain access to the systems and the required information as soon as possible.

In the last step, the interviewees are identified and appointments with them agreed upon. Now the audit can begin.

1.4.3   Assessment phase

The detailed audit steps require an understanding of methods for obtaining the necessary data/information and for analyzing it. Not all testing methods are feasible in every environment; therefore, an auditor must carefully select from the following:

▶ Document review (i.e., manuals, meeting minutes, system logs, configuration tables)

▶ Interviews

▶ Observations (including walkthroughs or the reperformance of controls)

Once the information has been collected and prioritized, methods are applied to test and analyze the information. Such methods might be:

▶ Sampling

▶ Computer-assisted audit techniques (CAAT)

Assessment of a PAM audit

 For the PAM audit, diverse activities were defined to test the operational effectiveness of controls concerning the risks of inappropriate access management, credential management, and other risks. One risk is that the solution is not comprehensive enough and does not cover all privileged accounts in Oracle databases. This could mean critical accounts not being managed, the password being subject to a cyberattack, and systems being exposed to privilege escalation. Controls are in place to address this risk, such as:

▶ Standard operating procedures that require all Oracle admins to onboard privileged accounts in the PAM solution

▶ An automated scan of accounts and systems in scope

▶ Automated onboarding procedures

▶ Reconciliation runs to compare managed accounts with all existing accounts

To test the effectiveness of these controls, an auditor can request reports from both the PAM system and the Oracle databases and compare all privileged accounts covered by PAM with those available in the databases. Specific tests may confirm the correctness of these accounts. The SQL statements for creating the report are validated as well as the listed accounts themselves. If there are unmanaged accounts (not connected to PAM), this would be a gap in the solution and would mean that the controls are not effective. The root cause might be:

Organizational: e.g., the operations unit centrally responsible may not manage all Oracle databases; the policy may not cover diverse administrators.

Processual: e.g., new administrative accounts within databases are not detected or automatically onboarded into PAM.

Technical: e.g., not all accounts can be managed through PAM or not all Oracle databases can be onboarded into PAM; the scan does not detect all systems or accounts.

By analyzing documents like the PAM policy, analyzing reports, and taking samples, as well as interviewing some of the administrators, an auditor obtains the information needed to evaluate control effectiveness and efficiency.

Before data can be used, its validity must be confirmed. Completeness and correctness are central elements of this confirmation.

By testing hypotheses, the auditor proposes a hypothesis and assumes a particular situation. By collecting evidence and using mathematical rules of probability, an auditor can then either confirm or discard a hypothesis.

The results of the data collection, prioritization, validation, and testing through different methods are called *findings*. Findings are the deviations from standards and ineffectiveness in controls that an auditor has identified by applying appropriate techniques and has supported with evidence.

An auditor must support every finding with evidence and make sure that the information underlying the finding is as valid as the methods used to test and analyze it.

1.4.4   Audit reporting

Before the audit findings are summarized in a final report and submitted to the audit committee, all findings are agreed upon in QA processes within the audit department/team and in final discussions with the auditees. This allows the auditor to perform a dual control of the findings, thereby ensuring that the findings are correct and valid. Auditees usually have a different understanding of the auditor's conclusions. It is crucial to discuss the conclusions before the final presentation of the results and submission of the report.

The most important factor for the auditee is the criticality of the findings, as this is crucial for prioritizing measures that need to be taken to counteract them. To a certain extent, an auditor takes on the role of a consultant by recommending and discussing actions for all of the findings. Both the findings and the measures must be agreed upon with the auditors.

The final deliverable is the audit report, which includes the following:

- ▶ An introduction to the audit objectives, background, team, timeline, audit environment, and methods applied
- ▶ A summary of the results and an assessment by the auditor of the overall situation and outcome
- ▶ The detailed findings, including their impact and the rationale behind them
- ▶ Recommendations mapped to the findings

Usually, the auditee also receives further details backing up the findings and analysis work of the audit team.

With the final audit report, the auditee must decide whether to implement all, selected, or none of the measures recommended. If there is no mandatory requirement behind a recommendation or finding, the management might well reject the recommendation to reroute budgets in other directions and into other undertakings.

1.4.5 Follow-up

The measures recommended lead to undertakings that are realized via projects or activities within the line organizations. However, there must be concrete plans for resolving the issues and fulfilling the measures. Even more important from the auditor's perspective is the overarching process of monitoring to ensure that the auditees do indeed perform the actions required.

The auditee and auditor agree on milestones. Along with specific deliverables, these milestones are used for monitoring and follow-up activities. An auditor might regularly assess the milestone fulfillment or the quality of the deliverables. Furthermore, the auditor could conduct an entire post audit when the auditee has completed the measures.

In this chapter, we have looked at the process steps for IS audits in general. Starting with Chapter 2, we will discuss SAP systems in more detail, applying what you have learned so far specifically in the world of SAP.

2 The basic principles of auditing SAP systems

In this chapter, the focus moves from audit basics to the specifics of the SAP world. We also discuss the business relevance of SAP systems and introduce the general architecture of SAP systems to prepare for the SAP audit universe and its components. Furthermore, we also discuss two particular audit scenarios in an SAP environment. By the end of this chapter, you will know how to scope and prepare an SAP-specific audit.

2.1 Business relevance of SAP systems

Tens of millions of people around the world use SAP systems. Why? One apparent reason is that a lot of companies find it challenging to manage their business using hundreds or thousands of different systems. Once you separate the material and value flow of the factories in different systems, for example, it might be difficult to bring them back together and align them with each other. The higher the number of relevant systems with subsets of the required data that exist within a company, the more cumbersome a month-end or year-end process becomes.

Having separate sales, production, or accounting processes can quickly lead to inconsistencies and difficulties—a factor that motivates companies to invest in highly integrated systems instead.

This is where SAP comes into play: it offers an integrated business solution that ties together disparate procurement, sales, production, consolidation, and many other processes. Its market-leading *Enterprise Resource Planning (ERP)* systems are only one aspect. Other solutions offered by SAP include (*https://www.sap.com/products.html*; 01/01/2018):

▶ ERP (for large, medium, and small enterprises)

▶ Cloud and data platforms (e.g., SAP HANA platform, big data)

▶ Procurement and networks (e.g., Supplier Management, Strategic Sourcing)

▶ Analytics (e.g., Business Intelligence, Predictive Analytics)

▶ Customer engagement and commerce (e.g., Sales, Marketing)

▶ IoT and the digital supply chain (e.g., Manufacturing, Asset Management)

▶ Human resources (e.g., Core HR and Payroll, Time and Attendance Management)

▶ Finance (e.g., GRC, Financial Planning, Treasury Management)

SAP is most famous for its Enterprise Resource Planning solutions. Its market share within the ERP market has declined in recent years, but SAP still holds the top position with an estimated 19% of the entire market. According to the data available, SAP achieves the highest customer satisfaction by realizing more than 50% of the business benefits anticipated in an implementation. Every time a company requires an ERP solution, it is very likely that SAP will be shortlisted. Once SAP is shortlisted, the likelihood of being finally selected for the job is even higher (*https://www.panorama-consulting.com/comparison-between-sap-oracle-and-microsoft-dynamics/*).

As mentioned above, SAP offers far more than only ERP solutions. To support a company's customer management and communication, the use of customer data, and other aspects, the CRM market evolved with an estimated volume of roughly $30 billion (*http://www.crmsearch.com/crm-software-market-share.php*). The big shot here is Salesforce. However, SAP holds a leading position even in this market and is a top player with a market share of around 5% (*https://www.appsruntheworld.com/top-10-crm-software-vendors-and-market-forecast-2015-2020/*).

By 2020, the global market for HR solutions will eventually reach more than $9 billion. HR solutions range from core administrative and payroll solutions to learning platforms, benefits administration, compensation, and much more. With its HR solutions, SAP became one of the market leaders and ranked first in 2015 with an overall market share of 14% (*https://www.appsruntheworld.com/top-10-core-hr-software-vendors-market-forecast-2015-2020-and-customer-wins/*).

Data is essential to support business decisions and optimize processes. Within the rapidly growing business analytics market, top players offer data mining solutions, statistical analyses, as well as predictive analytics. In 2015, SAP was one of the market leaders in this field (*https://www.forbes.com/sites/louiscolumbus/2016/08/20/roundup-of-analytics-big-data-bi-forecasts-and-market-estimates-2016/#4e7b06356f21*), with the highest year-to-year growth rate (*https://www.appsruntheworld.com/top-10-analytics-and-bi-software-vendors-and-market-forecast-2015-2020/*).

SAP has also become a leader in many more business areas. According to Gartner, SAP became a market leader in the combined enterprise information management tools market in 2016, offering solutions such as master data management and data quality, as well as data integration solutions (*https://news.sap.com/sap-leads-in-the-database-and-data-management-solutions-industry-based-on-market-share-revenue-growth-in-gartner-report/*).

As you can see, SAP ranks top in a myriad of markets and tool classes. It has significant business relevance in terms of market share and usage.

There are SAP landscapes that use more than 1,000 systems, or immense single implementations with hundreds of thousands of employees. Companies rely on SAP for their most essential business processes. Switching costs in the field of ERP are enormous. Furthermore, the more comprehensive a solution is, and the more widely it is used, the more difficult it becomes to switch. For this reason, even in cases where SAP implementations might not be best-of-breed anymore, high switching costs may cause companies to be locked in to SAP (the same applies for other ERP vendors as well).

However, SAP tools, especially the ERP software, are in fact among the most relevant systems in a lot of companies. The more than 365,000 customers of SAP include 87% of the Forbes 2000, 98% of the 100 most valued brands, and 100% of the Dow Jones top-scoring sustainability companies (see *https://www.sap.com/corporate/de/documents/2017/04/4666ecdd-b67c-0010-82c7-eda71af511fa.html*).

An SAP system is the centerpiece of a company's IT landscape; in most cases, disrupting it would have a devastating business impact. Efficient system operation and a stable security posture are therefore crucial to achieving business targets and ensuring the welfare of the company.

2.2 Technical design of SAP systems

SAP runs on a three-tier client-server architecture including a presentation tier, application/business logic tier, and a data tier (a tier can also be referred to as a layer).

The presentation layer is the front end. It has a variety of user interfaces, including the well-known SAP GUI (see Figure 2.1), the SAP NetWeaver Business Client, WebDynpro ABAP, SAP FIORI (2.0), SAP Screen Personas, and others. Here, the user can input data queries and display the system output in a usable fashion. The user requests are transmitted to the application and database servers on the subsequent tiers via the front end. The front end is the only part of the SAP system that resides on the end user's PC.

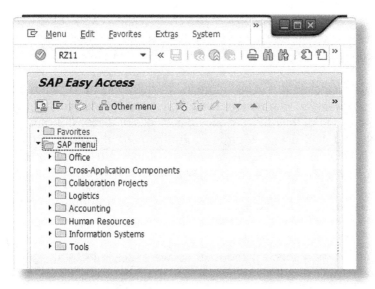

Figure 2.1: SAP GUI

The application/business logic layer controls the system functionality and processes requests. It executes the business logic and is the connecting piece between the front end and the database layer and communicates in both directions. A user enters a request in the front end, which the application server then translates into a database request. The application server thus requests data from the database, processes the data, and sends it back to the presentation layer. Multiple application servers are set up to share the workload requested through the presentation layer and to provide fast output. The technical name of SAP's software for this tier is *SAP NetWeaver Application Server*. SAP supports several operating systems and derivatives for the installation of SAP NetWeaver Application Server, such as Windows, AIX, HP-UX, and Solaris.

Transactional data, customer information, program code, function modules, etc. are examples of the data in the data tier. This tier comprises a *database management system (DBMS)* and the database itself, which retrieves the SQL queries and provides the requested data. SAP supports a variety of different DBMS, such as Oracle, DB/2, and of course Sybase and HANA. Depending on the database system, the DBMS can be either installed on derivatives of Unix/Linux or Windows Server (see Figure 2.2).

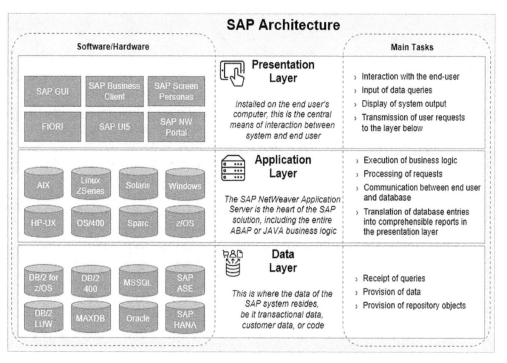

Figure 2.2: Rough SAP three-tier client-server architecture

SAP NetWeaver Application Server contains a variety of components. To keep things concise, we will discuss only some of the components in further detail. One critical element, for example, is the enqueue server. This provides a lock mechanism and prevents database entries from being manipulated by two requests simultaneously. Another element is the message server, which is responsible for distributing requests. However, from our perspective, most audit scopes will suffice without considering these components of SAP NetWeaver Application Server.

You have now learned about the concept of the three-tier client-server architecture within SAP systems. But there is another three-/four-/five-tier architecture we need to discuss. As with any software, the following major activities should be separated:

► Development

► Test

► Quality assurance

► Pre-production/migration

► Production use

It is not only SAP that recommends that you build up at least a three-tier system architecture; there are also hard regulatory requirements for segregation of duties. A typical example is that developers should not be able to access the production system and data. Therefore, you will typically find a setup of at least three different SAP systems. Administrators frequently segregate development, testing, and production activities into three separate systems. This way, development tasks or customizing activities can be fulfilled without the risk of hampering production. Once development activities have been finalized, the changes are transported into the test/QA system and thoroughly validated before being transported into the production system. Dual-control and approval processes flank this procedure.

The advantages of this procedure are obvious:

► Separation of development and production

► Change management with due care

► Production systems are locked for changes

▶ Traceability of changes

▶ Easy utilization of controls such as approval processes

▶ Test and training without the risk of jeopardizing production

▶ Separation of production data from developers

Three-tier architectures are widely used, but four-tier or five-tier architectures are also common (see Figure 2.3). In these architectures, an ERP system with five clients (explained further in this chapter), for example, has four additional installations, separated from each other, resulting in five ERP systems with a total of 25 clients. The administrative effort increases in favor of security and traceability.

Even in a three-tier architecture, the number of systems would at least triple (development, test/QA system, and production system), whereas characteristics of each system and herewith required infrastructure components may differ based on the purpose of each system. An example of a prominent characteristic is the sizing of each tier. Because the development system does not necessarily manage hundreds of thousands of requests and tons of data, fewer applications servers are required to operate the system in comparison to production environments.

From the perspective of an auditor, it is extraordinarily important to consider the following potential differences between the tiers, depending on the company's setup and the maturity and coverage of its control processes. Tiers might differ in (see Figure 2.3):

▶ The type of data (production data is typically located not only in production but also in pre-production and QA)

▶ The type of users and authorizations (while developers use the development tier and project members the middle tiers, end users will use the production system)

▶ The integration of control processes (e.g., access to pre-production systems might be gained without adequate approval processes)

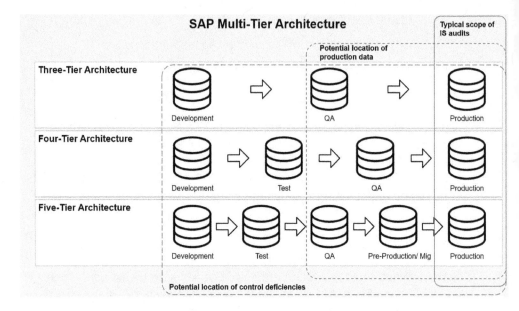

Figure 2.3: SAP multi-tier architectures

The primary means of supporting this method of segregation is SAP's integrated *transport management*, which allows changes to be exported and imported over an entire landscape. Transport management will be addressed further in Section 4.1.

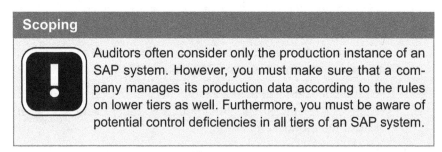

Scoping

Auditors often consider only the production instance of an SAP system. However, you must make sure that a company manages its production data according to the rules on lower tiers as well. Furthermore, you must be aware of potential control deficiencies in all tiers of an SAP system.

In a previous example, we mentioned the *clients*. SAP allows customers to manage various business units within one system. To do so, it uses an architecture with multiple clients. But what is a client?

A client is a logical entity of the SAP database with independent data. It usually resembles a business entity that may comprise multiple company codes. Every company code is subject to separate financial statements. A company code contains further organizational entities, all of which segregate data into business entities within one client:

▶ **Company code**
  ▶ Cost centers
  ▶ Profit centers
  ▶ Business units
  ▶ Plants
    ▶ Storage locations, numbers, types
    ▶ Shipping points
  ▶ Purchasing organizations
  ▶ Purchasing groups
    ▶ Sales organizations
    ▶ Sales offices
    ▶ Divisions
    ▶ Distribution channels
    ▶ Plants

The client concept in SAP allows users to manage multiple vendors or business units with different data efficiently on one physical system, one shared database. Furthermore, within every client, a separate organizational setup is possible, including the fields of Finance/Controlling, Procurement, Sales & Distribution, Production, and further modules of the ERP system.

With this concept, every client is a system within the system, and the auditor has to take this into account. Which clients will be audited, which business entity, which customer base?

Client concept

 Let us assume there is a private German bank called Masterbank which focuses on wealthy customers. It uses the SAP client 200 to manage these wealthy customers. However, management decided to expand the business and embrace the future of commercial and retail banking. In the aftermath of this decision, Masterbank bought the commercial bank Compbank and the retail bank Consbank to expand its business. It now serves three types of customers in Germany: wealth management, business, and commercial customers. The client concept of the SAP system helps Masterbank to avoid duplicates and to merge the data into one central system. Everything resides on one physical machine, but different clients separate the data:

▶ Client 200: Masterbank (management of wealth management customers)

▶ Client 300: Compbank (management of business customers)

▶ Client 400: Consbank (management of commercial customers)

Through the separation of its customer base into different clients, Masterbank has achieved a clear separation of data and can easily allow its customers to be accessed and managed by authorized personnel only. In addition to the concept of separating discrete business groups, it might also be possible to separate the business by geography and manage these geographical groups through different clients. In this case, Masterbank could define its SAP setup as follows:

▶ Client 200: Masterbank Group—Germany

▶ Client 300: Masterbank Group—Southern Europe

▶ Client 400: Masterbank Group—Asia

▶ Client 500: Masterbank Group—USA

To log in, the employee enters the three-digit number and his client-specific user account name and credentials to access the system.

In addition to the clients used in production, every SAP system has standard clients for further application scenarios:

▶ Client 000: The *golden client*, used as a template for all additional clients and in part for support package installations

▶ Client 001: A configuration client with all SAP standard customizing, a copy of client 000

- ▶ Client 066: Client used by SAP itself for monitoring and perform-ance check reasons with the standard account **Earlywatch**

As we have learned, a company can use clients to manage several entities within one system. Companies can use client-specific data, such as user accounts, transactional data, customer master records, number ranges, or client-specific programs. There is also cross-client data which is indepen-dent of the client. This data includes, for example, dictionary objects such as views and tables, and repository objects such as programs, tables, or function modules.

You can check SAP table DD02L and field CLIDEP to assess the character of the relevant data/tables (i.e., whether the data/tables is/are client-spe-cific or cross-client).

When we talk about an SAP system, we are referring to a system with dif-ferent layers (presentation, application, data), multiple machines (at least development, QA, production), and various clients on each machine.

The communication between such a variety of layers, systems, and clients requires the auditor to consider further control mechanisms, which leads us into the network part of SAP.

Ideally, layers of the client-server architecture are separated by differ-ent network zones. However, sensitive data should already be protected against unauthorized access at a network level, which requires robust net-work segmentation, firewalling, encryption, and further security measures.

As with any other system, you must protect the SAP landscape from mali-cious traffic from the outside world.

One central medium for doing this is the *SAProuter*, which is a program that serves as an application level gateway between SAP systems or be-tween an SAP system and the outside world.

An SAProuter complements firewalls by fulfilling tasks such as:

- ▶ Allowing and denying access via a route permission table that states specific ports and host names

- ▶ Allowing communication between SAP systems

▶ Allowing special support connections from the SAP system to the customer network

▶ Supporting firewalls, by, for example, allowing communication only via SAP-specific protocols

▶ Increasing security by enforcing encrypted connections (via SNC)

Web communication

 The SAProuter does not manage web communication/ HTTP(s) connections.

The *SAP Web Dispatcher* is an additional application level gateway. It manages HTTP(s) traffic to your SAP system—a task that the SAProuter cannot fulfill. Like the SAProuter, SAP Web Dispatcher can grant and deny access connections. It can also, amongst other things, increase security by converting incoming HTTP requests into SSL encrypted connections, enforce end-to-end encryption, or terminate incoming SSL connections so that they can be filtered and re-encrypted before being forwarded. Furthermore, SAP Web Dispatcher serves as a load balancer if multiple application servers are used (see Figure 2.4).

One paramount aspect of communication between SAP systems and from an SAP system to a non-SAP system is the technology of *Remote Function Calls (RFC)*, which is a proprietary interface of SAP. You can use RFC to execute functions remotely in other systems, thereby enabling you to perform cross-system transactions. Data can thus be requested from or even inserted into remote systems. An RFC connection always requires an **RFC server (the called system)** and **RFC client (the calling system)**.

As mentioned previously, a company should establish transport layer security for communication via the SAP protocol and web traffic, which it could do via SNC and SSL respectively. Otherwise, the clear-text information sent within the SAP systems or in the case of HTTP requests is subject to a variety of types of attack, such as eavesdropping or man-in-the-middle attacks.

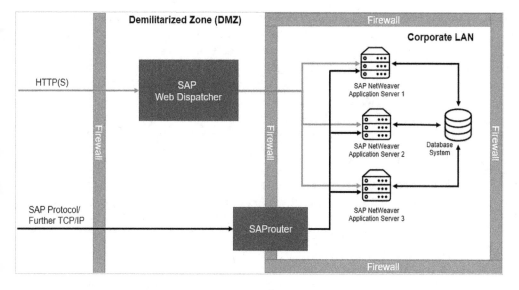

Figure 2.4: SAProuter and SAP Web Dispatcher

SAP systems and their landscapes are a complex environment to audit and to manage. One crucial point that justifies thousands of consultants and operation team members around the world is the way user accounts and authorizations are created and maintained. The authorization concept of SAP, which comprises around 127,000 transaction codes, thousands of authorization groups, and a billion ways to combine them, may be one of the most complex systems that exists.

The more complex a system landscape becomes, the more cumbersome the administrative efforts become, such as the management of user accounts and their permissions. One of the most tedious tasks is the management of similar user accounts required in multiple systems or clients of one system. Just imagine a controller who needs access to ten different SAP systems or clients, all set up for various locations or business entities. The controller always requires the same user account and account information in these systems. However, to set this controller up correctly, an administrator has to log in to ten different systems to fulfill the same tasks of account creation, etc. This has led to the establishment of *central user administration (CUA)*.

CUA introduces the concept of user master records and allows an administrator to manage the records from a central system. The central system is just another SAP system that already exists. If available, companies typically choose *SAP Solution Manager* as the CUA. A relationship between a central system and child systems is defined. The CUA distributes changes to an account to all child systems that were deemed relevant within this logical model. Not only does this make your administrative tasks more efficient, but you also get an overview of all user accounts distributed over a variety of systems.

While CUA logically supports the user administration, another entirely separate solution was developed by SAP to support user and access management, especially from a security perspective. This solution is called *SAP Access Control* and it is a module of the *SAP Governance Risk and Compliance (GRC)* solution.

SAP Access Control is a stand-alone solution that helps companies to execute, monitor and, in various processes, force authorization controls. Functions include:

- ▶ Analyzing users, roles, and profiles for any authorization risks that exist
- ▶ Creating and approving roles and users in a secure manner
- ▶ Providing an effective means for emergency access/break-glass procedures
- ▶ Recording mitigating controls for handling those risks

SAP Access Control must be installed as an overarching solution with interfaces to the rest of the SAP landscape, as roles and accounts etc. are managed via this product. If this product is used, an auditor should focus on this as it is the central security solution which impacts all connected systems.

Another overarching solution is SAP Solution Manager (SolMan). This is an IT management or IT service management solution which provides processes such as:

▶ Portfolio and project management (e.g., KPIs, dashboards)

▶ Software development lifecycle (e.g., documented requirements, test case fulfillment, automated test planning, change management process)

▶ Service management (e.g., catalog of services, management of cost of service, SLA fulfillment)

▶ Incident management (e.g., monitoring, resolution)

Once SolMan is highly integrated into the SAP landscape, an auditor should focus on this solution, as it may be the integral component for the change management processes of the actual SAP system in scope.

You should now understand the multi-tier character of SAP systems and the client-server architecture, including the method of splitting business data into several clients within one associated database, essential network level components and communication interfaces, as well as overarching methods and tools (CUA, SAP Access Control, SolMan) that are common in vast SAP landscapes. We can now turn this into an audit approach.

2.3   SAP audit universe

To define the approach and scope for an SAP audit, you have to be aware of the entire SAP audit universe. The SAP audit universe is a model, comprised of seven clusters, which has been developed to describe the SAP-specific and non-SAP-specific elements, all of which can be relevant for auditing SAP systems depending on the detailed scenarios and scope.

The seven elements that will be portrayed in the next sections form the SAP audit universe (see Figure 2.5).

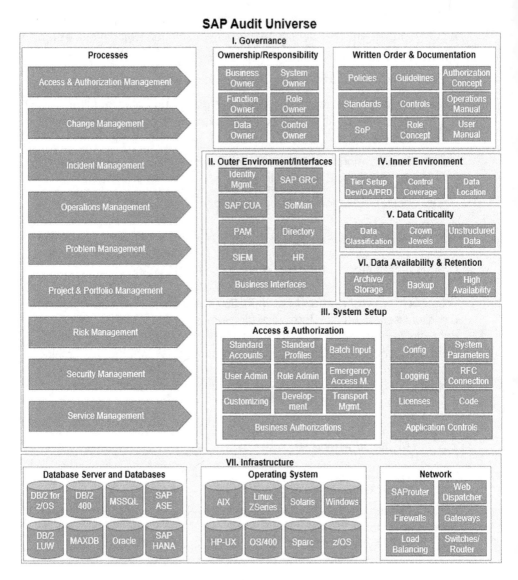

Figure 2.5: SAP audit universe

In the following sections, this depiction will serve as an orientation between the technical, processual, and organizational elements of SAP systems.

2.3.1 Governance

The first and overarching cluster of the SAP audit universe is **Governance**, which includes the following sub-clusters: **Processes**, **Ownership/responsibility**, and **Written order/documentation**. The detailed components of these clusters are introduced below along with a typical question which could be relevant from an auditor's perspective.

The three sub-clusters combined allow an auditor to gain an understanding of how a company wants to run according to its policies and assigned responsibilities. You get an understanding of the desired state of the company. However, a more in-depth look at the actual processes and clusters in the six subsequent sections may reveal notable deviations to the descriptions given below and the desired state.

Elements of the governance cluster

Processes:

▶ **Access & authorization management**
The entirety of operations related to identities, user accounts, and their authorizations, such as joiner, mover, leaver, or re-certification processes.
Does the process ensure a traceable and sustainable user and permissions base in the system?

▶ **Change management**
The process to push changes in functionality or upgrades of the system into the production instance.
Is there a guarantee that no one can push changes into production without adequate tests and approvals?

▶ **Incident management**
Organizational and technical processes to prepare for and react to system failures or security incidents.
Are the processes implemented sufficient to respond to a major incident in time?

▶ **Operations management**
Processes to keep the system up and running.
Are patches installed? Is a decrease in performance identified promptly?

▶ **Problem management**
The analysis of root causes of incidents and the management of resolution of incidents.
Were adequate actions taken to avoid a problem occurring again?

▶ **Project & portfolio management**
The methods and tools for initiating, planning, conducting, monitoring, and closing projects or a portfolio of activities.
Are the project management processes sufficient to ensure the secure development of new functionality or implementation of new systems?

▶ **Risk management**
The family of processes for identifying, assessing, analyzing, handling, and monitoring events that could negatively or even positively impact business objectives.
Are risks concerning the SAP landscape identified and adequately managed?

▶ **Security management**
Processes for securing the availability, confidentiality, and integrity of a company's assets.
Is sensitive data adequately classified and protected?

▶ **Service management**
Processes for supporting the end-to-end delivery of IT services to the customers.
Are SLAs fulfilled and are actions taken if SLAs are not fulfilled?

Ownership/responsibility:

▶ **Business owner**
Responsible for a system from a business perspective, as such in charge of allocating budgets and equipped with decision-making authority.
Is the business owner in place to make decisions if necessary?

▶ **System owner**
Responsible for the well-being of the system itself, and therefore for operations and engineering.
Is a system owner in place who manages the operations of the system?

▶ **Function owner**
Responsible for and knowledgeable about a function. The person to approach if changes to a function are needed.
Is a function owner defined for a critical function to ensure that knowledge stays available and further development is possible?

▶ **Role owner**
Responsible for an SAP role, and as such knowledgeable about re-certifying its content and ensuring technically that the role can only grant the rights it is supposed to allow.
Are role owners available to explain the content of their roles?

▶ **Data owner**
Responsible for a specific set of data and knowledgeable about who should access this set of data.
Is the data owner involved in approval processes to grant access?

▶ **Control owner**
Responsible for conducting controls and adopting changes if required.
Was the weekly failed login list exported and analyzed?

Written order & documentation:

▶ **Policies**
Provide a blueprint, rough controls, and the general targets of a company in a field, such as a security policy or data protection policy. Policies describe the desired state at a high level.
Are policies aligned with business objectives and do they cover all relevant topics, currently known developments, and business entities?

▶ **Guidelines**
Include optional steps and recommendations on how to fulfill standards and comply with policies.
Do guidelines cover recent developments and still provide valid recommendations?

▶ **Standards**
Provide mandatory actions to be taken and specific rules to support a policy.
Are the encryption algorithms allowed as standard still considered secure?

▶ **Standard operating procedures (SoP)**
The desired process and its steps, including who is responsible for conducting which step, thereby following the requirements of the policy.
Are SoPs written and published for all relevant processes?

▶ **Controls**
Definition of internal controls, the detailed control activities, their frequency, and who needs to conduct them.
Are controls defined and do the right persons know how to perform them?

▶ **Role concept**
Definition of which business entity, department, or unit can be assigned which roles and thus authorizations.
Does the concept cover all relevant business units and roles?

▶ **Authorization concept**
Definition of mechanisms and specific authorization objects and fields within the SAP system that are used for authorization management.
Are the custom Z* and Y* authorization objects explained in the authorization concept?

▶ **Operations manual**
Description of specific monitoring, back-up, patching, or other maintenance activities for the system.
Does the patching process comply with the company's policies and leading practices and ensure timely remediation of vulnerabilities?

▶ **User manual**
Description of how to use the system and its functionalities.
Do the workflows described comply with the internal standard, for example, regarding approval instances?

The governance cluster is extremely important for elaborating the desired state of a company and getting a detailed look at process descriptions and the coverage of owners and responsible persons. The content of this cluster is relevant to the six subsequent clusters.

2.3.2   Outer environment/interfaces

An SAP system is seldom alone—a business never uses just one SAP system. Instead, there is a variety of supportive tools or systems for monitoring the SAP landscape. Both may change some audit procedures and may determine where to focus on what.

The outer environment/interfaces cluster includes the most common interfaces to other systems, be they SAP systems or non-SAP systems.

Elements of the outer environment/interfaces cluster

▶ **Identity management (IdM)**
Central gateway for identity management within the company. Ideally, user accounts and permissions of all kinds are requested here and run through adequate approval workflows. Furthermore, provision of user accounts and roles into the SAP systems is automated. Do the accounts and roles within the SAP system match the officially requested and approved accounts and roles documented in the IdM?

▶ **SAP GRC**
An overarching SAP tool that integrates security measures into day-to-day administrative processes such as automated risk assessments for role assignments.
How was the ruleset for performing risk assessments on authorizations defined?

▶ **SAP CUA**
A central client takes over the user administration for all connected systems and thus saves administrators time.
How secure is the setup and how secure are the processes around user administration in the CUA client?

▶ **Solution Manager (SolMan)**
Overarching tools that provide functionality to support, for example, service management or change and transport management. Does the change process set up prevent unauthorized changes from being pushed into production?

▶ **Privileged account management (PAM)**
Methods and tools to lock down the credentials of privileged accounts, monitor sessions of privileged users, and analyze anomalies in the usage of these accounts.

Does the PAM system include privileged accounts on servers, databases, and the application layer of the SAP system?

▶ **Directory**
Directories provide a central repository for user and account data and provide means of authentication and authorization. How is the central server that provides these directory services secured against unauthorized access?

▶ **Security information and event management (SIEM)**
A system that correlates log data from a variety of hosts, such as servers, databases, firewalls, and switches to identify and provide alerts for security breaches.
Is the SAP log data integrated into the log management and SIEM architecture of the company?

▶ **Human resources (HR)**
A central system that manages, among other things, the start and end dates of employees' work contracts and job assignments. How is the HR information aligned with the SAP system regarding contract dates or the synchronization between official job assignments and actual authorizations within the system?

▶ **Business interfaces**
The vast number of SAP systems or non-SAP systems connected that exchange data or call function modules across systems. What assurance is there that data cannot be altered in transit between these systems?

2.3.3   System setup

The centerpiece of an SAP system from an end user's perspective is the application layer, the configuration of the application, and the authorizations that grant the end user access to specific functions. Through the front end, an end user interacts with the SAP system, enters transactions, displays and changes data, runs through workflows and controls, obtains and answers messages, performs approvals, etc. These elements have been incorporated within the cluster.

Elements of the system setup cluster

Access and authorization:

► **Standard accounts**
Built-in accounts that are available in every SAP system by default, such as DDIC or SAP*.
Have the standard passwords of the built-in accounts been changed?

► **Standard profiles**
Powerful standard profiles that grant wide access to the system and its most sensitive functions, such as SAP_ALL.
Is someone assigned to the profile SAP_ALL or a similar profile?

► **Batch input**
Method of entering data en masse and simulating user activities without using the GUI.
Who is allowed to run batch inputs?

► **User administration**
Authorizations that allow a user to create or maintain accounts that allow a user to assign roles or profiles to a user and thus finally grant the rights.
Are user admin rights provided in the production system?

► **Role administration**
Authorizations that allow a user to create or maintain roles within the SAP system.
Who can administer roles within which system tier and ensure that role changes are tested and approved before they are assigned?

► **Emergency access management**
Extensive access rights that can be used by a user in case of an emergency.
Who is allowed to use emergency access accounts?

► **Customizing**
Authorizations that allow access to customizing functions.
Is any user capable of changing settings in the production system without an adequate change management process?

▶ **Development**
Authorizations that allow access to development functions or system debugging.
Can any user alter ABAP programs directly in the production system?

▶ **Transport management**
Authorizations to perform transport management and thus push changes into the production system via the landscape.
Who can perform changes in the SAP system?

▶ **Business authorizations**
Authorizations deemed critical by business units, such as the maintenance of posting periods or maintenance of automated payments.
Have business units defined what authorizations are critical and introduced effective means to protect their most vital functions?

Further areas of interest:

▶ **Configuration**
The myriad of possibilities for changing system functions, such as workflows or reports, or for customizing organizational units.
How is the system changeability set up?

▶ **System parameters**
Further system-wide settings that require a restart of the application instance.
Do the password parameters comply with internal policies and leading practices?

▶ **Logging**
Mechanisms for logging table changes and events.
Is logging active and does it include changes to business-critical tables?

▶ **RFC connections**
The setup of SAP to SAP or SAP to non-SAP remote function module calls.
Are specific user accounts used for every single RFC connection?

▶ **Licenses**
The management of licenses to comply with the agreed license terms.
Are license reviews performed on a regular basis?

▶ **Code**
The program code, either ABAP or Java, that executes the system's functions.
What assurance is there that programmers are complying with coding policies?

▶ **Application controls**
Technical controls within the SAP system to mitigate risks.
What application controls are used to prevent financial misstatements?

2.3.4 Inner environment

The inner environment is the fourth cluster of the SAP audit universe and dives deeply into the multi-tier setup of the SAP installation.

Elements of the inner environment cluster

▶ **Tier setup: Dev/QA/PRD**
A way of separating one SAP system into multiple installations to allow for more secure change management, development, etc.
Are development, test, and production activities separated efficiently?

▶ **Control coverage**
Coverage of the company's controls on all tiers.
Are critical controls, such as account approval processes, also applied to the QA tier and test tier for critical systems?

▶ **Data location**
Examination of which type of data is located in which tier.
Is production data available unaltered on tiers lower than production?

2.3.5 Data criticality

The fifth cluster of the SAP audit universe addresses the sensitivity of data and the way a company is aware of its most critical data and information.

Elements of the data criticality cluster

▶ **Data classification**
The process of classifying data in a structured way and imposing security measures accordingly.
Is the data in the SAP system classified and have adequate security measures been taken?

▶ **Crown jewels**
The most critical data, such as secret recipes or secret strategies of a company.
Is the company aware of its crown jewels and has it taken adequate measures to protect them?

▶ **Unstructured data**
Data that is not located in a structured way within relational databases but rather in the form of documents, photographs, etc.
Is the company aware of critical information that might be in unstructured data and has it taken measures to identify and protect such information?

2.3.6 Data availability and data retention

To comply with legal regulations and to ensure proper continuity of business in case of an interruption, data retention, backup management, and high availability are crucial elements which have been summarized in the sixth cluster.

Elements of the data availability and data retention cluster

▶ **Archive/storage**
The processes and tools for storing and archiving data according to legal regulations and business needs.
How long are critical logs stored?

▶ **Backup**
The processes and tools for copying data and restoring it if necessary.
What assurance is there that all data is backed up and restorable after a data loss event?

▶ **High availability**
Processes and tools to ensure a very high level of availability of a system.
Which actions have been taken to ensure that the system is highly available?

2.3.7　Infrastructure

Section 2.2 introduced various components of the technical architecture and foundation of an SAP system. These are at least as relevant for an SAP audit as the other clusters. Any manipulation in the server or database may have a severe impact on system operation.

Elements of the infrastrucure cluster

Database server and databases:

▶ **Database server**
The server on which the database and DBMS resides.
Is the database server subject to the PAM infrastructure of the company or similar control means?

▶ **Databases (DB/2, MaxDB, MSSQL, Oracle, SAP ASE, SAP HANA)**
The location of the data.
How is unauthorized access to the database prevented?

Operating system:

▶ **AIX, HP-UX, Linux ZSeries, OS/400, Solaris, Solaris Sparc, Windows, z/OS**
The system on which SAP Application NetWeaver Server or the Web server runs.
Are adequate processes in place to request, approve, and frequently rotate secure shell (SSH) keys on Unix servers?

Network:

▶ **SAProuter**
An application level gateway that is located between SAP systems or between an SAP system and the outside world.
How often is the route permission table checked and reconciled?

▶ **SAP Web Dispatcher**
An SAP program that manages HTTP(s) traffic to the SAP system and distributes the workload to various application servers.
How is incoming web traffic secured?

▶ **Firewalls**
A network security system that controls inbound and outbound traffic.
What assurance is there that only formally requested and approved firewall rules and port activations are maintained?

▶ **Gateways**
Hardware or software that enables a connection between two systems.
How are insecure gateways detected and prevented?

▶ **Load balancing**
Hardware or software to divide the workload over multiple computing resources.
How are unauthorized connections prevented?

▶ **Switches/router**
Tools for connecting devices within a network and enabling communication between them.
How are the management, data, and control planes of your devices secured?

2.4 General approach and prerequisites for auditing SAP systems

"We are going to audit your SAP ERP system." Forget it. If you hear such a sentence, you should ask for more details. The audit team is definitely not equipped with enough resources and time to conduct an audit of an entire SAP ERP system. To lay the foundation for a successful audit undertaking, scoping may be even more critical than the audit steps themselves.

Therefore, the most crucial part of an SAP audit is the initiation and planning process steps. The first step is to define the approximate audit boundaries, followed by the precise controls/risks that will drive the audit. To illustrate this, two typical scenarios are discussed on the following pages.

2.4.1   Scenario 1: SAP audit with a focus on ITGC

Audits of the *IT general controls (ITGC)* of a system are widespread. Unlike application controls, ITGC are independent of a system's business functions but are related to IT controls, which fall under the responsibility of the IT department. ITGC typically address data availability, confidentiality, integrity, and traceability.

ITGC most notably cover the following topics:

- ▶ Access and authorization management
  - ▶ Joiner, mover, leaver processes
  - ▶ Re-certification and reconciliation processes
  - ▶ Role management
  - ▶ Emergency access management
  - ▶ Credential management
  - ▶ Physical access and protection
  - ▶ Convergence
- ▶ Operations management
  - ▶ Logging and monitoring
  - ▶ Incident and problem management
  - ▶ Backup and archiving
- ▶ Change management
  - ▶ Change request process
  - ▶ Change approval process
  - ▶ Change fulfillment process
- ▶ Software development
  - ▶ Requirements engineering
  - ▶ Development process

▶ Test management

▶ Migration process

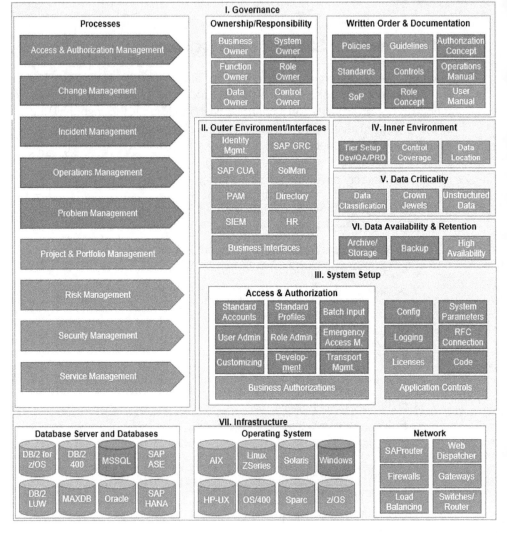

Figure 2.6: SAP audit environment with a focus on ITGC

The most important step in the scoping for an SAP ITGC audit is the definition of the systems and clients to be tested. This is because the topics presented above are relevant not only to the SAP Application NetWeaver layer, but also to underlying operating systems and databases. The same applies to network components. Based on its experience, related incidents, and recent developments, a company should either include the infrastructure systems in the scope or not. The recommendation is to include the operating system and database system as well. Assuming the company uses an MSSQL database on a Windows machine, as well as the NetWeaver application, this would lead to the audit environment depicted in Figure 2.6.

Some of the audit activities are relevant to multiple clients—if the audit scope itself covers multiple clients. For example, the analysis of authorizations granted may be cumbersome depending on the landscape. If a variety of different clients are in scope, you should calculate the effect of the multiplication of some efforts.

2.4.2   Scenario 2: SAP audit with a focus on GDPR

Imagine the scenario of an audit that focuses on *General Data Protection Regulations (GDPR)*. The EU regulation has been in force since May 25, 2018 and is relevant to all companies that process data of citizens of the European Union. Let us assume a company has to include its customer data processing SAP ERP system in the overall audit environment to examine compliance with GDPR requirements and the ERP system use an Oracle database.

The following is a list of probable elements of interest from the SAP audit universe when the audit focusing on data protection is about to commence.

Governance
  ▶ Identify the desired means of enforcing data protection and incorporating the GDPR requirements through data protection-related policies, standards, and procedures, as well as controls (for example, an external data privacy policy to detail the data collection and processing activities)

► Identify the desired state regarding who should be allowed to access customer data by analyzing the role and authorization concept

► Assess the adequacy of the access and authorization management processes with regard to preventing unauthorized access to customer data

► Assess the security processes that directly or indirectly influence data protection, such as data inventory management and data classification on the one hand, and vulnerability management and PAM on the other hand

► Assess the integration of privacy impact assessments in the change management and software development lifecycles

► Assess the test procedure incident responses to data breaches

Outer environment/business interfaces

► Check the business interfaces to understand the transmitter and recipient of customer data transfers

► Assess the integration with PAM and SIEM; ideally, behavior is analyzed and log information is correlated

System setup

► Analyze the appropriateness of authorizations for accessing and maintaining sensitive customer data through business authorizations or super authorizations (such as SAP_ALL)

► Analyze the availability of audit trails, especially for data transfers, for example, to foreign countries

► Check customizing samples to determine whether only required customer data is processed in accordance with the principle of data minimization

Inner environment

- ▶ Check the setup of the multi-tier landscape and where to find sensitive customer information

- ▶ Assess the coverage of all related controls to ensure that it does not differ in intensity on minor tiers where customer data resides

Data criticality

- ▶ Assess the data classification scheme and coverage

- ▶ Check that sensitive customer information requires adequate controls

Data availability and data retention

- ▶ Assess how the company can search for and provide requested customer data to respond to a data subject access request (DSAR)

- ▶ Assess how customer data can be deleted permanently upon request subject to the right to erasure (right to be forgotten)

- ▶ Assess the retention periods and deletion mechanisms for situations in which customer data is no longer needed

Infrastructure

- ▶ Check the existence of controls for data protection, such as encryption of data in transit (firewalls, SAProuter, SAP Web Dispatcher)

- ▶ Assess data-at-rest encryption on the Oracle database

- ▶ Check for adequate network segmentation

A GDPR audit requires more than a system audit, as data protection policies, processes, or even user awareness are paramount across the entire company and system landscape. However, once the SAP system is a centerpiece in the processing of customer data, the system will become

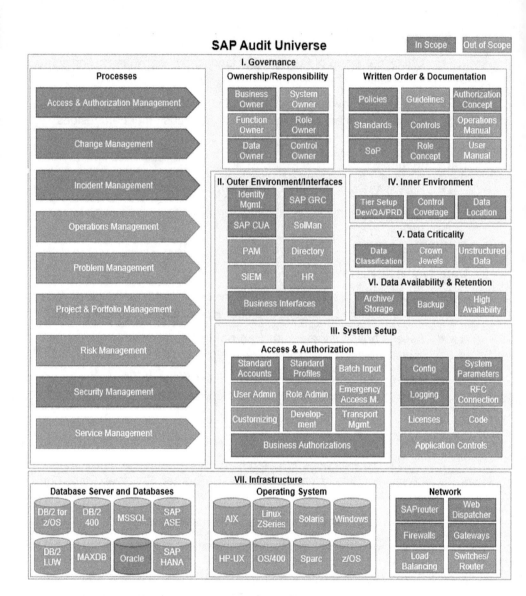

Figure 2.7: SAP audit environment with a focus on GDPR

2.4.3   Information request

Once the audit environment, its boundaries, and precise scope are clear, the auditor creates the audit plan. The deliverable of this process is the risk control matrix (see Section 1.4.2).

The audit planning then ends with a kick-off meeting with the auditees, sponsors, and auditors to communicate the scope of the audit and agree on timelines and procedure. The auditor usually submits an information request after the kick-off and before the assessment phase. This request usually covers:

▶ A user account and specific authorizations to allow access to the system and performance of the audit steps

▶ The policies, guidelines, standards, SoPs, etc. relevant to the audit steps

▶ Tables or specific reports needed from the SAP systems

▶ Further documentation that is not specific to the SAP system (such as a list of all incidents from ServiceNow's tool **IT Service Management**, all test cases from HP's tool **Application Lifecyle Management**, or all controls from RSA's tool **Archer**)

You must communicate your requirements to the auditees as precisely as possible.

Give me a list of all authorizations

 Tell your auditees precisely what you need. If you tell them you need a "list of all authorizations", you will most probably get something that you neither need nor expect. From an administrator point of view, a "list of all users" from the SAP system could be interpreted as:

▶ The assignment of roles to users (table AGR_USERS)

▶ The user master authorizations (table USR04)

▶ The user master authorization profiles (table USR10)

▶ The assignment of roles to users in a CUA environment (table USLA04)

> Even with all of the above tables, you may not be able to distinguish critical accounts with privileged access rights, as the names of roles and profiles will not help you gain insight into the specific transaction codes, authorization objects, and field values.

The attention to detail required in an SAP environment makes having SAP-related experience crucial. To perform an audit with any scope in an SAP system successfully, specific knowledge is required. The superordinate process knowledge of an IS audit will not be sufficient.

The best solution for meeting your requirement is to get the user accounts and authorizations, query the information you need, and export the required reports yourself.

Therefore, Chapter 3 will introduce some useful tools that will help SAP auditors to work with SAP systems. When portraying the most common or the most important controls in all SAP systems, the tables, authorizations, reports, etc. required are explicitly stated. This will give you what you need to self-confidently start the next audit.

You have now learned about the bandwidth of an SAP audit through the presentation of the SAP audit universe. You have also received an initial introduction into the extraordinarily important step of audit scoping. You should now be aware that you have to communicate the audit requirements precisely with regard to documents, reports, authorizations, etc. In the next chapters, we will introduce the tools and detailed controls you need to help you through your audit.

3 Useful tools for an SAP auditor

This chapter introduces crucial transactions and the functionalities behind them. Transactions SE16/SE16N, SUIM, SA38, and SAIS are an integral part of an auditor's everyday life. They can be used for comprehensive analysis and execution of important audit-related programs. Without a comprehensive understanding of these tools, auditing SAP systems is an almost insurmountable challenge.

3.1 Transaction SE16/SE16N: Data Browser

In principle, all data and information in an SAP system is stored in tables. Transaction SE16 is used to provide access to tables and their contents. To access the contents of a table, enter the technical name of the table in transaction SE16 (as shown in Figure 3.1 for table USR02—a table that stores user information).

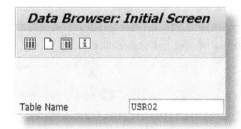

Figure 3.1: Transaction SE16—initial screen

Once you enter the technical name of a table in transaction SE16, you can display either the entire contents of a table or contents filtered according to specific attributes by entering the relevant selection criteria in one of the available selection fields ❶ (Figure 3.2).

Selection fields

 The selection screen in transaction SE16 does not always display all fields that can be used to select values. To check which fields are available and to also enable them for selection, open the SETTINGS menu and select the FIELDS FOR SELECTION option.

The SELECTION OPTIONS button ❷ allows you to choose more than one selection value or to specify selection ranges. To ensure that the output contains all available results, in the MAXIMUM NO. OF HITS field ❸, enter a value that is either to equal or greater than the number of entries in your selection.

Maximum number of hits

 The value in the MAXIMUM NUMBER OF HITS field cannot be changed dynamically on the results screen within transaction SE16. Therefore, make sure that you enter a suitable number in this field before running your selection. If you forget to do this, from the results, go back to the selection screen, change your input, and execute the data collection again.

You can initiate the data collection by clicking EXECUTE ❹ or by pressing F8 .

The results screen has various options that allow you to assess your data further. For example, you can sort data in ascending or descending order, determine totals and subtotals, and set further filters. You can also download data within transaction SE16 to analyze it further. (Figure 3.3)

In addition to transaction SE16, SAP provides an evolution of this transaction: transaction SE16N. To access the selection criteria in transaction SE16N, enter the technical name of a table in the TABLE field and press Enter (Figure 3.4).

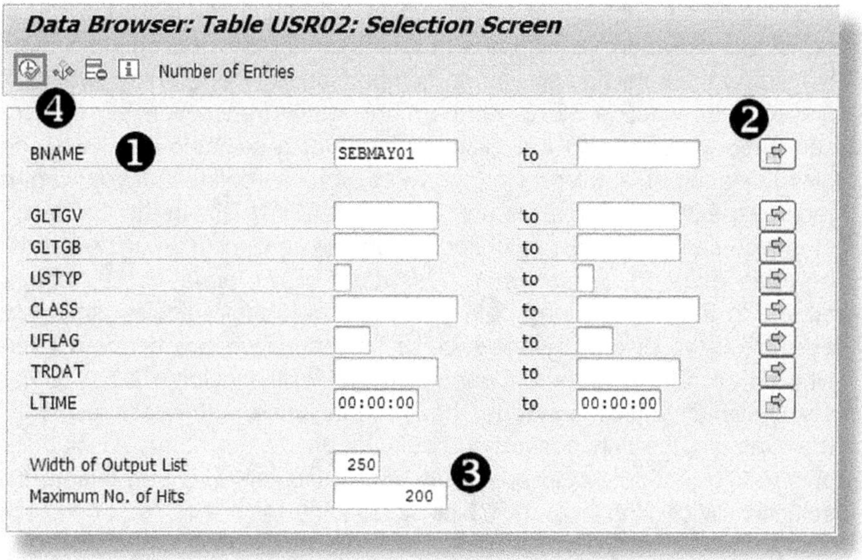

Data Browser: Table USR02: Selection Screen

⊕ ⊹ ⧉ ⓘ Number of Entries

❹

BNAME ❶	SEBMAY01	to	❷ ⇨
GLTGV		to	⇨
GLTGB		to	⇨
USTYP		to	⇨
CLASS		to	⇨
UFLAG		to	⇨
TRDAT		to	⇨
LTIME	00:00:00	to	00:00:00 ⇨

Width of Output List   250   ❸

Maximum No. of Hits   200

Figure 3.2: Transaction SE16—general selection screen

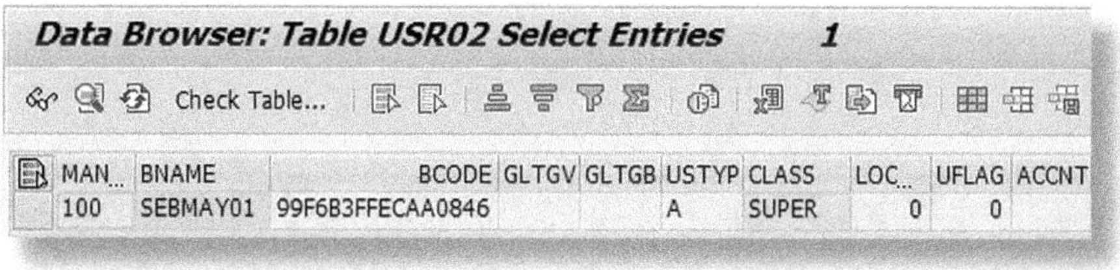

Data Browser: Table USR02 Select Entries   1

&⁊ ⧉ ⧈ Check Table…   ⧉ ⧉ | ⬁ ⬆ ⬇ Σ | ⊕ | ▤ ⬅ ⬆ ▽ | ▦ ▦ ▦

🗅	MAN..	BNAME	BCODE	GLTGV	GLTGB	USTYP	CLASS	LOC..	UFLAG	ACCNT
	100	SEBMAY01	99F6B3FFECAA0846			A	SUPER	0	0	

Figure 3.3: Transaction SE16—results screen

General Table Display

⊕ Background   Number of Entries   ⧉ ⧉ ⧉ ⧉ All Entries   ▦ ⇨

Table	USR02	
Text table		☐ No texts
Layout		
Maximum no. of hits	500	☐ Maintain entries

Figure 3.4: Transaction SE16N—initial screen

The biggest advantage of this transaction is that both the technical names of fields (equivalent to columns in tables) and their description are displayed on the selection screen. In comparison, only one of the two is displayed in transaction SE16. Furthermore, within transaction SE16N, you can already specify on the initial screen which columns should be displayed as output. As shown in Figure 3.5, you can define that you want to receive the information stored on user *SEBMAY01* ❶. In the OPTION column, you can specify the selection options. For example, you can choose between *equal to*, *greater than*, *less than*, or *not equal to* ❷, among others. In the MORE column ❸, you can add further selection lines—for example, if you would like to receive the output on two or more users who do not fit into a specific range. In the OUTPUT column ❹, you can specify which selection criteria should be included in the data results. In the example, the only desired output is the user's lock status (USER LOCK) and validity period (VALID FROM and VALID THROUGH). You can initiate the selection by clicking EXECUTE ❺ or by pressing F8.

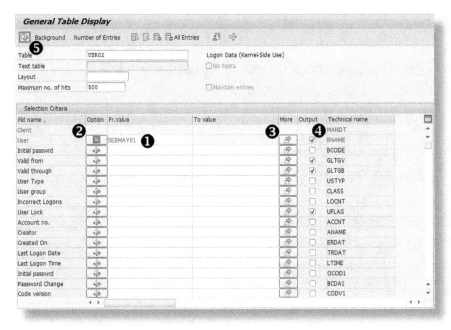

Figure 3.5: Transaction SE16N—general selection screen

The results screen in transaction SE16N (Figure 3.6) differs slightly from that of transaction SE16. First, the number of entries in the table that meet the selection criteria is displayed more clearly in the NUMBER OF HITS field

1. In transaction SE16, this is displayed less clearly within the header of the table. In addition, in transaction SE16N, you have the option of adjusting the maximum number of hits (MAXIMUM NO. OF HITS) **2** shown on the results screen without having to return to the selection screen. Similar to transaction SE16, you can also use various additional functions in transaction SE16N. For example, you can sort data in ascending or descending order, determine totals and subtotals, and set further filters **3**.

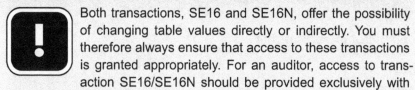

Figure 3.6: Transaction SE16N—results screen

Permission within transaction SE16/SE16N

Both transactions, SE16 and SE16N, offer the possibility of changing table values directly or indirectly. You must therefore always ensure that access to these transactions is granted appropriately. For an auditor, access to transaction SE16/SE16N should be provided exclusively with read-only authorization and only for relevant tables. This can be controlled via authorization object S_TABU_DIS or S_TABU_NAM.

Finally, if you do not know the technical name of a table, the following advice may help. Figure 3.7 shows transaction PFCG. You want to find out which table the derived roles are stored in. Therefore, in the DERIVE FROM ROLE field, open the SAP help functionality either by right-clicking the field and selecting the HELP menu or by pressing F1.

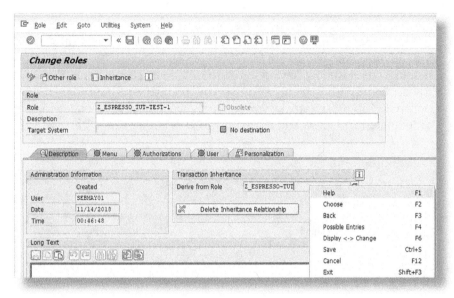

Figure 3.7: Technical name determination—step 1

In the PERFORMANCE ASSISTANT window that opens, select the icon outlined in Figure 3.8.

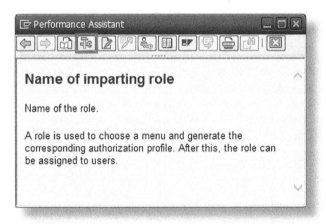

Figure 3.8: Technical name determination—step 2

The TECHNICAL INFORMATION screen appears (see Figure 3.9). Here, the TABLE NAME field ❶ contains the technical name of a table. If you enter this name in transaction SE16 or SE16N, you can access the table and all stored values directly. Sometimes, instead of a transparent table, the names of structures are displayed. These cannot be opened directly in transactions SE16 and SE16N. In this case, you have to perform another step using the FIELD NAME field ❷.

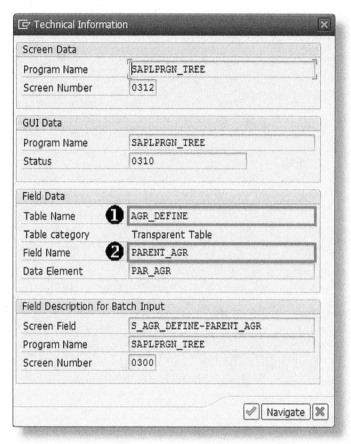

Figure 3.9: Technical name determination—step 3

Open transaction SE15 and navigate through the menu: REPOSITORY INFORMATION SYSTEM • ABAP DICTIONARY • FIELDS • TABLE FIELDS, as shown in Figure 3.10. Enter the relevant name in the FIELD NAME field ❶. Initiate the selection by clicking EXECUTE ❷ or by pressing F8.

The result is a display of all tables containing this field. In this example, in addition to table AGR_DEFINE, tables /ISDFPS/AGR_DEF and WP3RO-LEHIER are also displayed (Figure 3.11)

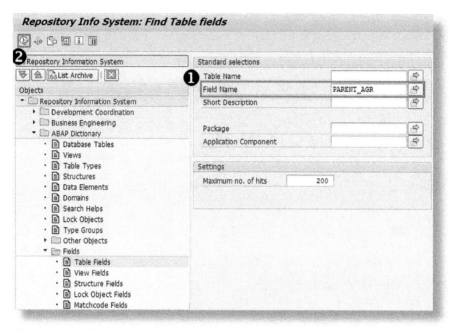

Figure 3.10: Technical name determination—step 4

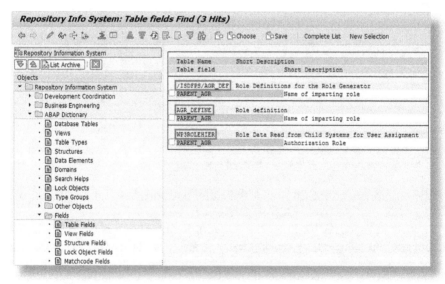

Figure 3.11: Technical name determination—step 5

Transactions SE16H and SE16S

 In addition to the previously introduced transactions SE16 and SE16N, there are two further transactions in this context: SE16H and SE16S. Transaction SE16H exists only in SAP ERP systems (including S/4HANA) and corresponds to transaction SE16N, with the additional functionality of merging tables. Transaction SE16S was introduced with S/4HANA and the SAP HANA database and, unlike the other transactions, allows you to search for specific values in tables.

3.2 Transaction SUIM: User Information System

Transaction SUIM is a comprehensive tool for evaluating users and roles and their authorizations. This transaction offers a variety of filter tools that will be used sooner or later in every audit. This section introduces the basic functions of the transaction and provides you with useful tips and tricks. If certain functions of transaction SUIM are necessary in the context of specific control testing, these are explained in detail in the respective sections of Chapter 4.

Transaction SUIM consists of a large number of reports in the area of user, role, and authorization management (Figure 3.12). The most relevant reports from an audit perspective are listed below. There are, of course, other reports that may be of use for your audit.

❶ Users by Complex Selection Criteria
Allows you to analyze users against different criteria. From an audit perspective, you can use this report to determine access risks at user level.

❷ Roles by Complex Selection Criteria
Allows you to analyze roles against different criteria. From an audit perspective, you can use this report to determine access risks at role level.

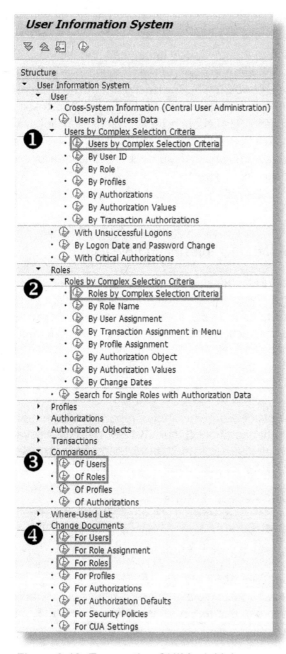

Figure 3.12: Transaction SUIM—initial screen

❸ Comparisons: Of Roles/Of Users

Allow you to compare roles and users across the system. From an audit perspective, you can use these reports, for example, to assess the consistency of roles in a development, quality, and production system to identify direct changes to roles which bypass change management controls.

❹ Change Documents: For Users/For Roles

Provide access to change logs with varying levels of detail. From an audit perspective, you can use these reports, for example, to understand the root cause of access risks identified and to determine the responsibilities.

Users by Complex Selection Criteria

You use the **Users by Complex Selection Criteria** report to evaluate users and their authorizations. It is helpful in audits, especially when you are checking whether critical authorizations are assigned to end users (Figure 3.13).

The LOGON DATA tab appears first. On this tab, you filter relevant users. In the STANDARD SELECTION area, you can specify which user groups are or are not to be included in the analysis ❶. You do this, for example, for **Basis administrators** where you know in advance that they have more far-reaching permissions than the **normal** end users. Since this is the default setting and in the best case, mitigating controls are in place for administrative accounts, these administrative accounts are often excluded to avoid false positives. You can also determine which user types are to be included in the analysis ❷. When it comes to analyzing the authorizations of end users, it is often appropriate to restrict the search to the user types *Dialog* and *Service*, since the remaining user types (*System*, *Communication*, and *Reference*) do not allow a logon dialog at all. Furthermore, you can choose to exclude users that are locked ❸ or users that are no longer valid ❹. It is common practice in companies that users of SAP systems are not deleted; instead, their accounts are disabled when an employee leaves the company. In this case, you must make sure such users are not involved in user assessments, as the account can no longer be used.

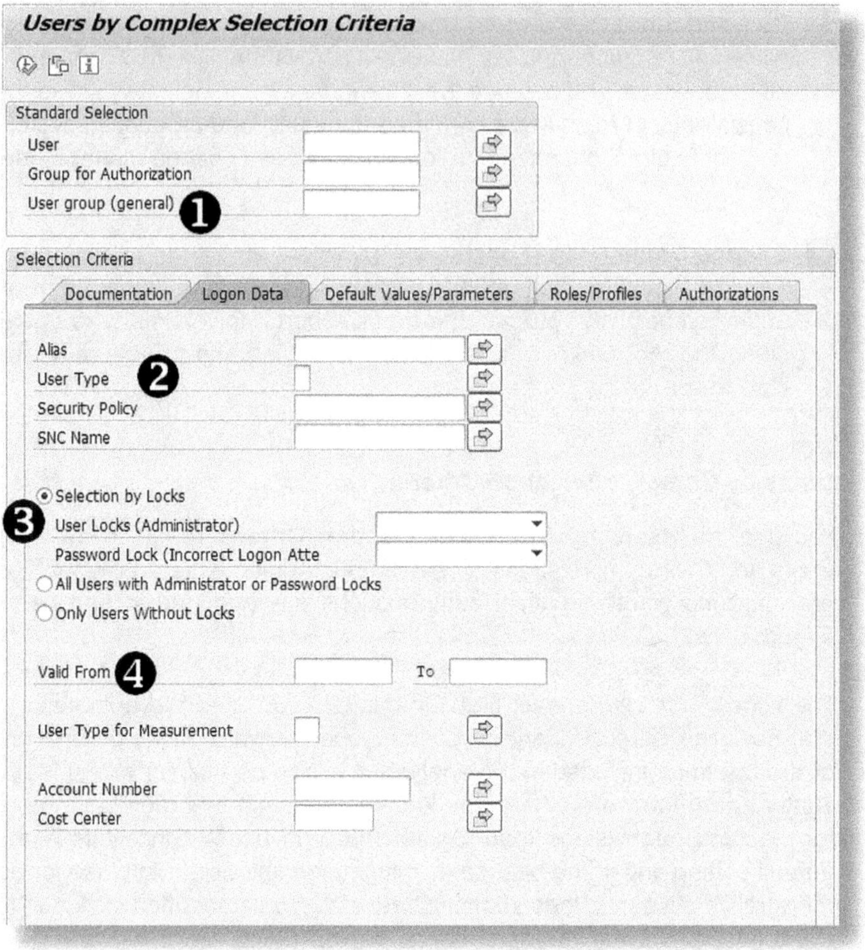

Figure 3.13: Users by Complex Selection Criteria—Logon Data tab

The second important tab within this report is AUTHORIZATIONS. On this tab, you define the authorizations to be assessed. The decisive factor here is the SELECTION BY VALUES section: here you can define authorization objects that are to be analyzed, along with their field values. In the example in Figure 3.14, you want to determine which user the authorizations for user administration are granted to. To do this, you have to check who has access to transaction *SU01* (authorization object *S_TCODE*) with activity *01* and/ or *02* in the authorization object *S_USER_GRP*.

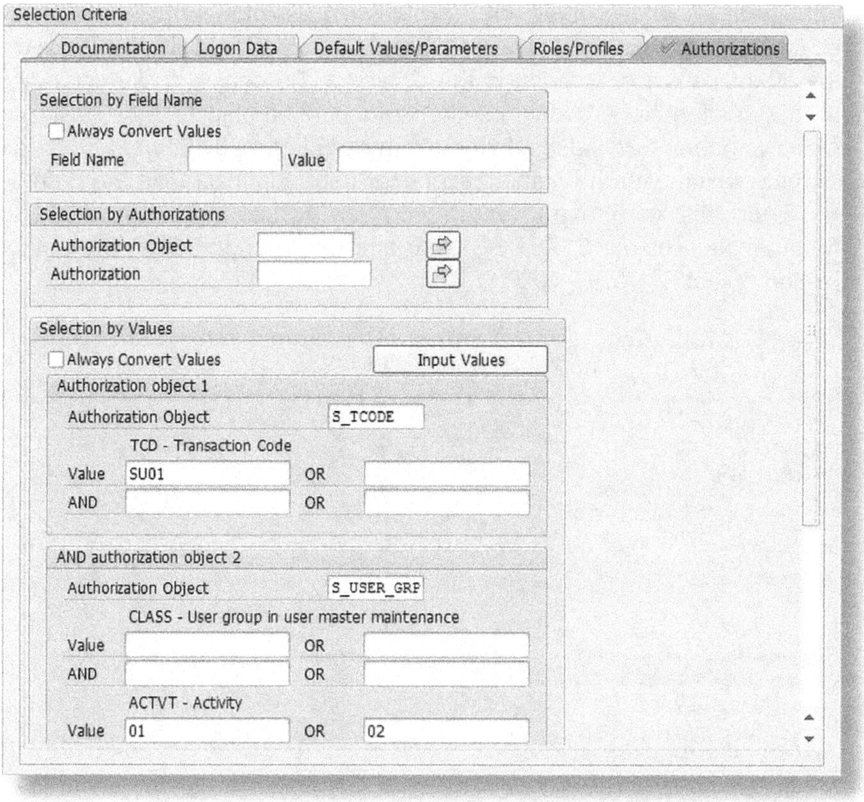

Figure 3.14: Users by Complex Selection Criteria—Authorizations tab

Once you have entered your filter criteria, initiate the analyses by clicking
EXECUTE or by pressing [F8].

Roles by Complex Selection Criteria

The **Roles by Complex Selection Criteria** report is very similar to the
report previously presented at user level.

In the STANDARD SELECTION section, you first determine which roles you want
to analyze. You can examine both individual roles and a variety of roles at
the same time. In the analysis, you can also exclude roles or include roles
that follow a specific naming scheme. Standard SAP roles that are not
used are often excluded. You can also specify the role type to include in
the analysis by selecting SINGLE ROLES or COMPOSITE ROLES. You can then

choose to show only roles that have a valid assignment to a user. However, as for the report **Users by Complex Selection Criteria**, the most important selection criterion is the SELECTION ACCORDING TO AUTHORIZATION VALUES section: here, you can define authorization objects to be analyzed, along with their field values. In the example in Figure 3.15, you want to determine which user the authorizations for user administration are granted to. To do this, you have to check who has access to transaction *SU01* (authorization object *S_TCODE*) with activity *01* and/or *02* in the authorization object *S_USER_GRP*.

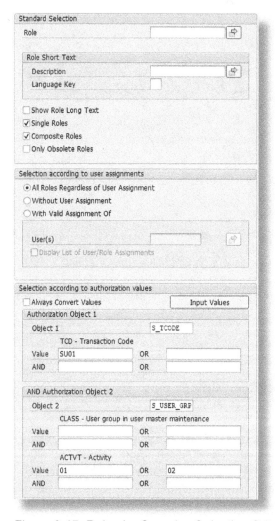

Figure 3.15: Roles by Complex Selection Criteria

Comparisons: Of Roles/Of Users

The COMPARISON, as the name suggests, allows you to compare different components of the authorization system, such as users, roles, or profiles. The exciting thing about the comparison functionality within transaction SUIM is that it also works across systems. We will introduce this in the following example (Figure 3.16). In this analysis, for one role the status in the quality assurance system is compared with the status in the production system. To do this, in the RFC DESTINATION FOR SYSTEM A field, enter *P-SYSTEM* and in the RFC DESTINATION FOR SYSTEM B field, enter *D-SYSTEM* ❶. Then, in the ROLE A and ROLE B fields, enter the role name. In this example, *Z_ESPRESSO_TEST* ❷ in both systems. After completing the selection, run the report by clicking EXECUTE ❸ or by pressing F8 .

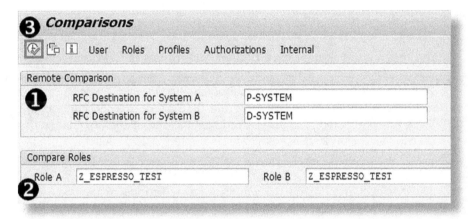

Figure 3.16: Role comparison selection screen

The result of the role comparison, shown in Figure 3.17, shows similarities and differences between the roles analyzed. A green light in the COMPARISON column means that the respective authorization object is contained in both roles with identical field values. A yellow light ❶ here means that the respective authorization object is contained in both roles, but that the field values are not identical. A red light ❷ means that in one of the two systems, the respective authorization object does not exist at all in the role.

Selection Overview as Table

	Role:	Client:	System:
Role A	Z_ESPRESSO_TEST	100	P-SYSTEM
Role B	Z_ESPRESSO_TEST	100	Q-SYSTEM

Comparison Object		Z_ESPRESSO_TEST	Z_ESPRESSO_TEST	Authorization Object Name
CC☐	PLOG	☐	☐	Personnel Planning
CC☐	S_SECPOL	☐	☐	Security Policy
CC☐	S_TCODE	☐	☐	Transaction Code Check at Transaction Start
C✕O **①**	S_USER_AGR	☐	☐	Authorizations: Role Check
CC☐	S_USER_AUT	☐	☐	User Master Maintenance: Authorizations
CC☐	S_USER_GRP	☐	☐	User Master Maintenance: User Groups
✕CO **②**	S_USER_PRO	☐	◉	User Master Maintenance: Authorization Profile
CC☐	S_USER_SAS	☐	☐	User Master Maintenance: System-Specific Assignments
CC☐	S_USER_SYS	☐	☐	User Master Maintenance: System for Central User Maintenance

Figure 3.17: Results of the role comparison

Change Documents: For Users/For Roles

The last area of transaction SUIM we will explain is CHANGE DOCUMENTS. The individual types of change documents and the respective analysis options are quite different. Here, we introduce the DISPLAY CHANGE DOCUMENTS FOR ROLE ADMINISTRATION screen (Figure 3.18). If one of the controls and test steps presented in Chapter 4 requires the use of another change document, this will be discussed in detail in the respective section.

On the DISPLAY CHANGE DOCUMENTS FOR ROLE ADMINISTRATION screen, you can initially select only change documents for specific roles or exclude certain roles via the selection (ROLE NAME field). You can also restrict the selection to documents changed by a specific person (CHANGED BY field). Finally, you can specify a period for which change documents are selected (FROM DATE/ FROM TIME and TO DATE/TO TIME fields).

In the case of roles, a wide variety of change documents is offered (Figure 3.18), containing either different information or different levels of detail. From an audit perspective, the following change documents are particularly useful: OVERVIEW OF CHANGE DOCUMENTS (basic overview of what was changed in a role), AUTHORIZATION DATA (overview of, amongst other things, changed transactions, authorization objects, and field values), or ROLE ASSIGNMENT FOR USERS (overview of when a role was assigned to a user).

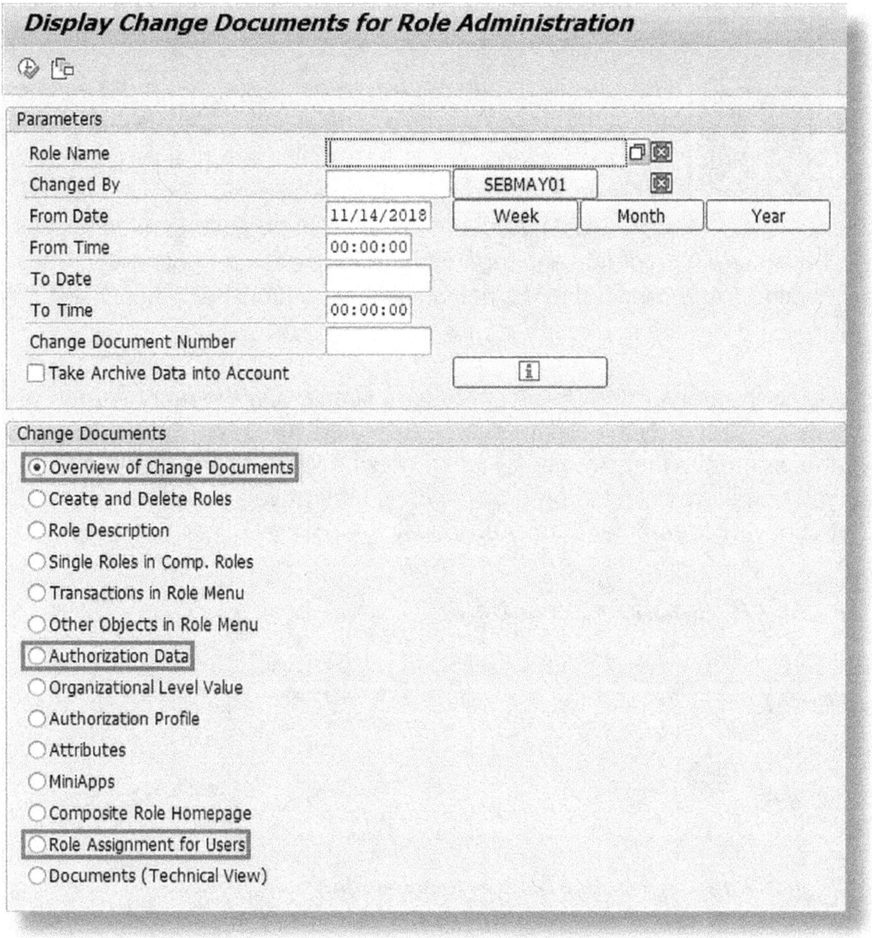

Figure 3.18: Change documents for role administration

3.3   Transaction SA38: ABAP program execution

Transaction SA38 is one of the most powerful transactions in an SAP system. With this transaction, you can execute any program provided you have the necessary permissions to do so. Since SAP offers a large number of audit-related and supportive programs, transaction SA38 offers an entry point to those programs.

Permission within transaction SA38

 From an audit perspective in particular, you must ensure that authorizations within transaction SA38 are adequate. The permissions in this transaction are mainly controlled by the authorization objects S_PROGRAM and S_ PROGNAM. Auditors should also be authorized to access only certain programs and reports. Extensive access rights within transaction SA38 can lead to the risk of system controls being bypassed.

Using the transaction, however, is very simple. On the entry screen (Figure 3.19), specify the program to be executed ❶. Then, you can execute the program either directly ❷ or by clicking WITH VARIANT ❸. In a variant, you can store selected program options so that you can reuse them without having to re-enter them individually.

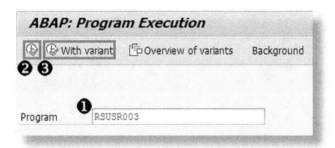

Figure 3.19: Transaction SA38—initial screen

Transaction SE38 in comparison with transaction SA38

 Transaction SE38 is even more powerful than transaction SA38 as this transaction allows you, for example, to create or change programs. Therefore, it is highly recommended on the one hand to not use this transaction for audit purposes, and on the other hand, to strictly restrict user access to and use of this transaction to production environments. This transaction should be used only by developers.

3.4 Transaction SAIS: Audit Information System

Finally, we would like to introduce transaction SAIS. This is the transaction for the *Audit Information System (AIS)*. The AIS was available in previous NetWeaver releases of SAP but has since been replaced by a role-based model and has now been reintroduced since SAP NetWeaver release 7.4. The AIS allows you to structure audit-related reports in menus, give auditors access to these reports, and to document the results of the audit tests performed.

To use the AIS, you have to first create an *audit structure*, also called an *area menu*. You use an audit structure to allocate reports and transactions that are required for specific audit purposes. To do this, open transaction SAIS and click AUDIT STRUCTURE (as shown in Figure 3.20) (alternatively, you can use transaction SE43).

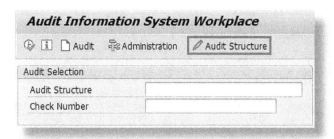

Figure 3.20: Creating an audit structure—step 1

On the AREA MENU MAINTENANCE screen, where you maintain audit structures, you have to create a new area menu. Specify a name for the area menu ❶ and then click CREATE ❷ (Figure 3.21).

Figure 3.21: Creating an audit structure—step 2

The next step is to fill the area menu with content. Two approaches are particularly worth mentioning in this context. Via the path EDIT • INSERT MENU ENTRY, you can integrate individual transactions and reports into the area menu. If, for example, you want to audit users and authorizations, you can integrate relevant reports and transactions, such as report RSUSR003 (standard user password status) or transaction SUIM (User Information System) into the area menu.

Since this approach is very time-consuming, you can also transfer the menu of specific roles to the area menu. In particular, you can use roles that have been provided by SAP for the role-based Audit Information System for this purpose. These are still available in newer releases. Follow the path EDIT • IMPORT • ROLE MENU. In the example shown in Figure 3.22, the menu of the role SAP_AUDITOR_SA was imported. The reports and transactions contained in the role menu were automatically added to the area menu Z_ESPRESSO_TUTORIALS_1.

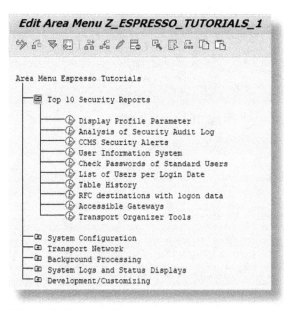

Figure 3.22: Creating an audit structure—step 3

Now that you have created the audit structure, you can initiate an audit. To do this, select the relevant audit structure ❶ (Figure 3.23). Then, define a check number ❷; this allows you to use audit structures multiple times (e.g., initial audit equals check number 1, follow-up audit equals check number 2). To create a new audit, click AUDIT ❸. Once you have created the audit, you can start it by clicking EXECUTE ❹.

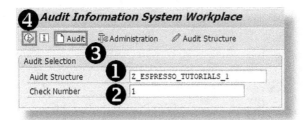

Figure 3.23: Initiating an audit

You are now in the *audit cockpit*. The audit cockpit lists all reports and transactions that have been added to the audit structure. By clicking EXECUTE ❶ next to the relevant report (Figure 3.24), you can go directly to the respective SAP report. For example, clicking EXECUTE next to CHECK PASSWORDS OF STANDARD USERS opens report RSUSR003 in a new session. After performing the analysis within the opened report or transaction, you can then document the results of the check in the audit cockpit. First, record the check status ❷, that is, whether findings or issues were identified and, if so, their weighting. Second, you can enter detailed information about the test step(s) in a free-text field ❸. Click SAVE ENTRY ❹ to save the documentation of the check results.

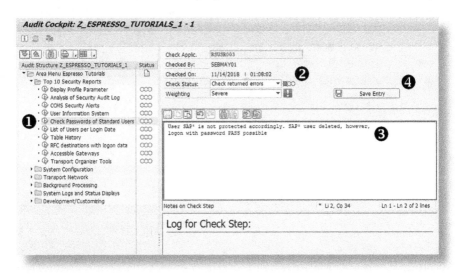

Figure 3.24: Audit cockpit—step 1

As soon as you have saved the entries, a log entry (LOG FOR CHECK STEP) ❶ (Figure 3.25) is created automatically. You cannot change this log entry. The status and date of execution are also displayed in the audit structure ❷.

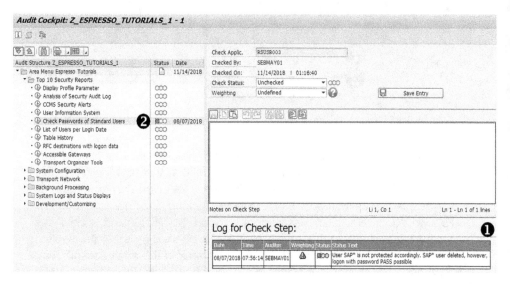

Figure 3.25: Audit cockpit—step 2

In our view, the Audit Information System is particularly interesting if you perform recurrent audits in an SAP environment, such as SOX management control testing, which is done, for example, every quarter, and which uses the same reports again and again. In this case, the relevant reports can be allocated to an audit structure and the respective executions can be documented with individual check numbers.

4 Technical steps for auditing SAP systems

This chapter is the core part of this book. It explains 12 of the most important audit steps in SAP systems with appropriate system walk-throughs. All of the audit steps described follow the same structure. The first part of each section looks at a specific control in the SAP system, provides background information, and explains the underlying risk to point out why an appropriate implementation of controls is necessary. We then demonstrate test steps for evaluating the effectiveness of the respective controls in SAP systems. Finally, we examine critical authorizations for each control area which should be checked during an audit.

4.1 Change management

4.1.1 Background to the control and associated risk

Change management is one of the key elements for ensuring that all IT adaptations are implemented in a controlled manner and that risks of negative impacts when running business services supported by information technologies are minimized. To accomplish this, a change management process must be defined and implemented. Typically, this process covers the following key process steps and controls:

- ▶ Change requests must be formally requested
- ▶ Change requests must be formally approved by the IT department as well as by business stakeholders
- ▶ Changes to information technologies must be tested by both the IT department and business stakeholders before going live
- ▶ Changes must be formally accepted before being deployed in a production environment

> ## Associated risk: Request for and testing and acceptance of changes
>
> If an appropriate IT change management framework is not established, changes to the SAP system may neither be performed efficiently nor are risks of negative impacts to the availability, confidentiality, or integrity of business-critical data sufficiently mitigated or managed.

In the following, we will introduce key controls in SAP systems for ensuring that steps and control points required by the change management process are enforced through the system:

▶ **System and client changeability**
SAP has an option that prevents direct changes to production systems and production clients. Appropriate implementation of this option in the SAP system is key to ensuring that changes are made using change management processes. If production systems and clients cannot be changed, developers have no other option than to make amendments in a development system.

> ## Associated risk: System and client changeability
>
> If there is no assurance that SAP production environments are protected against direct modifications, defined change management controls can be bypassed to implement unauthorized changes which may negatively impact productive systems.

▶ **System separation**
The development environment must be separated from the production environment either logically or physically. Good practices recommend using an environment consisting of development, test, and production systems which are either logically or physically separated.

Associated risk: System separation

 If productive and non-productive systems are not separated, the correctness of changes cannot be evaluated independently of productive systems. As a result, unknown errors that result in negative impacts on data integrity or system stability have a direct impact on productive systems.

▶ **Transport route**
To further facilitate change management processes, SAP provides the **Transport Management System**. Transports are used to transfer changes from a non-production environment to a production system without manual system adjustments. This mechanism ensures that changes can only be implemented in a non-production environment and transferred to a production instance using an automatic mechanism.

Associated risk: Transport route

 If no automated transportation mechanisms are used to support change control, change migration requires manual interaction, resulting in higher control efforts and higher susceptibility to errors. As a result, changes may be migrated erroneously and may negatively impact productive systems.

▶ **Segregation of duties**
Development and migration duties must be separated. If this were not the case, controls within the change management process, such as the dual control principle, could be circumvented by having the developer transport changes to subsequent systems without further testing or approval by an independent third party. The optimal solution is that an automated approval and release process for migrating transports into the production environment is implemented.

Associated risk: Segregation of duties

If there is no segregation of duties in the area of change development and customization as well as change migration, changes are not required to be independently reviewed and approved, thereby increasing the risk of fraudulent activities as well as negative impacts on productive systems due to unauthorized change migration.

4.1.2 Test steps in SAP systems

System and client changeability

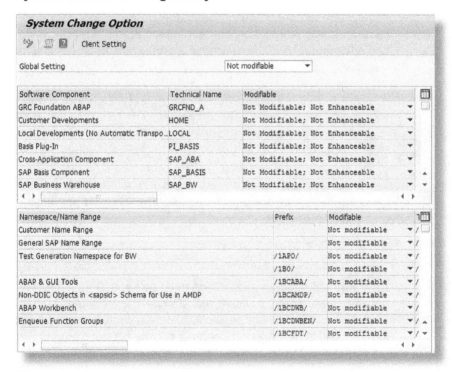

Figure 4.1: System changeability

To check whether an SAP production system has been set to *Not modifiable*, open transaction SE06, RSWBO004, or SCTS_RSWBO004, or execute program RSWBO004 in transaction SA38. In the GLOBAL SETTING field, as shown in Figure 4.1, you define whether or not an SAP system, or, more precisely, the repository and cross-client tables, can be changed.

In this field, the following two options are available:

▶ *Not modifiable*: No changes can be made to repository or cross-client tables.

▶ *Modifiable*: Changes to repository or cross-client tables are allowed, except for the software components and namespace/name ranges that are individually set to *Not Modifiable; Not Enhanceable*, or *Not modifiable*.

The changeability of client-specific tables is controlled within the client settings. These can be accessed by opening transaction SCC4, selecting your company-specific production client ❶, and clicking DETAILS ❷, as shown in Figure 4.2.

Display View "Clients": Overview

Client	Name	City	Crcy	Changed on
000	SAP AG Konzern	Walldorf	EUR	
001	Protiviti US	Houston	USD	08/14/2018
066	Test EarlyWatch Profiles	Walldorf	EUR	05/08/2018
100	Protiviti Europe	Frankfurt	EUR	08/27/2018
200	Protiviti Sandbox	Houston	USD	10/08/2018

Figure 4.2: Client changeability: overview of existing clients

Figure 4.3 provides an overview of the settings that you can choose in the client administration. As a first step ❶, you have to specify the client role:

▶ *Production*: Technical control that prevents clients being deleted or overwritten by client copies. **Mandatory for (all) production client(s)**.

▶ *Test*: Indicator of the test environment; no technical control assigned to this role.

▶ *Customizing*: Indicator of the test environment; no technical control assigned to this role.

▶ *Demo*: Indicator of the test environment; no technical control assigned to this role.

▶ *Training/Education*: Indicator of the training environment; no technical control assigned to this role.

▶ *SAP Reference*: Flag for clients delivered by SAP: 000 and 066.

Secondly ❷, you can determine how changes and transports for client-specific objects are handled:

▶ CHANGES WITHOUT AUTOMATIC RECORDING: Client-specific changes can be made but are not automatically recorded in a transport request. This can be done manually. **For sandbox or training systems only**.

▶ AUTOMATIC RECORDING OF CHANGES: Client-specific changes can be made and are automatically recorded in a transport request. **For development systems only**.

▶ NO CHANGES ALLOWED: Client-specific changes are not allowed and are technically prevented. **For production and test systems**.

▶ CHANGES W/O AUTOMATIC RECORDING, NO TRANSPORTS ALLOWED: Client-specific changes can be made but cannot be recorded in a transport request either automatically or manually. **For sandbox or training systems only**.

Thirdly ❸, the CROSS-CLIENT OBJECT CHANGES area contains the definition of whether cross-client objects can be changed. This setting only has a direct influence when the global system changeability is set to *Modifiable* (please refer to the previous control/paragraph).

▶ *Changes to repository and cross-client Customizing allowed*: No restrictions, changes to repository and cross-client customizing allowed. **For development, sandbox, or training systems only**.

► *No changes to cross-client customizing objects*: Changes to cross-client customizing objects are not allowed and are technically prevented. However, repository objects can be changed. **For development systems only**.

► *No changes to repository objects*: Changes to cross-client repository objects are not allowed and are technically prevented. However, cross-client customizing objects can be changed. **For development systems only**.

► *No changes to repository and cross-client customizing objs*: Changes to repository and cross-client customizing objects are not allowed and are technically prevented. **For production and test systems**.

Finally, the level for the CLIENT COPY AND COMPARISON TOOL PROTECTION setting ❹ must be defined. This setting allows the specification of whether the client is protected against being overwritten by a client copy and whether the client is protected against read access from other clients (e.g., table comparison):

► *Protection level 0: No restriction*: Client is not protected against being overwritten and external read access. **For sandbox or training systems only**.

► *Protection level 1: No overwriting*: Client is protected against being overwritten. However, external read access is not restricted. **Minimum protection level for production clients. Should also be chosen for development and test clients.**

► *Protection level 2: No overwriting, no external availability*: Client is protected against being overwritten and external read access. **To be chosen if very sensitive information is stored within a production client.**

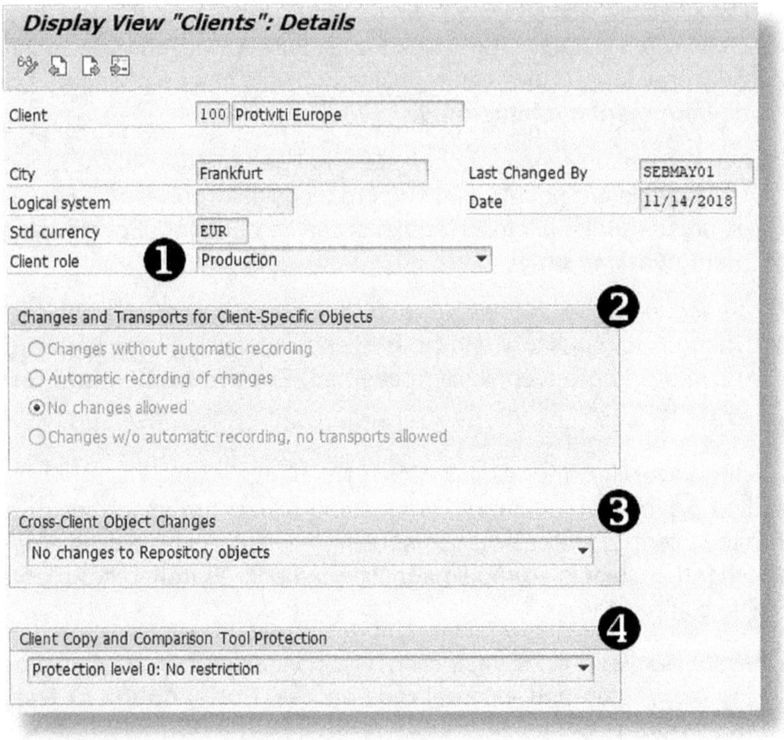

Figure 4.3: Client changeability settings

In addition to evaluating whether the system and client changeability settings are currently appropriate, you should also check whether these settings have been changed from protected to unprotected during the audit period. If this is the case, ask for documentation of the system or client opening, which should include at least an approval (e.g., by the system owner), a description of the need for opening, and documentation of the changes made. Assess the documentation for appropriateness and completeness.

To perform this test step, proceed as follows:

► **System changeability**
   Use transaction SE06, RSWBO004, or SCTS_RSWBO004, or execute program RSWBO004 in transaction SA38. Click on the log button (outlined in Figure 4.4) to access the system changeability change history. To see the exact change date and the user who performed the change, expand all entries in this overview.

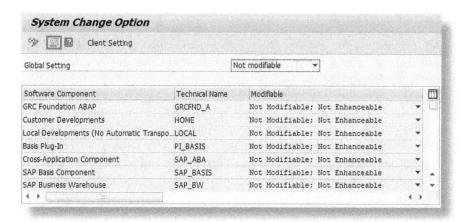

Figure 4.4: Transaction RSWBO004: change history

▶ **Client changeability**

Use transaction SCU3 (evaluation of change logs) and display changes to table T000. In particular, the fields CCCORACTIV/ CORR.SYS. (changes and transports for client-specific objects, recommendation = 2) and CCNOCLIIND/NoCRsCLI/No CROSS-CLI-ENT (maintenance authorization for objects in all clients, recommendation = 3) are relevant (Figure 4.5).

Evaluation of change logs

Techn. information   Logging: Display status

Customizing Objects: Change Logs

Clients
Technical Name: T000

Date :   11/14/2018   User: SEBMAY01

	Key Fields	Function Fields, Changed	
Time	Client	Field Name Old	New
01:30:50	100	Corr. sys.	2
		NoCrsCli	2
		CHANGEUSER MARGGE01	SEBMAY01
		CHANGEDATE 08/27/2018	11/14/2018
01:31:09	100	Role C	P

Figure 4.5: Transaction SCU3: changes to table T000

System separation

After analyzing the system changeability, you must check whether there are separate systems for developing and testing changes and for the production environment.

Ask whether the SAP environment at the party being audited contains dedicated systems for development, testing, and production. Open table TPFID within transaction SE16 or SE16N in each system. Compare the host of your production system (as depicted in Figure 4.6) with the host of your development and your test environment and check whether the systems are separate.

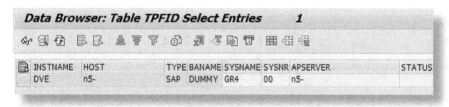

Figure 4.6: Review of system separation: table TPFID

Transport route

To find out whether the transport route has been defined appropriately, open transaction STMS and click TRANSPORT ROUTES (icon outlined in Figure 4.7).

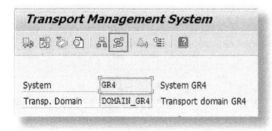

Figure 4.7: Transport Management System: opening a transport route

An overview showing the transport route(s) currently implemented is displayed, as illustrated in Figure 4.8. Transport routes should be implemented following your company's requirements and no unintended detours should be used to transport changes to a production system.

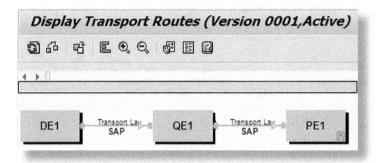

Figure 4.8: Transport route

Segregation of duties

To check whether an individual has the ability to implement changes in a development environment as well as to release or import changes into a production environment, first open transaction SUIM in your **development system** and navigate through the menu: USER INFORMATION SYSTEM • USER • USERS BY COMPLEX SELECTION CRITERIA • USERS BY COMPLEX SELECTION CRITERIA. Check who can either develop or customize your development instance (for further information regarding transaction SUIM and how to use the report **Users by Complex Selection Criteria**, please refer to Section 3.2).

▶ **Application development**

Authorization object	Field	Field value
S_TCODE	TCD	Various, e.g., SE80, SE38 (...)
S_DEVELOP	ACTVT	01 or 02 or 06 or 07 (...)
	OBJTYPE	PROG or TABL or TRAN or DEVC or DEBUG (...)

▶ **Customizing**

Authorization object	Field	Field value
S_TCODE	TCD	Various, e.g., SPRO, SM30 (…)
S_TABU_DIS	ACTVT	02

or

Authorization object	Field	Field value
S_TCODE	TCD	Various, e.g., SPRO, SM30 (…)
S_TABU_NAM	ACTVT	02

Then check who has the authorization to either release transports in the **quality assurance system**, if transports are automatically imported into production after they are released in this system, or who has the permission to manually import transports into the **productive system** if transports are imported manually rather than automatically.

▶ **Release of transports requests**

Authorization object	Field	Field value
S_TCODE	TCD	SE01 or SE09 or SE10
S_TRANSPRT	ACTVT	43
	TTYPE	DTRA

▶ **Import of transports requests**

Authorization object	Field	Field value
S_TCODE	TCD	STMS
S_CTS_ADMI	CTS_ADMFCT	IMPS or IMPA

or

Authorization object	Field	Field value
S_TCODE	TCD	STMS
S_CTS_SADM	CTS_ADMFCT	IMPS or IMPA

If an individual has the ability to do both—that is, develop or customize in your development environment and, based on your SAP setup, to either release transports or to import transports into the production environment—this constitutes an SoD violation.

Find out whether transports are imported automatically

 To find out whether transports are imported automatically within a specific SAP system, first open the menu EDIT • SYSTEM • CHANGE in transaction STMS. Check whether the transport strategy is set to *Queue-controlled transports/Mass transports*. If this is the case, open transaction SM37 and check whether the job TMS_*TMS_TP_IMPORT is scheduled periodically. If this is also the case, transports are automatically imported into this SAP instance.

In addition to the manual or automated transport of changes, SAP also offers the option of integrating a release process into transport management. Once implemented, all transports must be approved in the quality assurance system by one, two, or three different approvers before they can reach the production environment (again, either through automated or manual imports).

Quality assurance approval procedure

 The quality assurance approval procedure can be used only if the system landscape consists of at least three instances (development, quality assurance, and production)—referred to as a three-tier environment.

To check whether the quality assurance approval procedure is used in the SAP landscape of your company and to assess how this process has been designed, open transaction STMS and navigate through the menu OVERVIEW • SYSTEMS (Figure 4.9).

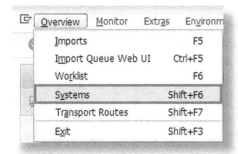

Figure 4.9: Navigating to the QA approval procedure—step 1

In the system overview, open the menu GOTO • TRANSPORT DOMAIN (Figure 4.10).

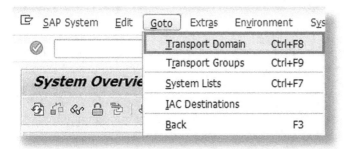

Figure 4.10: Navigating to the QA approval procedure—step 2

The TMS configuration of your transport domain is now displayed. Open the QA APPROVAL PROCEDURE tab, as shown in Figure 4.11. In this example, no QA system is defined ❶. This means that the QA approval procedure is not used in this SAP system. However, you can decide between three different approval types within the QA approval procedure that you can activate individually ❷:

▶ System administration: approval by the system administrator(s)

▶ Department: approval by the business department for which a change is implemented

▶ Request owner: approval by the technical owner of a transport request, often the developer; rarely used in practice, since the transport must already be released per se in the development system.

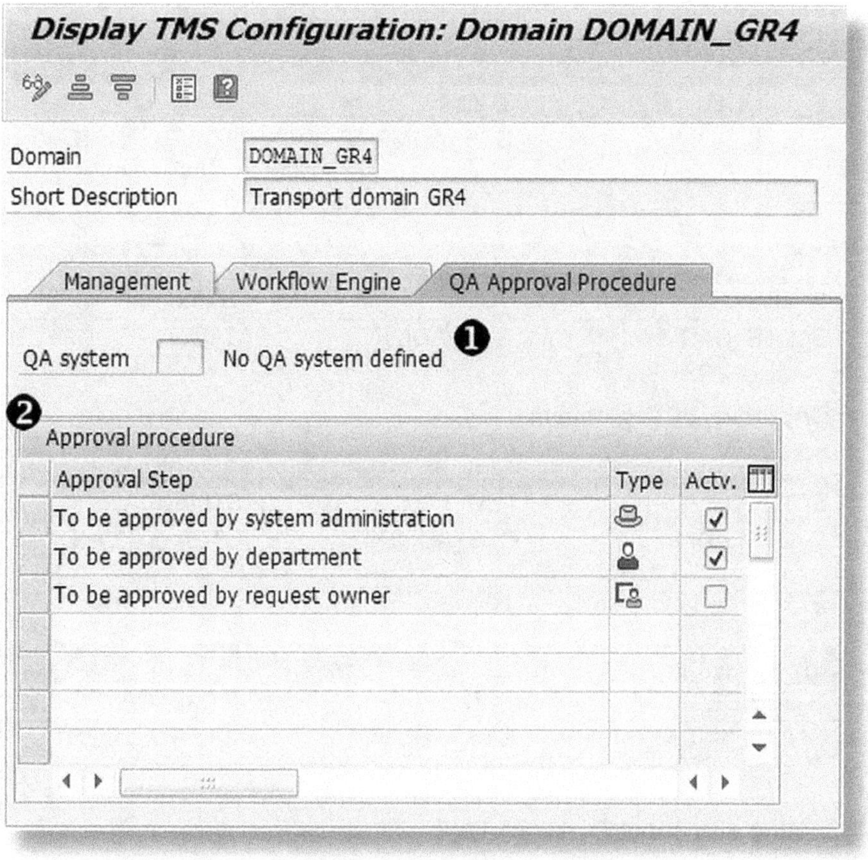

Display TMS Configuration: Domain DOMAIN_GR4

Domain	DOMAIN_GR4
Short Description	Transport domain GR4

Management **Workflow Engine** **QA Approval Procedure**

QA system [ ] No QA system defined ❶

❷ Approval procedure

Approval Step	Type	Actv.
To be approved by system administration	🖳	☑
To be approved by department	🧑	☑
To be approved by request owner	🗐	☐

Figure 4.11: TMS configuration—QA approval procedure

To be able to grant approvals as system administration or a department, the respective users must be provided with sufficient authorizations. To the previously presented assessment of the functional separation between developers and individuals who are able to release or import transports, we must now add the determination of who belongs to the system administration or department approval groups and who has the permissions to approve transports in the QA system (this applies to the approval stage system administration and department)—especially if transports are automatically imported into the production system after approval has been granted in the quality assurance system. Therefore, you must check whether a developer also has one of the following permissions:

▶ **Approval by system administration**

Authorization object	Field	Field value
S_TCODE	TCD	STMS_QA
S_CTS_ADMI	CTS_ADMFCT	TQAS

or

Authorization object	Field	Field value
S_TCODE	TCD	STMS_QA
S_CTS_SADM	CTS_ADMFCT	TQAS

▶ **Approval by department**

Authorization object	Field	Field value
S_TCODE	TCD	STMS_QA
S_CTS_ADMI	CTS_ADMFCT	QTEA or TQAS

or

Authorization object	Field	Field value
S_TCODE	TCD	STMS_QA
S_CTS_SADM	CTS_ADMFCT	QTEA or TQAS

Testing and approval of changes

Finally, you must check whether all transports that entered the production system have been sufficiently tested and approved beforehand. To do this, compare a sample of imported transports to the test and approval documentation. To extract the population of transports imported into a production system, open transaction STMS and click Import Overview (icon outlined in Figure 4.12).

Next, select your production system ❶ and click Import History ❷, as illustrated in Figure 4.13.

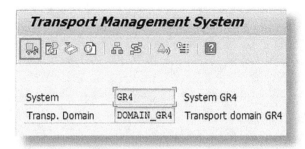

Figure 4.12: Transport Management System: opening the import overview

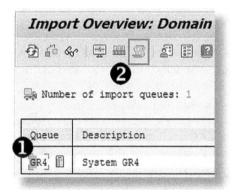

Figure 4.13: Transport Management System: opening the import history

An overview (Figure 4.14) of all transports is shown for a specified time interval (you can change the time interval to meet your requirements). The first two columns provide information on when the transport was imported into the production system. The REQUEST column shows a unique transport ID, which should be linked to external references so that appropriate testing and approval can be traced. In the last column, RC, the import status is presented. A green light indicates that a transport was imported without errors, a yellow light indicates an imported transport with warnings, and a red light shows that a transport was not successfully imported into the production system.

Import History: System GR4

Entries for GR4: 43   11/14/2018 02:12:17

Time Interval 06/06/16 00:00:00 to 11/14/18 24:00:00

Date	Time	Request	Owner	Short Text	RC
06/09/16	13:57:01	SAPKITAB9Q	SAPUSER	Servicetools for SAP Basis 731	△
06/09/16	15:36:50	SAPKD74061	SAP	SPAM/SAINT Update - Version 740/0061	△
06/09/16	15:52:37	SAPKD75061	SAP	SAP_OCS 750: SP 0061	△
07/23/16	10:04:46	LM1K000099	SAP	SUNM empty	▣
07/23/16	11:25:24	SAPK701EHP	SAP	EHP-Installer Toolimport - Version 17 Patch Level 31	▣
07/23/16	11:25:46	SAPK731EI2	SAP	ICNV tools - Version 17 Patch Level 1	▣
07/23/16	11:26:14	SAPK731ESQ	SAP	Upgrade SQL Templates - Version 17 Patch Level 4	▣
07/23/16	11:26:15	B5SK011625	SAP	rsupgrcheck for SUM	▨
07/24/16	09:20:44	SAPK742EDL	DDIC	Deletion request for upgrade components: 091707,20160724:Sup	△
07/25/16	17:51:35	SAPK-V1112INGRCFNDA	SAP	GRCFND_A V1100: SP 0012	△
07/25/16	17:55:32	SAPK-V1113INGRCFNDA	SAP	GRCFND_A V1100: SP 0013	△

Figure 4.14: Overview of the transport import history

Select a sample of transports and check whether they have been appropriately tested and approved—for example, by the requester or by a functional person responsible.

If the quality assurance approval procedure is as described in the previous section, you can check directly in the SAP system whether changes have been approved appropriately. To do so, select your QA system ❶ and click on the QA worklist icon ❷ (Figure 4.15).

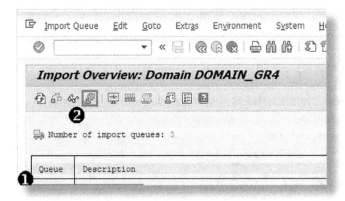

Figure 4.15 : QA worklist history—step 1

Then, click the QA history button (outlined in Figure 4.16).

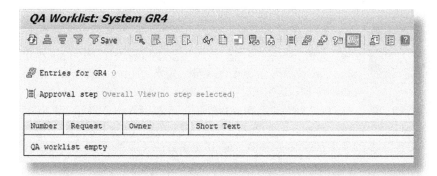

Figure 4.16: QA worklist history—step 2

Finally, select a transport ❶ and click the QA status ❷.

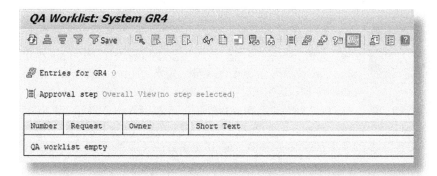

Figure 4.17: QA worklist history—step 3

The results will show whether a transport has been approved and, if yes, who the approver(s) was (were). This information can, on the one hand, be used to check whether transports have generally been approved, but on the other hand also to check whether the segregation of duties requirements described in the previous section are fulfilled by assessing if the persons that have approved a transport are not identical to the owner of the transport or to the persons that developed the content that is included in the transport.

> ### QA approval history table
>
> QA approvals are also stored centrally in a table. The name of the table is TMSQWLFH. Therefore, instead of the method shown here via transaction STMS, you can also simply open the content of this table through transactions SE16 or SE16N. Here, although the presentation is less lucid, you can view the approvals for a variety of transports in a single overview.

4.1.3   Critical access rights

The access rights listed in this section are considered as critical in the area of change management. Therefore, check that the transactions and associated authorization objects detailed below are granted only to appropriate users by using the report **Users by Complex Selection Criteria** in transaction SUIM (for further information, please refer to Section 3.2).

> ### Reporting transactions
>
> In addition to the transactions presented below (and in the following sections) which enable users to execute a certain functionality in SAP, you can also use these functionalities through one of the numerous reporting transactions (e.g., transaction SE38). The assessment of the combination of transaction (authorization object S_TCODE) and underlying authorization objects used should therefore be considered only the initial test step with regards to critical authorizations. However, the recommendation is that in a next step, you perform checks without focusing on transactions and instead, only on the underlying authorization objects—for example, to also catch reporting transactions or to cover customer-created transactions that allow the same functionalities as a standard SAP transaction.

▶ **Maintain system changeability**

Authorization object	Field	Field value
S_TCODE	TCD	SE06, RSWBO004, SCTS_RSWBO004, or S_ALR_87101269
S_CTS_ADMI	CTS_ADMFCT	SYSC

or

Authorization object	Field	Field value
S_TCODE	TCD	SE06, RSWBO004, SCTS_RSWBO004, or S_ALR_87101269
S_CTS_SADM	CTS_ADMFCT	SYSC

▶ **Maintain client changeability**

Authorization object	Field	Field value
S_TCODE	TCD	SCC4
S_TABU_DIS	ACTVT	02
	DICBERCLS	SS
S_TABU_CLI	CLIIDMAINT	X

or

Authorization object	Field	Field value
S_TCODE	TCD	SCC4
S_TABU_NAM	ACTVT	02
	TABLE	T000
S_TABU_CLI	CLIIDMAINT	X

▶ **Maintain transport route**

Authorization object	Field	Field value
S_TCODE	TCD	STMS or STMS_PATH
S_CTS_ADMI	CTS_ADMFCT	TABL

or

Authorization object	Field	Field value
S_TCODE	TCD	STMS or STMS_PATH
S_CTS_SADM	CTS_ADMFCT	TABL

► **Release of transport requests**

Authorization object	Field	Field value
S_TCODE	TCD	SE01, SE09, or SE10
S_TRANSPRT	ACTVT	43
	TTYPE	DTRA (workbench requests) or CUST (customizing requests)

► **Import of transports requests**

Authorization object	Field	Field value
S_TCODE	TCD	STMS, STMS_IMPORT, or STMS_QUEUES
S_CTS_ADMI	CTS_ADMFCT	IMPS or IMPA

or

Authorization object	Field	Field value
S_TCODE	TCD	STMS, STMS_IMPORT, or STMS_QUEUES
S_CTS_SADM	CTS_ADMFCT	IMPS or IMPA

► **Deletion of transport requests**

Authorization object	Field	Field value
S_TCODE	TCD	STMS
S_CTS_ADMI	CTS_ADMFCT	TDEL

or

Authorization object	Field	Field value
S_TCODE	TCD	STMS
S_CTS_SADM	CTS_ADMFCT	TDEL

4.2 Development management

4.2.1 Background to the control and associated risk

Closely related to the process and controls of change management, as described in the previous Section 4.1, is *development management*. Whereas change management aims to ensure that only approved, tested, and appropriate changes are made available in an SAP productive system, the goal of development management is to ensure that certain good practices are generally followed in developments in SAP systems.

Good practices in the field of SAP developments are as diverse as the configuration of a new car. Therefore, in this chapter, the focus is on essentials to bear in mind when developing and customizing in SAP systems.

> **Developments vs. customizing**
>
> The term **development** means the implementation of customer-specific code by programming in an SAP system (for example, developing your own report for uploading specific master data if SAP does not provide standard functionality for this). **Customizing** means setting SAP functionality in terms of company requirements (definition of a tax type to be applied or a specific depreciation method).

The first thing to clarify is the question of who is allowed to develop in an SAP system at all. In addition to the required authorizations described in Section 4.2.3, an end user needs a *developer key* to implement programs in SAP. A developer key can be requested via SAP Marketplace and enables a specific user in a particular SAP system to implement developments in general. In addition to developer keys, there are *object keys*.

Developer and object keys in the context of S/4HANA

 In the new SAP ERP system, S/4HANA, developer and object keys are no longer necessary (described in SAP Note 2309060). Therefore, in S/4HANA systems, developers need only appropriate access rights to implement changes and to update SAP standard objects.

For non-S/4HANA SAP systems, developer and object keys are generated via SAP Marketplace and are always required if an SAP standard object is to be changed. Here, an individual object key is generated for each SAP standard object.

Generating developer and object keys

 In addition to generating developer and object keys via SAP Marketplace, there are other (not quite legal) ways to generate such keys. Of course, these options will not be explained in detail here. Nevertheless, it is important to point out that in addition to the appropriate and very restrictive assignment of developer and object keys, associated authorizations must be handled appropriately to prevent unintended developments.

Both developer keys and object keys overlap the areas of change management and development management. On the one hand, you can control who is generally allowed to develop in a system and who can make changes to the SAP standard code. On the other hand, both types of keys should be assigned only in an SAP development system, ensuring that the change management processes and controls described above are actually adhered to.

Developer and object keys on non-development instances

 There are cases in which developer keys and object keys must also be assigned to individuals in a test or a productive system. This is the case, for example, when an SAP system is upgraded. For this purpose, follow-up tasks must be performed in the respective systems and cannot be transported following the standard change management processes. If necessary, the assignment of developer and object keys must be explicitly approved and the approvals must be retained.

The following risk is associated with developer keys not being appropriately controlled in an SAP system.

Associated risk: Developer keys in production systems

 Developer keys are the prerequisite for performing development activities in an SAP system. Assigning developer keys to individuals in productive systems may result in changes being performed directly in production and, therefore, without ensuring that defined change controls are adhered to. Unauthorized changes implemented may negatively affect the system or be used for fraudulent activities.

The following risk is associated with object keys not being appropriately controlled in an SAP system.

Associated risk: Object keys

 Object keys are the prerequisite for changing standard SAP logic. Changes to standard SAP logic may have an adverse impact on system stability and functionality.

The implementation of customer developments in an SAP system can include different components. In addition to classical programming—in the case of SAP, in the object-oriented programming language *ABAP*—the creation of new (database) tables as well as the implementation of customer-specific transactions must also be mentioned. Each of these components has its own specific features and associated good practices, which we will look at later.

In ABAP, just like in any other programming language, there are also ways to consciously or unconsciously incorporate vulnerabilities into the code. The number of potential vulnerabilities related to this is so great that they cannot all be addressed in this book. One example of an ABAP code vulnerability is explained below.

Missing authority check

 In SAP systems, programs and functionalities are protected via authorizations. Only users to which the required authorizations have been assigned receive access to a specific functionality. The authorizations required for a particular transaction, program, or functionality are specified in the ABAP code using the command AUTHORITY-CHECK. If, for example, the authorization object S_USER_GRP with the activity (ACTVT) = 01 and the user group (CLASS) = SUPER is required to access a program developed by a customer, the authority check within the ABAP code would look as follows:

```
AUTHORITY-CHECK         OBJECT       'S_USER AGR'
      ID    'ACTVT'     FIELD        01
      ID    'CLASS'     FIELD        Z*
```

Therefore, for SAP customer developments, you must always ensure that an authorization check is taken into consideration within the custom ABAP code. If no such check is implemented in the code, there is a risk that unauthorized persons might gain access to a (potentially critical) function in the SAP system.

Every new and every further development should generally be checked for code weaknesses. A corresponding test step can be integrated into the change management process, for example. This ensures that malicious code cannot reach a productive system.

How to analyze your ABAP code

 SAP provides standard functionality for automatically scanning your ABAP code for specific vulnerabilities—the *ABAP Code Inspector*. We will explain this report as part of the test steps in Section 4.2.2. In addition to the aforementioned standard functionality, there are numerous tools that provide automated ABAP vulnerability analysis—for example, the *CodeProfiler* from Virtual Forge or the *Code Vulnerability Analyzer* from SAP. These tools, however, are not free of charge and must be purchased at a cost.

If new tables are created in your SAP system, you must take particular care to assign them to an *authorization group*. Although you can also grant access for individual tables only (using the authorization object S_TABU_NAM), this is very time-consuming as each individual table has to be entered in the authorization object. The goal should therefore be to grant access to tables via authorization groups (using the authorization object S_TABU_DIS). However, if you do not assign tables to a specific authorization group during creation, they are automatically added to the group **&NC& (Not Classified)**, which contains per se several hundred SAP standard tables. If you authorize end users for the authorization group &NC&, they will receive access to a large number of unnecessary tables in addition to the desired table access—a violation of the principle of least privilege.

Associated risk: Table authorization groups

 If authorization groups are not assigned to customer tables, access to these tables cannot be granted to users without violating the principle of least privilege or without extensive manual efforts with a higher susceptibility to error. As a result, individuals may gain unauthorized access to data.

Customer transactions must also be protected. This type of transaction must always be backed up by an additional authorization object. This ensures that end users can only access a customer transaction if, in addition to the transaction, the corresponding authorization object has been assigned to their accounts.

Associated risk: Customer transactions

 If authorization objects are not assigned to customer transactions, access to underlying programs cannot be managed efficiently (especially if there are no appropriate authority checks within the ABAP code), thus increasing the risk that these transactions and the corresponding data can be accessed by unauthorized personnel.

4.2.2 Test steps in an SAP system

Developer keys in production systems

To find out who a developer key is assigned to, open table DEVACCESS in transaction SE16 or transaction SE16N. On the selection screen, specify either a user name or a user name range that you want to check for the assignment of developer keys (field: UNAME) ❶; alternatively, specify a specific developer key to find out who the key is assigned to (field: ACCESSKEY) ❷. If you want an overview of all developer keys available, simply click EXECUTE ❸ or press F8 without entering any values in the fields UNAME or ACCESSKEY (depicted in Figure 4.18).

The result is an overview of all users that developer keys have been assigned to (Figure 4.19). For a development system, check that developer keys are assigned only to appropriate individuals. If you detect developer keys in a quality assurance or production environment, ask whether there is valid reason for this and whether a documented approval is available.

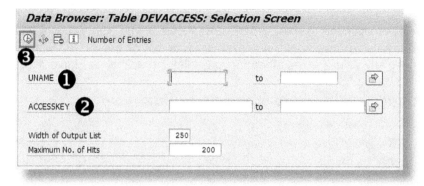

Figure 4.18: Table DEVACCESS: selection screen

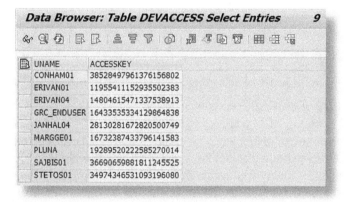

Figure 4.19: Table DEVACCESS: results

Object keys

The process for finding out who an object key is assigned to is similar to the process for developer keys. Open table ADIRACCESS in transaction SE16 or transaction SE16N. On the selection screen, specify either a program ID (field: PGMID) ❶, an object (field: OBJECT) ❷, or an object name (field: OBJ_NAME) ❸ that you want to check for object keys. You can also specify a specific object key to find out which object or program the key is assigned to (field: ACCESSKEY) ❹. If you want an overview of all available developer keys, click EXECUTE ❺ or press [F8] without entering any values in the aforementioned fields (depicted in Figure 4.20).

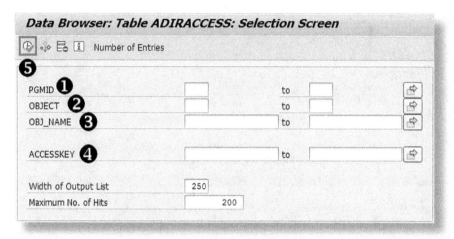

Figure 4.20: Table ADIRACCESS: selection screen

The result is an overview of object keys assigned (Figure 4.21). In a development system, check whether object keys are used appropriately. If you detect object keys in a quality assurance or production environment, ask whether there is a valid reason for this and whether a documented approval is available.

Figure 4.21: Table ADIRACCESS: results

Code vulnerabilities

As mentioned in Section 4.2.1, code reviews can be supported by a variety of tools. The two fundamental questions that need to be clarified in this test step are:

▶ Is there a company-specific design guideline that describes which principles have to be considered when developing customer-specific (ABAP) programs (e.g., naming conventions, control mechanisms to be considered, prohibited programming practices)?

▶ Is there a process in place to verify operational compliance with these defined requirements?

We will now introduce the *ABAP Code Inspector*, one of the tools that you can use to assess ABAP code. The tool is included as standard in SAP systems. You can use it to analyze ABAP code for predefined vulnerabilities and programming good practices. The ABAP Code Inspector can be accessed by opening transaction SCI. As a first step, create an inspection, as shown in Figure 4.22, and click NEW (the icon outlined).

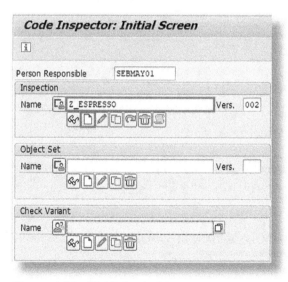

Figure 4.22: ABAP Code Inspector—step 1

You then have to define what you want the Code Inspector to review ❶. You can either choose an object set (to be defined in the previous step; consolidation of several single objects, Figure 4.22), a request/task (transport requests or task included in a request), or single objects (such as a program). In this example, we are analyzing program *Z_ESPRESSO*. The Code Inspector already contains a large number of predefined checks. Next, specify the check variant to be used ❷. In this step, you can also combine several individual check variants in one single variant (also defined on the previous screen; Figure 4.22). Initiate the code inspection by clicking EXECUTE ❸ or by pressing ⌷F8⌷, as depicted in Figure 4.23.

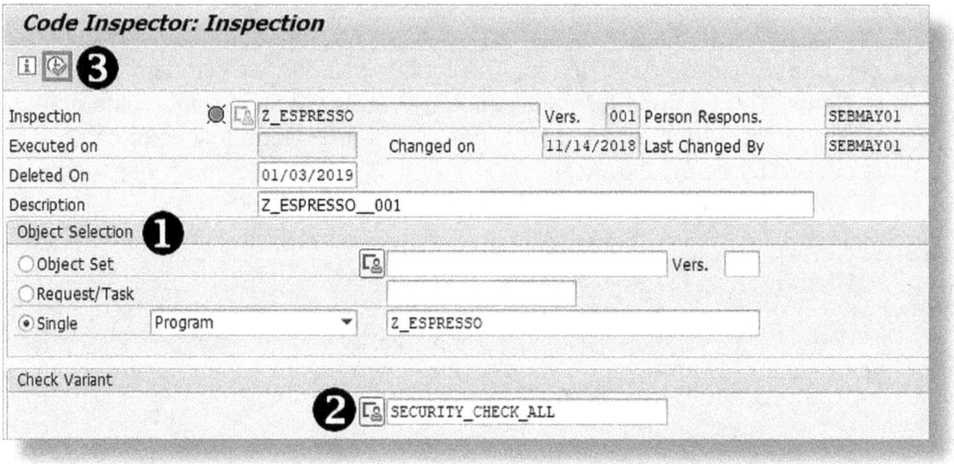

Figure 4.23: ABAP Code Inspector—step 2

Once the analysis is complete (green light next to the INSPECTION field ❶), you can display the results by clicking the RESULTS icon ❷ outlined in Figure 4.24.

As shown in Figure 4.25, the Code Inspector did not detect any code vulnerabilities or improvement opportunities.

Figure 4.24: ABAP Code Inspector—step 3

Figure 4.25: ABAP Code Inspector—step 4

Customer tables

To check whether customer tables are assigned to authorization groups, open table TDDAT in transaction SE16 or SE16N. On the selection screen, use a filter in the TABNAME field ❶, filtering by *Z** and *Y** transactions ❷ (namespace for customer tables), and confirm ❸. Furthermore, enter *&NC&* (authorization group) in the CCLASS field ❹.

Authorization group &NC&

Tables that have not been assigned to an authorization group are automatically assigned to the authorization group &NC&. The group &NC& can, therefore, be considered as a container for tables without authorization groups.

Initiate the selection by clicking EXECUTE ➎ or by pressing F8, as depicted in Figure 4.26.

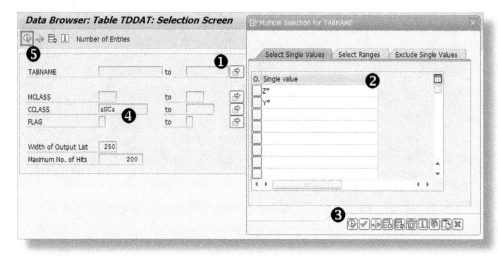

Figure 4.26: Table TDDAT: selection screen

The result (Figure 4.27) is a display of all customer tables without an assigned authorization group, or to be precise, customer tables assigned to the authorization group &NC&.

TABNAME	MCLASS	CCLASS	FLAG
Z_EEWWZ_APPLGRP		&NC&	
Z_EEWWZ_BUSOBJ		&NC&	
Z_EEWWZ_CONFIGGN		&NC&	
Z_EEWWZ_OBJDEF		&NC&	
Z_EEWWZ_PLACE		&NC&	
Z_EEWWZ_PLACEGP		&NC&	
Z_EEWWZ_PLACELN		&NC&	
Z_EEWWZ_SUBOBJ		&NC&	

Data Browser: Table TDDAT Select Entries   26

Figure 4.27: Table TDDAT: results

Customer transactions

To assess whether customer transactions have been protected sufficiently, open table TSTC in transaction SE16 or SE16N. On the selection screen, use a filter in the TCODE field ❶, filtering by *Z** and *Y** transactions ❷ (namespace for customer transactions), and confirm ❸. Initiate the selection by clicking Execute ❹ or by pressing [F8], as depicted in Figure 4.28.

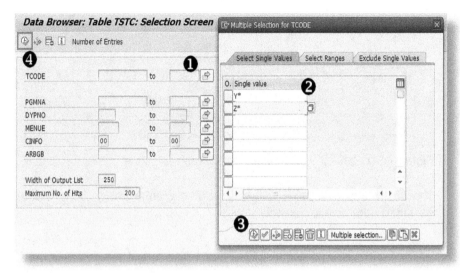

Figure 4.28: Table TSTC: selection screen

The result (Figure 4.29) is a display of all customer transactions.

Data Browser: Table TSTC Select Entries   3

TCODE	PGMNA	DYPNO	MENUE	CINFO	ARBGB	TTEXT
ZGRACFFLOG		0000		02		GRAC FF Log Report
Z_ESPRESSO	RSUSR200	0001		00		Report
Z_TEST	RSUSR200	0001		04		TEST

Figure 4.29: Table TSTC: results

To complete your assessment, open a new session in the SAP system and open table TSTCA in transaction SE16 or transaction SE16N. On the selection screen, use a filter in the TCODE field ❶, again filtering by *Z** and *Y** transactions ❷ and confirm ❸. Initiate the selection by clicking Execute ❹ or by pressing [F8], as depicted in Figure 4.30.

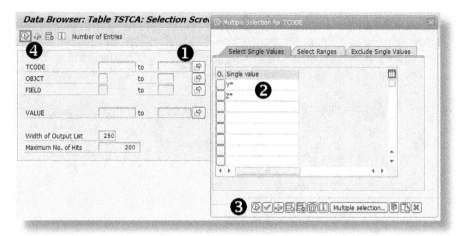

Figure 4.30: Table TSTCA: selection screen

The result (Figure 4.31) is a display of all customer transactions with an assigned authorization object.

Data Browser: Table TSTCA Select Entries   *5*

TCODE	OBJCT	FIELD	VALUE
Z_TEST	S_DEVELOP	ACTVT	01
Z_TEST	S_DEVELOP	DEVCLASS	
Z_TEST	S_DEVELOP	OBJNAME	
Z_TEST	S_DEVELOP	OBJTYPE	
Z_TEST	S_DEVELOP	P_GROUP	

Figure 4.31: Table TSTCA: results

Finally, check whether all customer transactions (Figure 4.29) have an authorization object assigned (Figure 4.31)—for example, by manually comparing the results or by exporting the results into Microsoft Excel and comparing the result through a VLOOKUP. In the current example, only transaction Z_TEST has an authorization object assigned; transactions ZGRACFFLOG and Z_ESPROSSO are missing an authorization object and, therefore, offer room for improvement.

4.2.3 Critical access rights

The access rights listed in this section are considered as critical in the area of development management. Therefore, check whether the following transactions and associated authorization objects are granted only to appropriate users by using the report **Users by Complex Selection Criteria** in transaction SUIM (for further information, please refer to Section 3.2).

▶ **Application development**

Authorization object	Field	Field value
S_TCODE	TCD	Various, e.g., SE80 (object navigator), SE11 (maintain tables), SE37 (maintenance of function modules), SE38 (ABAP editor), SU21 (maintenance of authorization objects), SE93 (maintenance of transactions)
S_DEVELOP	ACTVT	01 or 02 or 06 or 07 (...)
	OBJTYPE	Various, e.g., PROG (ABAP programs), TABL (tables), SUSO (authorization objects), TRAN (transactions), FGR (function modules) (...)

▶ **Maintenance of development packages**

Authorization object	Field	Field value
S_TCODE	TCD	Various, e.g., SM30, SM31, SE16, SE16N, SE16H, SE38, SE80 (...)
S_TABU_NAM	ACTVT	02
	OBJTYPE	STRW

or

Authorization object	Field	Field value
S_TCODE	TCD	Various, e.g., SM30, SM31, SE16, SE16N, SE16H, SE38, SE80 (...)
S_TABU_NAM	ACTVT	02
	OBJTYPE	TDEVC

▶ **Customizing**

Authorization object	Field	Field value
S_TCODE	TCD	Various, e.g., SPRO, SM30, SM31
S_TABU_DIS	ACTVT	02

or

Authorization object	Field	Field value
S_TCODE	TCD	Various, e.g., SPRO, SM30, SM31
S_TABU_NAM	ACTVT	02

▶ **Debug & replace**

Authorization object	Field	Field value
S_DEVELOP	ACTVT	02
	OBJTYPE	DEBUG

4.3 Table logging

4.3.1 Background to the control and associated risk

Changes to general system settings as well as to data relevant for financial statements must always be transparent, plausible, and traceable, especially if the changes are done without change management procedures, which is per definition the case for transactional data and sometimes even for configurations. Logs are the most fundamental part of IT systems for accomplishing this.

The central log in the SAP system for documenting changes to data is the *table logging* function. This function captures all changes made directly within tables that are flagged to be included in the log and, if the relevant feature is activated, also captures changes to SAP systems through transports.

Using table logging requires you to ensure the following:

▶ **Activation of table logging**
Table logging is activated in all SAP production environments and in all other relevant SAP systems.

▶ **Activation of logging of changes through transports**
Changes through transports are also captured within the table logging.

▶ **Include all relevant tables**
Relevant tables are flagged as to be included in the table logging in all SAP production environments and in all other relevant SAP systems. Tables deemed as relevant are either those leading to or reflecting financial statements or those containing system configuration settings.

Setting up table logging incorrectly leads to the following risk.

Associated risk: Table logging
If table logging is not set up appropriately, unauthorized activities may not be identified and followed up on in a timely manner. Moreover, analysis and forensic activities cannot be performed following an incident if audit log files do not exist.

4.3.2 Test steps in the SAP system

Activation of table logging

To determine whether table logging has been activated in the SAP system and to assess whether the control is effective, open transaction SA38 and execute program RSPARAM. This program shows all available system parameters. However, this option does not allow you to select specific parameters in advance. Alternatively, in transaction SA38, you can execute program RSPFPAR, as depicted in Figure 4.32. In comparison to program RSPARAM, this program allows you to select specific parameters.

Figure 4.32: Executing program RSPFPAR—parameter: rec/client

After executing either program RSPARAM or program RSPFPAR, the parameter *rec/client* is displayed (Figure 4.33). The display is comprised of five columns. Please refer to Section 4.9.2 for further details regarding the purpose of each column. In the context of table logging, you must check whether there is an entry in the USER VALUE column ❶. If no user value is specified in the second column, the system uses the value in the SYSTEM DEFAULT VALUE column ❷. In our example, this means that table logging is switched *OFF*.

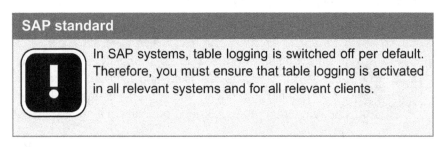

In the USER VALUE column, you can define either that a specific client is included in the table logging (as is the case for client 001 ❸), or you can include all clients of an SAP instance in the table logging. In this case, the value *All* is found in the second column rather than a specific client name.

Figure 4.33: Parameter rec/client

To prove the design effectiveness of the control **activation of table logging**, you must ensure that table logging is activated in all relevant SAP systems and for all relevant clients.

In which SAP clients should table logging be activated?

 In principle, the recommendation is to activate table logging in all clients of your SAP production environment. Furthermore, you should activate table logging in all clients of your SAP development environment from which transports—containing configurations and developments—to the production environment can be initiated.

Activation of logging of changes through transports

Changes through transports can be captured within table logging as well. Similar to the general activation of table logging, this must also be enabled in the respective SAP systems. To check whether changes through transports are included in the table logging, open transaction STMS and click OVERVIEW • SYSTEMS. Then, double-click a system as depicted in Figure 4.34.

System Overview: Domain DOMAIN_GR4

No. of systems: 3   11/14/2018 02:57:17

System	Typ	Short text	Release	Status	Conf
GR4		System GR4	740		
GR8		Test for STMS_QA	740		
GR9		Test for STMS_QA	740		

Figure 4.34: Transaction STMS: system overview

Determine whether the parameter RECCLIENT is set in the TMS configuration of the chosen system and whether all relevant production clients are included. Similar to the general activation of table logging, you can include all clients of an instance by choosing the value *ALL* (see Figure 4.35).

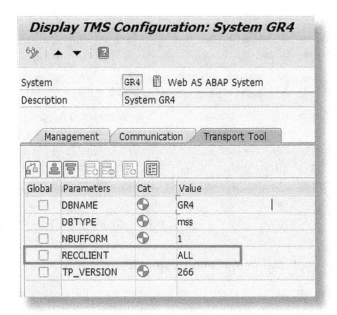

Figure 4.35: Transaction STMS: TMS configuration

Changed by

 If the logging of changes through transports has been activated, you will not see the person that has implemented the change in a development system in the table logging. However, the ID of the transport that led to the corresponding change is shown in the field USER in the log of a specific table.

Include all relevant tables

With SAP Note 112388, SAP provides an overview of tables that must be included in the table logging as mandatory from an audit point of view. As not all of the tables mentioned are flagged to be included within the table logging per default, you must check whether this has been implemented manually within your SAP instances. Furthermore, the recommendation is to also include the tables DEVACCESS (contains developer keys) as well as ADIRACCESS (contains object keys) within the table logging (for further information regarding developer and object keys, please refer to Section 4.2).

To assess whether the tables mentioned in SAP Note 112388 and tables DEVACCESS and ADIRACCESS are appropriately flagged, open table DD09L in transaction SE16 or SE16N. On the selection screen of table DD09L (depicted in Figure 4.36), paste all relevant tables to be assessed into the TABNAME field ❶. Also, specify that only tables that have no X in the PROTOKOLL field ❷ should be displayed. Execute the table selection ❸.

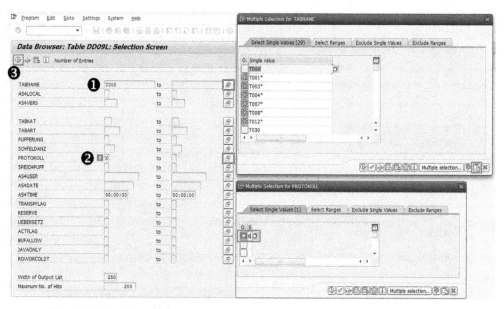

Figure 4.36: Table DD09L: selection screen

Figure 4.37 shows the results: all tables that have no flag (X) in the PROTOKOLL column. This means they are currently not included in the table logging.

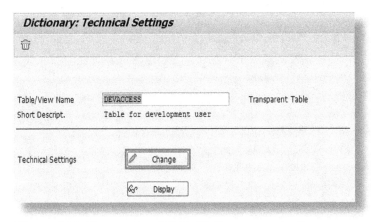

Data Browser: Table DD09L Select Entries   5

TABNAME	AS4LOCAL	AS4VERS	TABKAT	TABART	PUFFERUNG	SCHFELDANZ	PROTOKOLL	SPEICH
ADIRACCESS	A	0000	0	APPL0		000		
DEVACCESS	A	0000	1	APPL0		000		
TACTZ	A	0000	1	APPL0	G	001		
TASYS	A	0000	0	APPL2	X	000		
TSTC	A	0000	1	SSEXC	P	000		

Figure 4.37: Table DD09L: results

To set the logging flag for a specific table, open transaction SE13 and choose the corresponding table (field: TABLE/VIEW NAME). Open the table in CHANGE mode as shown in Figure 4.38.

Dictionary: Technical Settings

Table/View Name	DEVACCESS	Transparent Table
Short Descript.	Table for development user

| Technical Settings | Change |
| | Display |

Figure 4.38: Transaction SE13: Dictionary—selection screen

On the GENERAL PROPERTIES TAB, select LOG DATA CHANGES. Save, activate, and process these changes through your change management process (Figure 4.39).

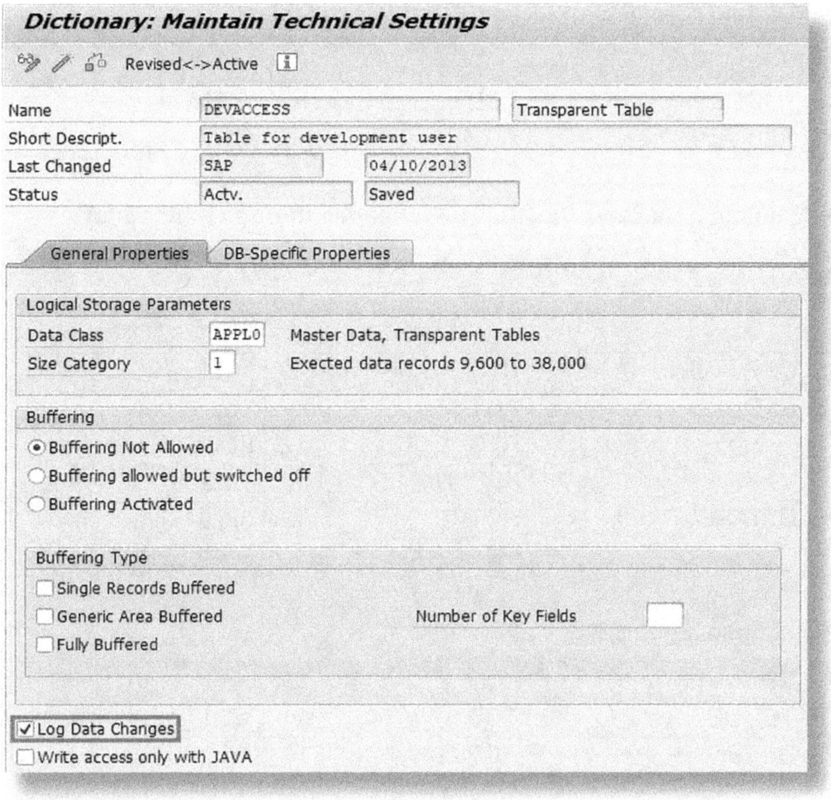

Dictionary: Maintain Technical Settings

≪ ∅ 🔒 Revised<->Active ⓘ

Name	DEVACCESS		Transparent Table
Short Descript.	Table for development user		
Last Changed	SAP	04/10/2013	
Status	Actv.	Saved	

General Properties · DB-Specific Properties

Logical Storage Parameters

Data Class	APPL0	Master Data, Transparent Tables
Size Category	1	Exected data records 9,600 to 38,000

Buffering

- ⦿ Buffering Not Allowed
- ○ Buffering allowed but switched off
- ○ Buffering Activated

Buffering Type

- ☐ Single Records Buffered
- ☐ Generic Area Buffered   Number of Key Fields ▢
- ☐ Fully Buffered

☑ Log Data Changes
☐ Write access only with JAVA

Figure 4.39: SE13: Dictionary—maintaining technical settings

4.3.3   Critical access rights

The access rights listed in this section are considered as critical in the area of table logging. Therefore, check whether the following transactions and associated authorization objects are granted only to appropriate users by using the report **Users by Complex Selection Criteria** in transaction SUIM (for further information, please refer to Section 3.2).

▶ **Maintain parameter rec/client (changes to tables)**

Authorization object	Field	Field value
S_TCODE	TCD	RZ10
S_RZL_ADM	ACVT	01

▶ **Maintain parameter RECCLIENT (changes through transports)**

Authorization object	Field	Field value
S_TCODE	TCD	STMS or STMS_DOM
S_CTS_ADMI	CTS_ADMFCT	TABL
S_RFC	ACTVT	16
	RFC_TYPE	FUGR
	RFC_NAME	TMSC
S_DATASET	ACTVT	33, 34
	PROGRAM	SAPLSTPP

▶ **Set table logging flag**

Authorization object	Field	Field value
S_TCODE	TCD	SE13 or SE13A
S_DEVELOP	ACTVT	02
	OBJTYPE	TABT

▶ **Deletion of table logs**

Authorization object	Field	Field value
S_TCODE	TCD	SCU3
S_TABU_DIS	ACTVT	02
	DICBERCLS	&NC& or SA (depends on which authorization group table DBTABLOG is assigned to)
S_TABU_CLI	CLIIDMAINT	X

or

Authorization object	Field	Field value
S_TCODE	TCD	SCU3
S_TABU_NAM	ACTVT	02
	DICBERCLS	DBTABLOG
S_TABU_CLI	CLIIDMAINT	X

4.4 SAP Security Audit Log

4.4.1 Background to the control and associated risk

Which events in an SAP system are wanted and which events possibly have a damaging background? This question is often a huge challenge for IT departments. Critical events must be detected and logged; they must be analyzed and proactive measures must be initiated. However, the real-time monitoring and detection of critical events in an SAP system lead to an effective early detection of cyberattacks.

The *SAP Security Audit Log (SAL)* provides the basis for such a functionality in SAP systems. It collects various data from different operational levels, cumulates the data as risk events, and allows reviewers to analyze the risk events based on a pre-configured risk rating or even to integrate the logs into a *security information and event management (SIEM)* solution. To enable comprehensive use of the Security Audit Log, the following prerequisites must be fulfilled:

▶ **Activation of the Security Audit Log**
The Security Audit Log is activated in all SAP production environments and in all other relevant SAP systems.

▶ **Definition of security incidents**
Company-specific system events that are considered as a security incident are defined. The functional definition of security incidents forms the basis for the decision on what needs to be technically captured within the Security Audit Log.

▶ **Capturing of all relevant system events**
All relevant system events are captured by the Security Audit Log

in all SAP production environments and in all other relevant SAP systems. System events deemed as relevant are either those that reflect a security incident itself or those that are the basis of security incidents that consist of various cumulated data and events.

▶ **Review of security incidents or integration of Security Audit Log into an SIEM solution**
The Security Audit Log is either reviewed on a regular basis and security incidents are followed up manually, or the Security Audit Log is integrated into an SIEM solution where at least the follow-up on security incidents is automatically initiated.

Inappropriate setup or use of the Security Audit Log is accompanied by the following risk.

Associated risk: Security Audit Log

 Without appropriate audit logging, unauthorized activities may not be identified and followed up on in a timely manner. Moreover, analysis and forensic activities cannot be performed following a security incident if audit log files do not exist.

4.4.2 Test steps in the SAP system

Activation of the Security Audit Log

To determine whether the Security Audit Log has been activated in an SAP system, open transaction SA38 and execute program RSPARAM. This program shows all available system parameters. However, this option does not allow you to select specific parameters in advance. Alternatively, in transaction SA38, you can also execute program RSPFPAR. In comparison to RSPARAM, this program allows you to select specific parameters, as depicted in Figure 4.40.

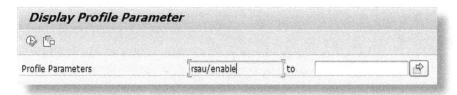

Display Profile Parameter

| Profile Parameters | rsau/enable| | | to | | |

Figure 4.40: Executing program RSPFPAR—parameter: rsau/enable

After executing either program RSPARAM or program RSPFPAR, the parameter rsau/enable is shown (Figure 4.41).

> ## Maintenance of Security Audit Log in SAP NetWeaver Release 7.5
>
> As of SAP NetWeaver Release 7.5, the Security Audit Log is managed centrally through transaction RSAU_CONFIG. However, the basic configuration options still match the settings subsequently introduced.

The display is comprised of five columns. Please refer to Section 4.9.2 for further details regarding the purpose of each column. In the context of the Security Audit Log, you must check whether there is an entry in the USER VALUE column ❶. If no user value is specified in the second column, the system uses the value in the SYSTEM DEFAULT VALUE column ❷, which in our example, means the Security Audit Log is switched off (equals value *0*).

> ## SAP standard
>
> In SAP systems, the Security Audit Log is switched off per default. Therefore, you must ensure that the Security Audit Log is activated in all relevant systems.

In the USER VALUE column, you can specify whether the Security Audit Log is activated by entering a value of *1*, as is the case for this client ❸.

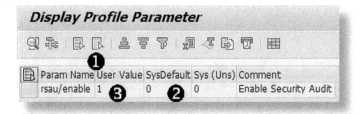

Figure 4.41: Parameter rsau/enable

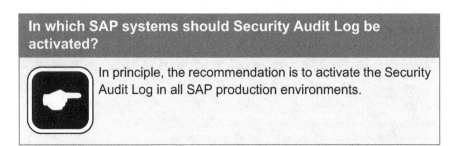

To prove the design effectiveness of the control **activation of Security Audit Log**, you must ensure that the Security Audit Log is activated in all relevant SAP systems.

Besides the parameter described above, there are further parameters, as described in Table 4.1, which must be defined in order to enable the use of the Security Audit Log.

Storing Security Audit Log files

Security Audit Log files are saved on the operating system. A new file is created every day. As standard, each file is named with the current date and the prefix *audit_*.

Parameter name	Description	Recommended value
rsau/selection_slots	Number of possible filters within the Security Audit Log (please refer also to the following paragraph)	10
rsau/user_selection	The value *1* allows the use of wildcard filters in the User Selection field within the definition of filters (please refer also to the following paragraph). You can, for example, define a filter for *SAP** which logs activities done by user SAP_1 and user SAP_2. The value *0* allows you to use only static filters. In this case, two individual filters must be set up for SAP_1 and SAP_2.	1
DIR_AUDIT	Defines the location where audit files are saved	No recommendation
FN_AUDIT	Defines the name (patterns) of audit files	No recommendation
rsau/max_diskspace/ local	Maximum size of the audit files. Once the size of the audit file reaches the specified maximum file size, logging stops.	1 Gigabyte (whereas the size of audit files must be monitored on a regular basis)
rsau/max_diskspace/ per_file	Maximum size of one audit file. If the size is reached, a new audit file is started. If the value is set to *0*, the parameter is not considered by the SAP system.	No recommendation
rsau/max_diskspace/ per_day	Maximum size of one or all security audit file(s) per day. This is an absolute maximum which must not be exceeded. If the value is set to *0*, the parameter is not considered by the SAP system.	No recommendation

Table 4.1: Security Audit Log parameters

Definition of security incidents

Defining security incidents is the key to only reporting events that actually present a threat to your company. This task is not done directly within the SAP system but represents a conceptual basis for the actual implementation of Security Audit Log filters in the SAP system. Furthermore, it is important to define security audit incidents based on a company's need and to not only focus on what is possible within the Security Audit Log. The evaluation of the technical feasibility is part of the next step.

Auditors must assess the functional definition of security incidents. For this purpose, the following implementation steps must be checked for appropriateness and completeness:

1. In order to define security incidents, firstly, you have to determine which issues are classified as security incidents.

2. The second step is the specification of thresholds. As soon as thresholds are exceeded, an alert must be raised and countermeasures initiated.

3. Finally, you have to determine which technical system activities have to be captured in the logging in order to ensure that the desired security incidents are actually caught by the Security Audit Log.

Failed login attempts and debug & replace

 Failed login attempts (e.g., when an incorrect user name or password is used) are one of the standard events companies want to use in their security incident monitoring. However, not every single failed login attempt should result in a security incident. Therefore, thresholds must be determined. A security incident must be raised in the event of:

▶ Ten failed login attempts

▶ Within one minute

A huge number of failed login attempts within a short period of time might be an indication of a brute force attack that must be reported and where countermeasures must be initiated. In contrast to failed login attempts, there are events in SAP that should result in a security incident immediately—that is, the first time they occur. For instance, the use of the debug and replace functionality, which can be used to manipulate business data and processes, should be reported as a security incident immediately: except for in very rare and specific cases, there is no reason to use this functionality in production environments.

Capturing all relevant system events

Based on the described definition of security incidents, you must determine system events that need to be captured within the Security Audit Log.

To check which events are actually captured by the Security Audit Log, open transaction SM20, which is the transaction for configuring audit profiles (depicted in Figure 4.42). Various audit profiles can be defined within an SAP system. However, only one of those profiles can be active at a time. The Security Audit Log differentiates between a *static configuration* ❶ and a *dynamic configuration* ❷.

- ▶ **Static configuration**: permanent change of the Security Audit Log, requires a restart of the application server

- ▶ **Dynamic configuration**: temporary change of the current Security Audit Log settings without the necessity to restart the application server

Depending on the configuration of parameter rsau/selection_slots, you can define up to ten different filters ❸. In addition, you can specify whether each filter is active (selected) or inactive (not selected) ❹. Each filter consists of selection criteria ❺, audit classes ❻, and events ❼.

- ▶ **Selection criteria**: definition of the clients and users in scope

- ▶ **Audit classes**: definition of the audit classes in scope, which consist of various events with different criticalities

- ▶ **Events**: definition of the events that should be considered for the selected audit classes based on criticalities

Finally, by clicking DETAILED DISPLAY ❽, you can flag whether dedicated events (as listed in Figure 4.42), should be included in the Security Audit Log regardless of the audit classes selected.

Figure 4.42: Transaction SM20—Security Audit: Administer Audit Profile

Recommendation—which events should be captured?

It is highly recommended that you include too much in a log rather than too little. Even if there are no security incidents assigned to a logged system event, this data can be used for forensic investigations. The recommendation is to include all events that are classified as critical for all users (i.e., user ID = *) in all clients (i.e., client ID = *) of your production systems.

To prove the design effectiveness of the control **capturing all relevant system activities**, you must ensure that all Security Audit Log events—as listed in detail below—relevant for your company are activated for users in scope on systems in scope and for clients in scope.

Security Audit Log events

Dialog logon

▶ **Critical**

Message ID	Message description (original SAP extract)
AU2	Logon failed (reason=&B, type=&A, method=&C)
AUM	User &B Locked in Client &A After Erroneous Password Checks
AUN	User &B in Client &A Unlocked After Being Locked Due to Inval.Password Entered
BUD	WS: Delayed logon failed (type &B, WP &C). Refer to Web service log &A.
BUE	WS: Delayed logon successful (type &B, WP &C). Refer to Web service log &A.
BUI	SPNego replay attack detected (UPN=&A)
CU4	OAuth 2.0: Logged-on client user &A not same as parameter client ID &B
CU6	OAuth 2.0: Client ID &A in SAML assertion not same as client ID &B in request
DU0	Invalid SAP GUI data

▶ **Severe**

Message ID	Message description (original SAP extract)
AU1	Logon successful (type=&A, method=&C)
AUO	Logon Failed (Reason = &B, Type = &A)
CU2	OAuth 2.0: Invalid access token received (reason=&A)
CU3	OAuth 2.0: Insufficient OAuth 2.0 scope for requested resource (user=&A)
CU5	OAuth 2.0: Client &A requested invalid access grant type &B
CU7	OAuth 2.0: Scope &B not permitted for client &C, user &D (cause=&A)
CUA	Rejected Assertion
CUB	&A: &B
CUC	&A
CUD	Name ID of a subject

Message ID	Message description (original SAP extract)
CUE	Attribute
CUF	Authentication Assertion
CUG	Signed LogoutRequest rejected
CUH	Unsigned LogoutRequest rejected

▶ **Non-critical**

Message ID	Message description (original SAP extract)
AUC	User Logoff
BUK	&A assertion used
BUL	&A: &B
BUM	Name ID of a subject
BUN	Attribute
BUO	Authentication assertion
BUP	&A
BUQ	Signed LogoutRequest accepted
BUR	Unsigned LogoutRequest accepted
CU8	OAuth 2.0: Access token issued (client=&A, user=&B, grant type=&C)
CU9	OAuth 2.0: Valid access token received for user &A

Report start

▶ **Severe**

Message ID	Message description (original SAP extract)
AUX	Start Report &A Failed (Reason = &B)

▶ **Non-critical**

Message ID	Message description (original SAP extract)
AUW	Report &A Started

Remote Function Call (RFC)

▶ **Critical**

Message ID	Message description (original SAP extract)
AUL	Failed RFC Call &C (Function Group = &A)
CUW	Failed Web service call (service = &A, operation = &B, reason = &C)
CUZ	Generic table access by RFC to &A with activity &B
DU3	Server &A is not contained in the whitelist
DU4	Connection to server &A failed
DU5	There is no logical file name for path &A
DU7	Validation for &A failed
DUJ	RFC callback rejected (destination &A, called &B, callback &C)
DUK	RFC callback in simulation mode (destination &A, called &B, callback &C)
DUT	Critical JSON RPC call of function module &A (S_RFC * authorization)

▶ **Severe**

Message ID	Message description (original SAP extract)
DU1	FTP server whitelist is empty
DU2	FTP server whitelist is non-secure due to use of placeholders

▶ **Non-critical**

Message ID	Message description (original SAP extract)
AUK	Successful RFC Call &C (Function Group = &A)
CUV	Successful WS Call (service = &A, operation &B)
DU6	Validation for &A successful
DU8	FTP connection request for server &A successful
DUI	RFC callback executed (destination &A, called &B, callback &C)
DUR	JSON RPC call of function module &A succeeded

Message ID	Message description (original SAP extract)
DUS	JSON RPC call of function module &A failed
FU1	RFC function &B with dynamic destination &C was called in program &A

RFC/CPIC logon

▶ **Critical**

Message ID	Message description (original SAP extract)
AU6	RFC/CPIC logon failed, reason=&B, type=&A, method=&C

▶ **Non-critical**

Message ID	Message description (original SAP extract)
AU5	RFC/CPIC logon successful (type=&A, method=&C)

System

▶ **Critical**

Message ID	Message description (original SAP extract)
AUE	Audit Configuration Changed
AUF	Audit: Slot &A: Class &B, Severity &C, User &D, Client &E, &F
AUG	Application Server Started
AUH	Application Server Stopped
AUI	Audit: Slot &A Inactive
AUJ	Audit: Active Status Set to &1
EU1	System change options changed (&A to &B)
EU2	Client &A settings changed (&B)

146

Transaction start

▶ Critical

Message ID	Message description (original SAP extract)
AU4	Start of transaction &A failed (Reason=&B)
CUJ	Failed to start application &A (reason =&B)

▶ Severe

Message ID	Message description (original SAP extract)
AUP	Transaction &A Locked
AUQ	Transaction &A Unlocked
BUX	Test message

▶ Non-critical

Message ID	Message description (original SAP extract)
AU3	Transaction &A Started
CUI	Application &A started
DU9	Generic table access call to &A with activity &B (auth. check: &C)

User master change

▶ Critical

Message ID	Message description (original SAP extract)
AU7	User &A Created
AUU	Authorization/Authorization Profile &B Activated
BUV	Invalid hash value &A. The context contains &B.
BUW	A refresh token issued to client &A was used by client &B.

▶ **Severe**

Message ID	Message description (original SAP extract)
AU8	User &A Deleted
AU9	User &A Locked
AUA	User &A Unlocked
AUB	Authorizations for User &A Changed
AUD	User Master Record &A Changed
AUR	Authorization/Authorization Profile &B Created
AUS	Authorization/Authorization Profile &B Deleted
AUT	Authorization/Authorization Profile &B Changed
DUH	OAuth 2.0: Token declared invalid (OAuth client=&A, user=&B, token type=&C)

▶ **Non-critical**

Message ID	Message description (original SAP extract)
BU2	Password changed for user &B in client &A

Other events

▶ **Critical**

Message ID	Message description (original SAP extract)
AUV	Digital Signature Error (Reason = &A, ID = &B)
BU0	RAL configuration access: Action: &A, type: &B, name &C
BU1	Password check failed for user &B in client &A
BU3	Security check changed in export: Old value &A, new value &B
BU8	Virus Scan Interface: Virus "&C" found by profile &A (step &B)
BUG	HTTP Security Session Management was deactivated for client &A.
BUS	&A: Request without sufficient security characteristic of address &B.
BUU	Certificate check for subject "&A" with profile &B failed (status &C)

Message ID	Message description (original SAP extract)
BUY	Field contents changed: &5&9&9&9&9&9
BUZ	> in program &A, line &B, event &C
CU0	RAL Log Access: Action: &A
CUK	C debugging activated
CUL	Field content changed: &A
CUM	Jump to ABAP Debugger: &A
CUN	A manually caught process was stopped from within the Debugger (&A)
CUO	Explicit database commit or rollback from debugger &A
CUP	Non-exclusive debugging session started
DUN	Active whitelist &A changed (&B)
DUQ	Active scenario &A for switchable authorization checks changed – &B
EU3	&A change documents deleted without archiving (&B)

▶ **Severe**

Message ID	Message description (original SAP extract)
AUY	Download &A Bytes to File &C
AUZ	Digital Signature (Reason = &A, ID = &B)
BU5	ICF recorder entry executed for user &A (activity &B)
BU6	ICF recorder entry executed by user &A (&B, &C) (activity &D).
BU7	Administration setting was changed for ICF Recorder (Activity: &A)
BU9	Virus Scan Interface: Error "&C" occurred in profile &A (step &B)
BUA	WS: Signature check error (reason &B, WP &C). Refer to Web service log &A.
BUB	WS: Signature insufficient (WP &C). Refer to Web service log &A.
BUC	WS: Time stamp is invalid. Refer to Web service log &A.
BUH	HTTP Security Session of user &A (client &B) was hard exited
BUJ	Non-encrypted &A communication (&B)

Message ID	Message description (original SAP extract)
BUT	CRL download failed with error code &A
CU1	CU Test Message
CUQ	Logical file name &A not configured. Physical file name &B not checked.
CUR	Physical file name &B does not fulfill requirements from logical file name &A
CUS	Logical file name &B is not a valid alias for logical file name &A
CUT	Validation for logical file name &A is not active
DUA	EHS-SADM: Service &A created on host &B
DUB	EHS-SADM: Service &A started on host &B
DUC	EHS-SADM: Service &A ended on host &B
DUD	EHS-SADM: Service &A deleted on host &B
DUM	Check for &A in whitelist &B failed
FU2	Parsing of an XML data stream canceled for security reasons (reason = &A)

▶ **Non-critical**

Message ID	Message description (original SAP extract)
AU0	Audit – Test. Text: &A
BU4	Dynamic ABAP code: Event &A, event type &B, check total &C
BUF	HTTP Security Session Management was activated for client &A.
CUU	Payload of PI/WS message &A was read | &B
CUX	Payload of postprocessing request &A read
CUY	> &A
DUE	EHS-SADM: Configuration of service &A changed on host &B
DUF	EHS-SADM: File &A transferred from host &B
DUG	EHS-SADM: File &A transferred to host &B
DUL	Check for &A in whitelist &B was successful
DUO	Authorization check for object &A in scenario &B successful

Message ID	Message description (original SAP extract)
DUP	Authorization check for object &A in scenario &B failed
DUU	Authorization check for user &C on object &A in scenario &B successful
DUV	Authorization check for user &C on object &A in scenario &B failed
DUX	TEMP: Customer-specific event DUX &A &B &C &D
DUY	TEMP: Customer-specific event DUY &A &B &C &D
DUZ	TEMP: Customer-specific event DUZ &A &B &C &D
EU0	Test message

Failed logon attempts and debug & replace (cont.)

As described before, a security incident must be raised in the event of:

▶ Ten failed logon attempts

▶ Within one minute.

Therefore, either the audit class **Dialog Logon** or the specific event **AU2 (Logon Failed)** must be activated within the Security Audit Log. This event even logs failed logon attempts if a user is already locked (e.g., as the account lockout threshold has been set to five failed logon attempts—refer to Section 4.7). To include the usage of the debug and replace functionality, in the Security Audit Log, either the audit class **Other Events** or the specific event **CUL (Field value changed (De-bugging & Replace))** must be added to the log.

Review of security incidents or integration of Security Audit Log into an SIEM solution

Security incidents raised must be either manually reviewed or transferred into an SIEM solution. To assess whether this is done appropriately, ask the auditee to provide sufficient evidence that the Security Audit Log is analyzed on a regular basis for security incidents and, in the case of any incidents, that appropriate follow-up measures have been initiated. For the integration of the results of the Security Audit Log into an SIEM solution, check whether the alerting has been set up appropriately and assess how alerts are followed up.

4.4.3   Critical access rights

The access rights listed in this section are considered as critical in the area of the Security Audit Log. Therefore, check whether the following transactions and associated authorization objects are granted only to appropriate users by using the report **Users by Complex Selection Criteria** in transaction SUIM (for further information, please refer to Section 3.2).

▶ **Maintain Security Audit Log**

Authorization object	Field	Field value
S_TCODE	TCD	SM19
S_ADMI_FCD	S_ADMI_FCD	AUDA

▶ **Maintain Security Audit Log (through new functionality of SAP Net-Weaver Release 7.5)**

Authorization object	Field	Field value
S_TCODE	TCD	RSAU_CONFIG
S_SAL	SAL_ACTVT	EDIT_PARAM (change parameter), EDIT_CONFD (change dynamic configuration), EDIT_CONFS (change static configuration)

▶ **Deletion of Security Audit Logs**

Authorization object	Field	Field value
S_TCODE	TCD	SM19
S_ADMI_FCD	S_ADMI_FCD	AUDA

► **Deletion of Security Audit Log (through new functionality of SAP NetWeaver Release 7.5)**

Authorization object	Field	Field value
S_TCODE	TCD	RSAU_CONFIG
S_SAL	SAL_ACTVT	DELE_LOG_F

4.5 Role management

4.5.1 Background to the control and associated risk

In SAP systems, programs, services, information, and tables are protected against unauthorized access through authorizations (also known as permissions). End users therefore need appropriate authorizations in the form of transactions and adequately defined authorization objects in the SAP system to do their daily work. The SAP authorization concept distinguishes between the following entitlements:

► Authorization profile (also known as simply: profile)

► Single role

► Composite role

► Derived role

In the SAP system, permissions are bundled using authorization profiles. If an end user is to be granted access to specific information or programs, the authorization profiles with the necessary authorizations must be assigned to that user's account.

For easy administration of authorization profiles, SAP has introduced the *Profile Generator* (transaction PFCG). In the Profile Generator, you can create and manage roles, define their attributes, and assign authorizations to them. Once you have created or maintained a role, you can use the Profile Generator to automatically generate an authorization profile. Similar to authorization profiles, roles can also be assigned directly to a user account in an SAP system. However, along with the role, the corresponding authorization profile belonging to the role is automatically assigned to the account.

As previously stated, there are three different types of roles. A *single role*, described very simply, contains various transactions and authorization objects that users need to access, for example, programs or information. *Composite roles* allow you to bundle single roles. You do this, for example, to reduce the maintenance effort required for user management. If you were to use only single roles, you would always have to manually assign all single roles required by a user in the SAP system. In composite roles, you can group functionally linked single roles together and assign only the higher-level composite role to the user. *Derived roles* are created by defining specific organizational values as part of role derivation, such as company codes (in SAP terminology, BUKRS), which are not defined in detail in a single role. Single roles that serve as templates in this operating principle are often referred to as *master roles* or *parent roles*. Derived roles are automatically generated by the system, including the respective organizational values, and technically also belong to the role type single roles. Figure 4.43 shows how the role derivation functionality generally works.

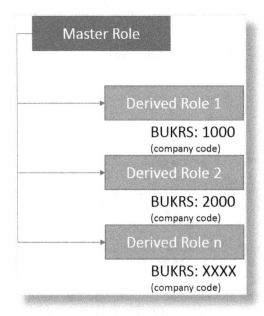

Figure 4.43: Role derivation functionality

Figure 4.44 provides an overview of the interaction of the various parts of the authorization concept described above in the SAP system.

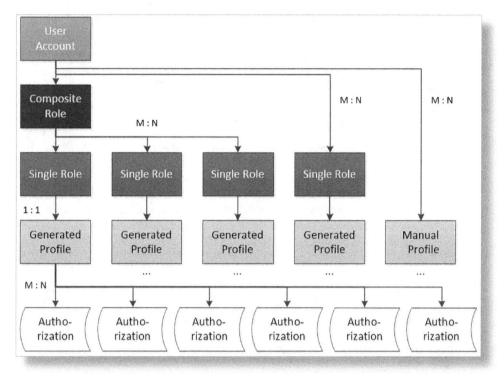

Figure 4.44: Interaction of roles, profiles, and authorizations

Role management and the authorization system itself are relevant for IT audits both from a data protection perspective as well as from a data security perspective. On the one hand, unauthorized persons could gain access to sensitive data as a result of incorrectly assigned authorizations and could even be authorized to extract this data from SAP systems. On the other hand, permissions control who can use which functions in the SAP system. In this case, authorizations can even allow users to go so far as to fraudulently interfere in ongoing business transactions.

Therefore, you must first ensure that roles and associated access rights are set up appropriately. This includes the following controls:

▶ **Role change management process**
Role changes must always be compliant with the standard change management process.

Associated risk: Role change management process

 If key controls are not embedded in the role change management process to ensure that role creation and role changes are formally requested and approved, revoked as required, and regularly recertified, the appropriateness of authorizations in the SAP system cannot be guaranteed.

▶ **Role concept**
A role concept must be in place to document existing roles, their business purpose, and authorizations granted. Furthermore, a role owner must be defined for each role to be responsible for approving all role changes.

Associated risk: Role concept

 Without an appropriate and approved role concept, there may be a lack of transparency around existing roles, their business purpose, and access levels granted and user groups allowed to be assigned to those roles. Therefore, roles may grant access that is too broad or may be assigned to inappropriate user groups, thus resulting in unauthorized access to business-critical data. In addition, segregation of duty conflicts could arise due to incompatible access rights being assigned to users. These segregation of duty conflicts may grant users extensive access which enables them to circumvent segregation of duties for fraudulent activities.

▶ **Role recertification**
Roles and their authorizations must be reviewed periodically by appropriate personnel (e.g., by the role owner).

Associated risk: Role recertification

If user access to the SAP application is not reviewed regularly, inappropriate or obsolete access rights may remain undetected and could result in unauthorized access to business-critical data.

▶ **Segregation of duties (SoD) and critical authorizations**
Roles must be preventively analyzed for SoD conflicts and critical authorizations when roles are changed or created.

Associated risk: Segregation of duties and critical authorizations

If SoD conflicts and inappropriate critical authorizations are not resolved or removed prior to becoming effective in the SAP system, these access rights may be exploited to manipulate, compromise, or delete business-critical data or to bypass implemented segregation of duty controls in the system.

4.5.2 Test steps in the SAP system

Role change management process

To check whether changes to roles or the creation of new roles comply with the requirements of the change management process, open the view V_E071EU in transaction SE16 or SE16N. On the selection screen (Figure 4.45), choose the corresponding audit period ❶ and the object *ACGR* ❷ (transport object to which role changes are linked). Initiate the selection by clicking Execute ❸ or by pressing ⌷F8⌷, as depicted in Figure 4.45.

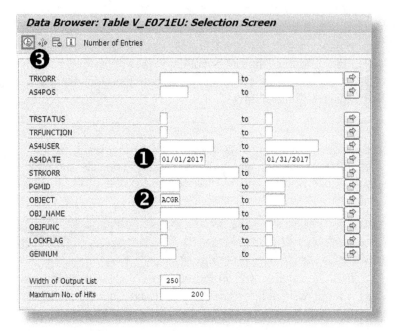

Figure 4.45: View V_E071EU: selection screen

The result is a display of all transports containing role changes, as the example in Figure 4.46 shows. You can check whether the roles for a sample of changes have been appropriately tested and approved before they have been transported to the production environment (please refer to Section 4.1).

Data Browser: Table V_E071EU Select Entries   47

TRKORR	AS4POS	TRSTATUS	TRFUNCTION	AS4USER	AS4DATE	STRKORR	PGMID	OBJECT	OBJ_NAME	OBJFUNC	LOCKFLAG	GENNUM
GR4K900133	000001	R	W	DUSKWE01	01/09/2017		R3TR	ACGR	GR_AC_01	K		
GR4K900133	000002	R	W	DUSKWE01	01/09/2017		R3TR	ACGR	GR_AC_02	K		
GR4K900133	000003	R	W	DUSKWE01	01/09/2017		R3TR	ACGR	GR_AC_03	K		

Figure 4.46: View V_E071EU: results

Role concept

The aim of reviewing a role concept is to find out whether the roles and associated authorizations of an SAP system are adequately document-ed. Therefore, the auditee must hand over the role concept and you must check whether the following points are taken into account in the concept and are sufficiently documented:

▶ List of all existing roles in the relevant SAP system

▶ Purpose of the roles

▶ Assigned access rights

▶ User group/job function authorized to use the role

▶ Role owner

▶ Segregation of duties (e.g., which roles should not be assigned together as the combination of roles would lead to a segregation of duties conflict)

Role recertification

You typically recertify users by first extracting all roles and their assigned authorizations from the SAP system. Therefore, open table AGR_1251 in transaction SE16 or SE16N. If relevant, specify a role name pattern to only assess roles that are in scope (e.g., to exclude SAP standard roles) ❶. Initiate the selection by clicking EXECUTE ❷ or by pressing ⌈F8⌋, as depicted in Figure 4.47.

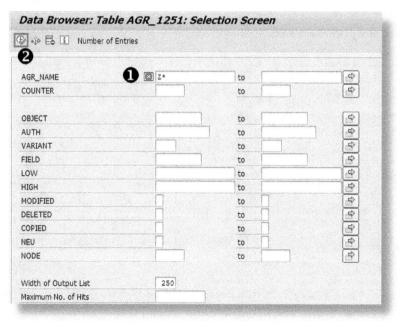

Figure 4.47: Table AGR_1251: selection screen

The result is a display of all roles and their corresponding authorization data. This example shows a role named *Z_TEST_RSUSR008009_1* ❶ (Figure 4.48). The authorization values consist of three different authorization objects ❷: *S_TCODE*, *S_USER_AGR*, *S_USER_GRP*. The field values (column: FIELD) ❸ and the values in the LOW and HIGH columns ❹ define the authorization objects further. In this example, the values *PFCG* and *SU01* are contained in the *TCD* field of the authorization object *S_TCODE*, which means that the role is generally authorized to access transactions SU01 (User Management) and PFCG (Role/Profile Management). The MODIFIED column ❺ shows whether an authorization object:

- Is kept in the standard form as maintained in transaction SU24 (*S*)
- Is modified (*G*), that is, implemented through SU24 comparison but the authorization values have not been fully defined and therefore need to be updated
- Is modified (*M*), that is, implemented through SU24 comparison but authorization values have been updated
- The object has been added manually (*U*)

The DELETED column ❻ indicates whether a specific authorization object has been marked as to be deleted. In this case, the authorization would still be in the role but corresponding authorizations are no longer taken into account during the authorization check.

Data Browser: Table AGR_1251 Select Entries 21

Check Table...

MAN...	AGR_NAME ❶	COUNTER	OBJECT ❷	AUTH	VARIANT	FIELD ❸	LOW ❹	HIGH	MODIFI... ❺	DELETED ❻	COPIED	NEU	NODE
100	Z_TEST_RSUSR008009_1	000026	S_TCODE	T-G478002700		TCD	PFCG		S			O	000005
100	Z_TEST_RSUSR008009_1	000027	S_TCODE	T-G478002700		TCD	SU01		S			O	000005
100	Z_TEST_RSUSR008009_1	000028	S_USER_AGR	T-G478002700		ACTVT	01		S			O	000013
100	Z_TEST_RSUSR008009_1	000029	S_USER_AGR	T-G478002700		ACTVT	02		S			O	000013
100	Z_TEST_RSUSR008009_1	000030	S_USER_AGR	T-G478002700		ACTVT	03		S			O	000013
100	Z_TEST_RSUSR008009_1	000031	S_USER_AGR	T-G478002700		ACTVT	06		S			O	000013
100	Z_TEST_RSUSR008009_1	000032	S_USER_AGR	T-G478002700		ACTVT	08		S			O	000013
100	Z_TEST_RSUSR008009_1	000033	S_USER_AGR	T-G478002700		ACTVT	21		S			O	000013
100	Z_TEST_RSUSR008009_1	000034	S_USER_AGR	T-G478002700		ACTVT	22		S			O	000013
100	Z_TEST_RSUSR008009_1	000035	S_USER_AGR	T-G478002700		ACTVT	36		S			O	000013
100	Z_TEST_RSUSR008009_1	000036	S_USER_AGR	T-G478002700		ACTVT	64		S			O	000013
100	Z_TEST_RSUSR008009_1	000037	S_USER_AGR	T-G478002700		ACTVT	DL		S			O	000013
100	Z_TEST_RSUSR008009_1	000038	S_USER_AGR	T-G478002700		ACTVT	UL		S			O	000013
100	Z_TEST_RSUSR008009_1	000039	S_USER_AGR	T-G478002700		ACT_GROUP	*		G			O	000014
100	Z_TEST_RSUSR008009_1	000043	S_USER_GRP	T-G478002700		ACTVT	01		M			O	000022
100	Z_TEST_RSUSR008009_1	000044	S_USER_GRP	T-G478002700		ACTVT	02		M			O	000022
100	Z_TEST_RSUSR008009_1	000045	S_USER_GRP	T-G478002700		ACTVT	03		M			O	000022
100	Z_TEST_RSUSR008009_1	000046	S_USER_GRP	T-G478002700		ACTVT	05		M			O	000022
100	Z_TEST_RSUSR008009_1	000047	S_USER_GRP	T-G478002700		ACTVT	06		M			O	000022
100	Z_TEST_RSUSR008009_1	000048	S_USER_GRP	T-G478002700		ACTVT	78		M			O	000022
100	Z_TEST_RSUSR008009_1	000049	S_USER_GRP	T-G478002700		CLASS	*		G			O	000023

Figure 4.48: Table AGR_1251: results

Download the data (e.g., to a spreadsheet). Send the spreadsheet to appropriate personnel (e.g., role or data owners) who can review the roles and assigned authorizations.

From an audit perspective, check whether the control described above is in place, whether feedback is provided appropriately by reviewers, and whether feedback provided is implemented in a timely manner (e.g., by checking whether roles have been deleted or updated).

Segregation of duties and critical authorizations

There are various possibilities and tools for analyzing roles with regard to segregation of duties conflicts and critical authorizations. At this point, we will introduce one of the SAP default resources, report RSUSR008_009_ NEW (Users or Roles with Combinations of Critical Authorizations), to give you an idea of how such a tool works and what should be considered during an audit. The explanation below does not provide detailed instructions on how to perform test steps in the SAP system; instead, it demonstrates and specifies how you can implement the control described in Section 4.5.1 in an SAP environment. Furthermore, you can use this report to automate the assessment of critical access rights documented at the end of each control section in Chapter 4.

To open the previously mentioned report, execute program RSUSR008_009_ NEW in transaction SA38. This report allows you to analyze roles as well as users with regard to critical authorizations (a transaction and/or an authorization that is considered as risky by itself) or segregation of duties conflicts (combinations of transactions and/or authorizations that allow implemented controls to be circumvented). However, before you can perform such analyses, critical authorizations and segregation of duties conflicts must be defined. As segregation of duties conflicts build on **critical authorizations**, as a first step, open the Critical Authorizations menu (Figure 4.49).

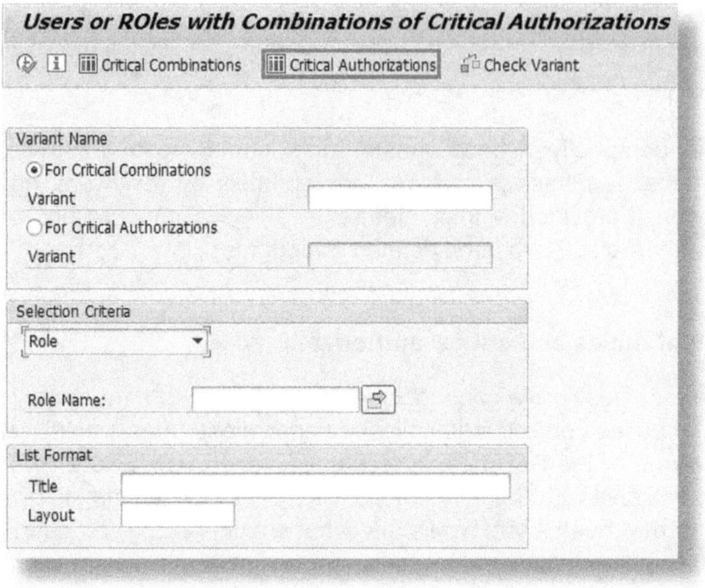

Figure 4.49: RSUSR008_009_NEW: selection screen

The first folder in the menu, VARIANTS FOR CRITICAL AUTHORIZATIONS, can be understood as a ruleset that contains all the rules to be tested. SAP provides a standard ruleset with a total of 21 predefined critical authorizations. However, for demonstration purposes, we will create our own set of rules with two critical authorizations:

- ▶ User maintenance (equivalent to user management) (S_TCODE with field TCD = SU01; S_USER_GRP with field ACTVT = 01 (create), 02 (change); S_USER_AGR with field ACTVT = XX (assign roles to users))

- ▶ Role maintenance (equivalent to role management) (S_TCODE with field TCD = PFCG; S_USER_AGR with field ACTVT = 01 (create), 02 (change))

Create a new entry in the folder VARIANTS FOR CRITICAL AUTHORIZATIONS by clicking NEW ENTRIES (Figure 4.50).

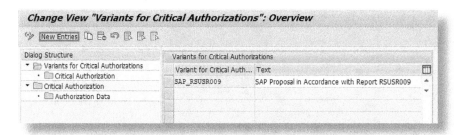

Figure 4.50: RSUSR008_009_NEW: creating critical authorizations—step 1

Define a technical ID (column: VARIANT FOR CRITICAL AUTHORIZATIONS) as well as a description (column: TEXT) for your ruleset (Figure 4.51). Save your entries.

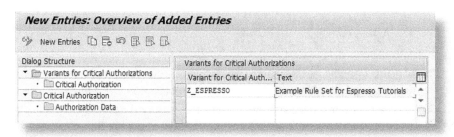

Figure 4.51: RSUSR008_009_NEW: creating critical authorizations—step 2

Add two entries in the second main folder, CRITICAL AUTHORIZATION—one for *User maintenance* and one for *Role maintenance* (Figure 4.52). Each transaction must be assigned to a color which can be used, for example, to document the criticality of a specific risk. Furthermore, you can add a transaction (column: TRANSACTION CODE) to be used as a reference for the critical authorization. If you do this, default values are added in the sub-folder AUTHORIZATION DATA based on information contained in transaction SE93. Save your entries. In this folder, you will also find the pre-configured standard critical authorizations provided by SAP.

Change View "Critical Authorization": Overview

New Entries

Dialog Structure	Critical Authorization				
▼ ☐ Variants for Critical Authorizations	Authorization ID	Text	Color	Transaction Code	Transaction text
• ☐ Critical Authorization	SAP_ABAA	Administration: All Rights for Background Jobs	Red ▼		
▼ ☐ Critical Authorization	SAP_ABJA	Administration: Release Background Jobs	Red ▼		
• ☐ Authorization Data	SAP_ABMA	Administration: Start Background Jobs with Any User	Red ▼		
	SAP_ABNI	Use Background Jobs	Yellow ▼		
	SAP_ADM01	Administration: Network, Processes, Update Admin., and so on	Red ▼		
	SAP_ALOG	Execute Logical Operating System Commands	Red ▼		
	SAP_ARIM	Administration: CCMS Maintenance	Red ▼		
	SAP_ASPA	Administration: Operations on Secured Print Requests	Yellow ▼		
	SAP_ASPO	Administration: Print on All Printers	Yellow ▼		
	SAP_ASPT	Administration: Operations on Other TemSe Objects	Yellow ▼		
	SAP_AUAM	Administration: Authorization Maintenance	Red ▼		
	SAP_AUAS	Auditing: Display Authorizations	Yellow ▼		
	SAP_AUPM	Administration: Profile Maintenance	Red ▼		
	SAP_AUPS	Auditing: Display Profiles	Yellow ▼		
	SAP_AUUM	Administration: User Maintenance	Red ▼		
	SAP_AUUS	Auditing: Display Users	Yellow ▼		
	SAP_CTBA	Customizing: Table Maintenance	Red ▼		
	SAP_CTBC	Customizing: Cross-Client Table Maintenance	Yellow ▼		
	SAP_CTBS	Customizing: Table Maintenance of All Basic Tables	Red ▼		
	SAP_DEVD	Development: Program and ABAP Dictionary Maintenance	Red ▼		
	SAP_DEVT	Development: Transport System	Red ▼		
	Z_PFCG	Critical Authorization Data for Transaction PFCG	Red ▼	PFCG	Role Maintenance
	Z_SU01	Critical Authorization Data for Transaction SU01	Yellow ▼	SU01	User Maintenance

Figure 4.52: RSUSR008_009_NEW: creating critical authorizations—step 3

To add the specific authorization data relevant for a critical authorization, mark the respective line in the CRITICAL AUTHORIZATION overview and open the subfolder AUTHORIZATION DATA. Implement the authorization data for the critical authorization as depicted in Figure 4.53. Finalize this step by saving your entries.

Change View "Authorization Data": Overview

New Entries

Dialog Structure		
▼ ☐ Variants for Critical Auth	Authorization ID	Z_SU01
• ☐ Critical Authorization	Color	Yellow ▼
▼ ☐ Critical Authorization	Transaction Code	SU01
• ☐ Authorization Data	Text	Critical Authorization Data for Transaction SU01

Authorization Data						
Group	Object*	Field Name	From	To	AND/OR*	Text
	S_TCODE	TCD	SU01		AND ▼	Transaction Code Check at Transaction Start
	S_USER_AGR	ACTVT	78		AND ▼	Authorizations: Role Check
	S_USER_GRP	ACTVT	01	02	AND ▼	User Master Maintenance: User Groups

Figure 4.53: RSUSR008_009_NEW: creating critical authorizations—step 4

The last step is to link the critical authorization to your implemented variant—that is, to the relevant ruleset. Open the sub-folder CRITICAL AUTHORIZATIONS (part of the main folder VARIANTS FOR CRITICAL AUTHORIZATI-

ONS) as shown in Figure 4.54. Add all relevant critical authorizations and save your entries.

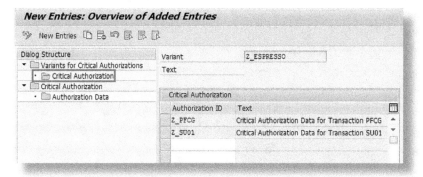

Figure 4.54: RSUSR008_009_NEW: creating critical authorizations—step 5

We will now focus on the implementation of segregation of duties (SoD) rules, referred to as **critical combinations**, which can be implemented in a similar way to the critical authorizations introduced above. In the following paragraphs, you will learn how to set up a rule to detect roles and users authorized to perform user management and role management at the same time.

Open the CRITICAL COMBINATIONS menu from the initial screen of report RSUSR008_009_NEW (Figure 4.49). The first folder, VARIANTS FOR CRITICAL COMBINATIONS OF AUTHORIZATIONS, can be understood as a ruleset that contains all the rules to be tested together. Firstly, create a new entry in the folder VARIANTS FOR CRITICAL COMBINATIONS OF AUTHORIZATIONS by clicking NEW ENTRIES (Figure 4.55). Define a technical ID (column: VARIANT FOR CRITICAL COMBINATIONS OF AUTHORIZATIONS) and a description (column: TEXT) for your ruleset and save your entries.

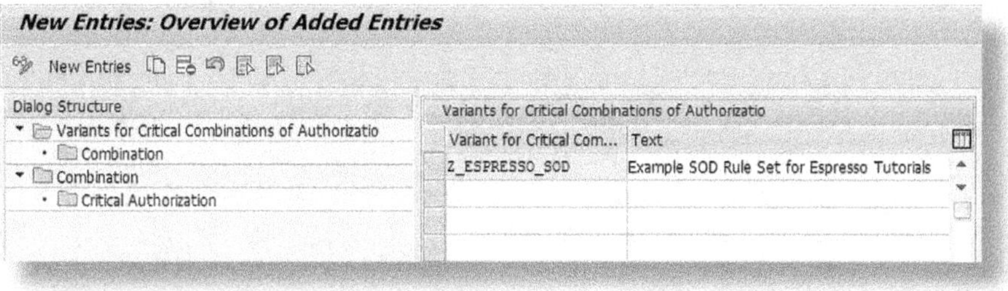

Figure 4.55: RSUSR008_009_NEW: creating an SoD conflict—step 1

The next step is to define a critical combination. Add an entry in the second main folder, COMBINATION, as a container for the critical authorizations reflecting user management and role management (Figure 4.56). The critical combination must also be assigned to a color. Save your entries.

Figure 4.56: RSUSR008_009_NEW: creating an SoD conflict—step 2

The next step in setting up critical combinations differs from the implementation of critical authorizations. At this point, you cannot define specific authorization data but you must select critical authorizations that have already been set up as part of the implementation of critical authorizations (Figure 4.57). Therefore, before you create critical combinations, it is important to have critical authorizations already defined. Once you have chosen the critical authorizations that lead to a risk if both are assigned to a single user or to a role, save your entries.

New Entries: Overview of Added Entries

Dialog Structure		
▾ ☐ Variants for Critical Combinations of Authorizatio	Authorization ID	Z_SOD_01
• ☐ Combination	Text	User Management (SU01) with Role Management (PFCG)
▾ ☐ Combination		
• ☐ Critical Authorization		

Critical Authorization		
Authorization ID	Text	
Z_PFCG	Critical Authorization Data for Transaction PFCG	
Z_SU01	Critical Authorization Data for Transaction SU01	

Figure 4.57: RSUSR008_009_NEW: creating an SoD conflict—step 3

Finally, you have to link the critical combinations to your implemented variant—that is, to the relevant ruleset. To do this, open the sub-folder COMBINATION (part of the main folder VARIANTS FOR CRITICAL COMBINATIONS OF AUTHORIZATION) as shown in Figure 4.58. Add all relevant critical combinations and save your entries.

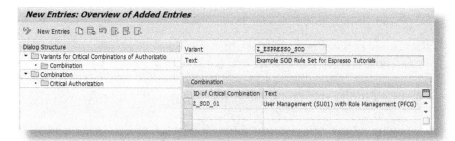

Figure 4.58: RSUSR008_009_NEW: creating an SoD conflict—step 4

You can now use your implemented critical authorizations and critical combinations to analyze roles. Now you can start a critical authorization analysis. In the VARIANT NAME section, select FOR CRITICAL AUTHORIZATIONS, as depicted in Figure 4.59, and specify the variant that you want to use **❶**. Next, define the role you want to analyze **❷**. You can also analyze several or all roles in one system in parallel. Start the analysis by clicking EXECUTE **❸** or by pressing [F8].

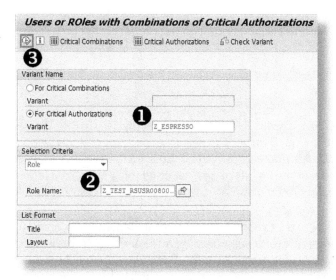

Figure 4.59: RSUSR008_009_NEW: performing a critical authorizations analysis

The result is a display of all the critical authorizations contained in the variant (Figure 4.60). If the ROLE column contains a value for a specific critical authorization, as is the case for the critical authorization *Z_PFCG* in the example shown, this means that the critical authorization exists in the role displayed. You now have to decide whether the critical authorization is included in the role legitimately—for example, if transaction PFCG is included in a role for role administrators—or if the critical authorization is inappropriate for a role—for example, if transaction PFCG is included in a role for the finance module. Depending on the decision, the underlying permissions can remain in the role or they must be removed.

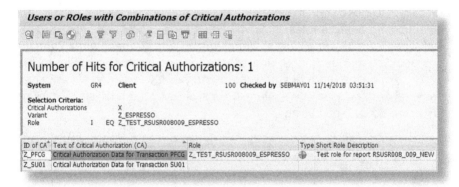

Figure 4.60: RSUSR008_009_NEW: results of the critical authorizations analysis

You can also perform a critical combinations analysis. In the VARIANT NAME section, select FOR CRITICAL COMBINATIONS and specify the variant that you want to use ❶ (Figure 4.61). Next, determine the role you want to analyze ❷. You can also analyze several or all roles in one system in parallel. Start the analysis by clicking EXECUTE ❸ or by pressing F8.

Just as for the critical authorizations analysis, all the critical combinations contained in the variant are initially displayed (Figure 4.62). If the ROLE column contains a value for a specific critical combination, as is the case for the critical combination *Z_SOD_1* in the example shown, this again means that the critical combination exists in the role displayed. Unlike critical authorizations, critical combinations must always be avoided at role level and are only allowed in exceptional cases (for example, roles for emergency or technical users). If end user roles already contain SoD conflicts (i.e., critical combinations), SoD conflicts can no longer be prevented at the user level.

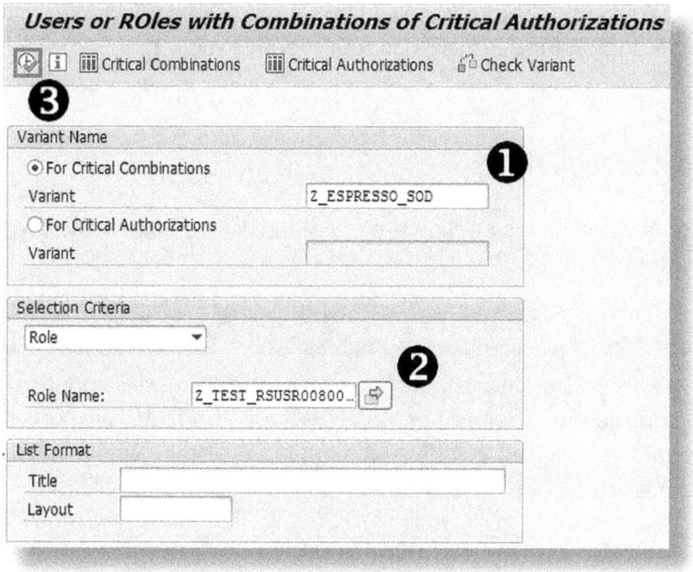

Figure 4.61: RSUSR008_009_NEW: performing a critical combinations (SoD) analysis

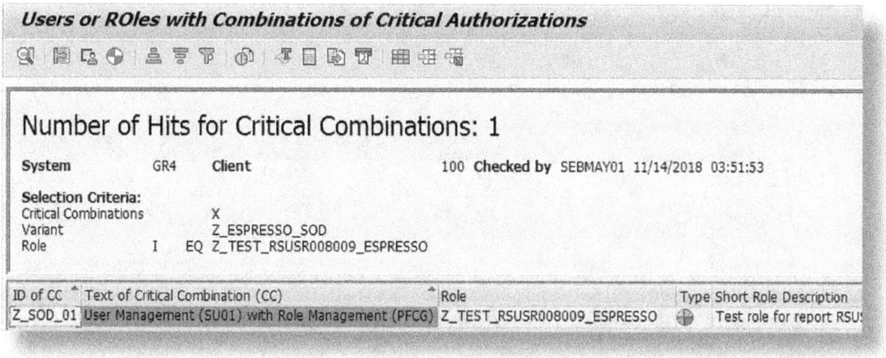

Figure 4.62: RSUSR008_009_NEW: results of the critical combinations (SoD) analysis

You have now seen how the assessment of critical permissions and segregation of duties conflicts (critical combinations) could be built into your role management. However, as this is just one of many ways to do this, as outlined earlier, take into account your company-specific actions performed to ensure the appropriateness of critical permissions and to avoid

SoD conflicts at role level. These reviews should always be integrated into the role creation and change process as a preventive measure.

4.5.3 Critical access rights

The access rights listed in this section are considered as critical in the area of role management.

> ### Authorizations for maintaining roles
>
> As role changes should always be performed through a change management process, these authorizations should not be assigned to individuals but only to emergency users in a production environment.

Therefore, check whether the following transactions and associated authorization objects are granted only to appropriate users by using the report **Users by Complex Selection Criteria** in transaction SUIM (for further information, please refer to Section 3.2).

▶ **Maintain roles**

Authorization object	Field	Field value
S_TCODE	TCD	PFCG
S_USER_AGR	ACVT	01 (create), 02 (change), or 06 (delete)

▶ **Generate authorization profile (through role maintenance)**

Authorization object	Field	Field value
S_TCODE	TCD	PFCG
S_USER_AGR	ACVT	64

▶ **Maintain profiles**

Authorization object	Field	Field value
S_TCODE	TCD	SU02
S_USER_PRO	ACVT	01 (create), 02 (change), 06 (delete), or 07 (activate, generate)

4.6 User access management

4.6.1 Background to the control and associated risk

Together with role management (please refer to Section 4.5), *user access management* is one of the central processes for granting, maintaining, and removing access to SAP systems for individuals and is therefore key to ensuring that users have access to the data they need to perform their job (*need-to-know principle*), but that they have no further access to data not necessary to fulfill their daily tasks (*principle of least privilege*). From an auditor's perspective, user management is therefore one of the essential fields for assessing whether both *data security* and *data privacy* can be ensured in SAP systems.

The first step, and this is independent of SAP or any other application used, is to ensure that users and their authorizations are set up, approved, and assigned according to a standardized procedure. Figure 4.63 shows an example of a user creation process. It starts with the initiation of a user request. The request is then reviewed by the beneficiary's line manager and the target system owner, before the user is technically created within the application. In this example, each user creation request must be appropriately reviewed and approved before any kind of technical implementation takes place.

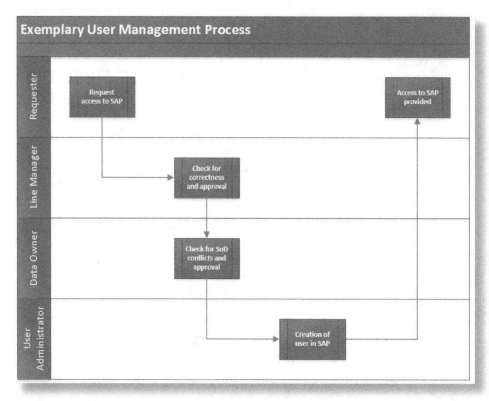

Figure 4.63: Exemplary user creation process

A similar process must be in place for adding (additional) authorizations to user accounts as well as for revoking users and authorizations.

Associated risk: User access management process

 If the user management process does not contain key controls to ensure that user access is formally requested and approved, revoked as required, and regularly recertified, the appropriateness of user access to the SAP system cannot be guaranteed.

In addition to the general user access management process, there are further non-SAP-specific and SAP-specific good practices that should be followed:

▶ **User deletion**

Accounts and users of employees who have left the company must be promptly disabled or deleted.

Associated risk: User deletion

If access granted to terminated employees remains active, this access may be used by the terminated employee or individuals with knowledge of the password for unauthorized or fraudulent activities.

▶ **User recertification**

Users and their assigned roles and authorizations must be periodically reviewed by appropriate personnel (e.g., by the line manager and/or the role owner).

Associated risk: User recertification

If user access to the SAP application is not reviewed on a regular basis, inappropriate or obsolete access rights may remain undetected and could result in unauthorized access to business-critical data.

▶ **Critical authorizations and segregation of duties**

Users must be preventively analyzed for segregation of duties conflicts and critical authorizations when changed or created.

Associated risk: Critical authorizations and segregation of duties

If SoD conflicts and inappropriate critical authorizations are not resolved or removed prior to becoming effective in the SAP system, these access rights may be exploited to manipulate, compromise, or delete business-critical data or to bypass implemented segregation of duty controls in the system.

▶ **No use of generic accounts**
Individuals must always work with unique user IDs. Generic accounts must be used only in exceptional cases—for example, for batch processing, for interfaces, or for emergency access.

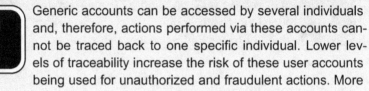

Associated risk: Generic accounts

Generic accounts can be accessed by several individuals and, therefore, actions performed via these accounts cannot be traced back to one specific individual. Lower levels of traceability increase the risk of these user accounts being used for unauthorized and fraudulent actions. Moreover, additional manual controls are required to ensure access to generic accounts remains appropriate, resulting in increased management effort and higher susceptibility to errors.

▶ **Use of the correct user types**
The SAP system provides five different user types. Password parameters are for instance only fully applied to the user type **Dialog**. Therefore, it must be ensured that the correct user type is chosen for specific kinds of users (e.g., end user accounts, technical user accounts).

Associated risk: User types

Inappropriate configuration of user types may result in either increased risk of unauthorized access (lower level of password rules, potential access to generic accounts) or increased risk of system availability impacts (lockout of technical users).

▶ **No use of reference users**
In the SAP system, access can be granted based on a reference user (specific user type). This means that everyone who is assigned to a reference user receives the same access that the reference user has or will ever receive.

Associated risk: Reference users

 By assigning access rights through reference user functionality, access rights are not assigned and approved specifically for each user individually. This may result in access being unintentionally assigned to multiple users, violating the principles of least privilege and need to know.

Furthermore, when an SAP system is installed, various built-in accounts are set up automatically. These accounts are used, for example, to perform post-installation tasks immediately after the SAP system has initially been implemented. In order to grant customers access to those standard accounts, many of the accounts have common and widely known passwords. As most of the built-in user IDs have very broad and extensive access rights, they are also considered *superuser accounts*. Table 4.2 provides an overview of the SAP built-in user IDs that exist along with their purpose.

SAP built-in user ID	Purpose
SAP*	Available in all SAP clients after installation. Has very extensive access rights (profile SAP_ALL) and a standard password (PASS). SAP* is used to perform post-installation tasks before unique user IDs for individuals are available. Accessibility is dependent on the password parameter login/no_automatic_user_sapstar.
DDIC	This is a user with specific authorizations for the installation, software logistics, and the ABAP Dictionary. SAP NetWeaver Application Server automatically creates the user master record in client 000 and client 001 when the SAP system is installed. The password must be defined individually within the installation process. DDIC is used to perform changes to the Data Dictionary during the installation or patching of SAP systems.
EAR-LYWATCH	This user is available only in old SAP releases (which also have client 066) and in that case, has a standard password (SUPPORT). The original purpose of this user was to enable remote system maintenance. The user EARLYWATCH as well as client 066 has been replaced by SAP Solution Manager.

SAP built-in user ID	Purpose
SAPCPIC	This user is created automatically during the installation of an SAP system and has a standard password (ADMIN). SAPCPIC is intended for the use of EDI interfaces. The standard authorizations of SAPCPIC are limited to RFC connections.
TMSADM	This user is created automatically in client 000 when the Transport Management System is set up in the SAP system and has a standard password (either PASSWORD or $1Pawd2&). This account is used for transferring transports from one instance into another.

Table 4.2: Overview of SAP built-in user IDs

SAP built-in accounts must be secured. This includes:

▶ Locking built-in user IDs

▶ Changing standard passwords of built-in user IDs

▶ Avoiding user types DIALOG and SERVICE for built-in user IDs

▶ Removing authorizations (i.e., profiles and roles) from built-in user IDs

Non-compliance with the setup of built-in user IDs is accompanied by the following risk.

Associated risk: Built-in user IDs

 If standard built-in accounts are not changed or deactivated, unauthorized personnel could be able to access these accounts and manipulate, compromise, or delete business-critical data as built-in standard user names and standard passwords are commonly known.

4.6.2 Test steps in the SAP system

User access management process

To analyze the creation of and changes to users, you have to first find out which users have actually been created or changed during the audit period. To do this, open transaction SUIM and navigate through the menu: USER INFORMATION SYSTEM • CHANGE DOCUMENTS • FOR USERS.

A selection screen opens (Figure 4.64). First, specify the audit period by using the fields FROM DATE/FROM TIME and TO DATE/TO TIME ❶. Secondly, select the USER CREATED option ❷ to include all users that have been created within the audit period in your query. Finally, select the ROLES and PROFILES options on the ROLES/PROFILES tab ❸ to also include changes made at user level regarding authorizations. If relevant, you can also include other options such as password changes or changes to the user type in the evaluation.

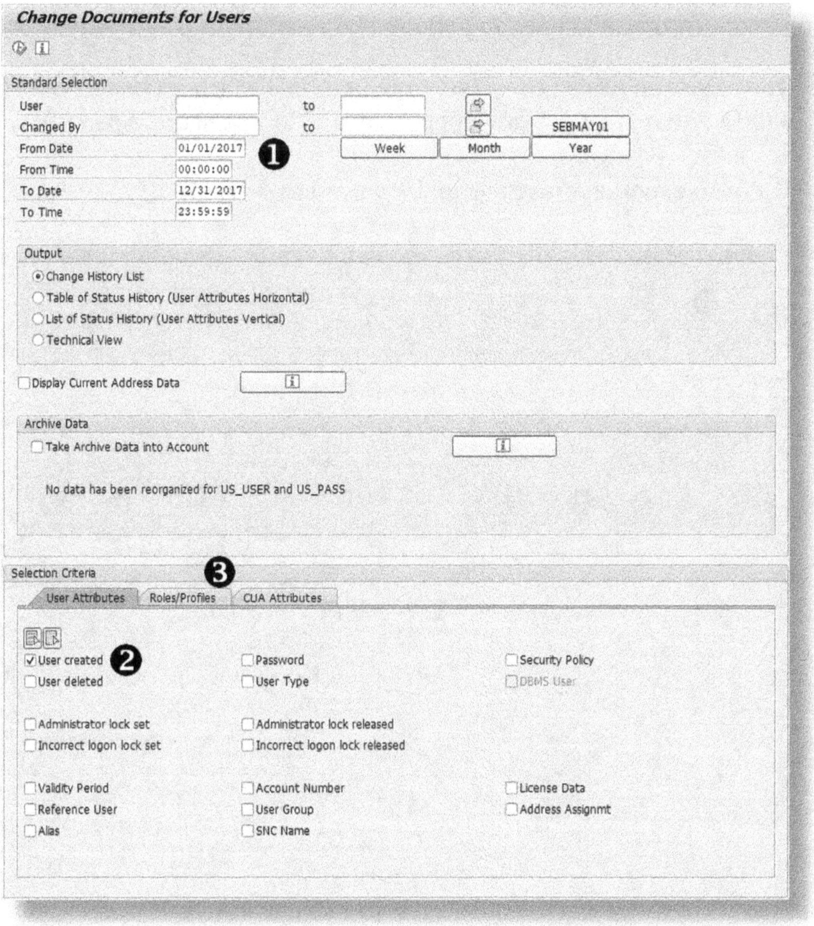

Figure 4.64: Change documents for users—selecting users that have been created or updated

The result is a display of all users that meet your criteria, as shown in the example in Figure 4.65.

❶ USER: ID of the user that has been changed

❷ DATE and TIME: Date and time on which the change took place

❸ CHANGED BY: ID of the user who performed the change

❹ ACTION: Description of what has actually been changed

❺ OLD VALUE and NEW VALUE: Values before and after the change

❻ TCODE: Transaction used to perform the change

❼ START DATE and END DATE: Date from and until which a change will be effective (e.g., role assignment can be limited to a specific period)

You can also export the results into, for instance, a .txt-file ❽.

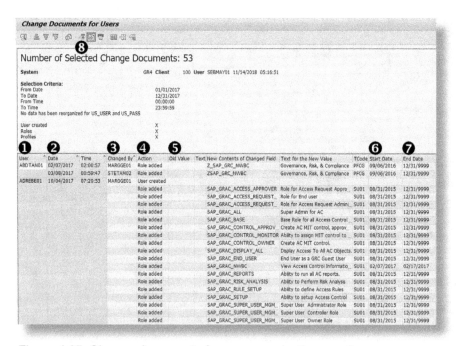

Figure 4.65: Change documents for users—selection results

Finally, request the documentation of the user access management process that is required in your company—such as the application form, approval of the line manager, or the data owner—for a representative sample of user creations or user changes.

Critical authorizations and segregation of duties

The analysis of users with regard to segregation of duties conflicts and critical authorizations is as diverse as the analysis at role level. Most tools that can analyze roles for these kinds of risks can also do so for users. This also applies to report RSUSR008_009_NEW, which was presented in Section 4.5.2. The only difference to consider is that *User* must be selected instead of *Role* as the SELECTION CRITERIA (see Figure 4.66). Since the variants are valid for both roles and users, there is no need for further updates.

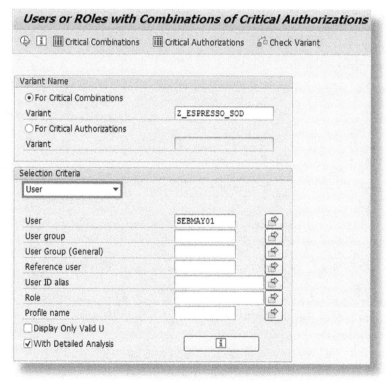

Figure 4.66: Report RSUSR008_009_NEW—user level

The presentation of the results is similar for roles and users, so please refer to Section 4.5.2 here as well.

As already stated in the analysis of roles, note that report RSUSR008_009_ NEW is just one of many ways to analyze users and roles for segregation of duties conflicts and critical authorizations. When auditing this specific control, always take into account your company-specific actions performed to ensure the appropriateness of critical authorizations and to avoid SoD conflicts. These reviews should always be integrated into the role creation and change process as a preventive measure.

User deletion

First, open transaction SUIM and again, navigate through the menu: USER INFORMATION SYSTEM • CHANGE DOCUMENTS • FOR USERS. However, instead of selecting USER CREATED and ROLES/PROFILES, select USER DELETED as shown in Figure 4.67.

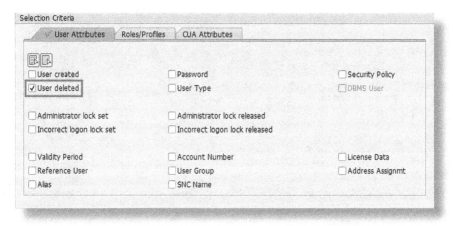

Figure 4.67: Change documents for users—selecting deleted users

The result is a display of all users deleted in the specified period, as shown in the example in Figure 4.68.

Request a list of all persons with SAP access that have left your company within the audit period—for example, from the HR department—and check whether, in all cases, the corresponding SAP account has been deleted in a timely manner.

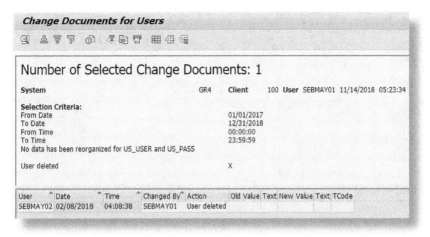

Figure 4.68: Change documents for users—results for deleted users

User recertification

You typically perform a user recertification by first extracting all users and their assigned roles and authorizations from the SAP system. However, before you can do this, you have to identify all the users that you want to review. The following users are usually excluded from a user recertification:

▶ Locked users

▶ Invalid users

▶ Technical accounts (users without the possibility to log on via SAP GUI)

To filter out these users, open table USR02 in transaction SE16 or SE16N. In the GLTGV field (valid from) ❶, choose *less than or equal to* today's date as well as the date *00/00/0000*. In the GLTGB field (valid through) ❷, choose *greater than or equal to* today's date as well as the date *00/00/0000*. This ensures that only users that are still valid and users for which the validity period has not been set are displayed. Next, select for example only dialog and service users—*A* and *S*—in the USTYP field (user type) ❸. Finally, ensure that only unlocked users are displayed by setting the value *0* in the UFLAG field (user lock status) ❹. Initiate the selection by clicking Execute ❺ or by pressing [F8], as depicted in Figure 4.69.

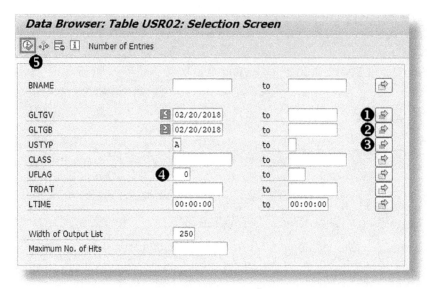

Figure 4.69: Table USR02: selection screen

The result is a display of all valid dialog and service accounts that are not locked. Download the data (e.g., into a spreadsheet) and copy the user names into the clipboard.

Next, open table AGR_USERS in transaction SE16 or SE16N. Paste the copied users from table USR02 into the UNAME field (user name) ❶ so that you only receive the role-to-user assignments for unlocked, valid dialog and service accounts. Initiate the selection by clicking EXECUTE ❷ or by pressing ⌐F8⌐, as depicted in Figure 4.70.

Download the results to enhance your spreadsheet. Send the spreadsheet to appropriate personnel (e.g., line manager or role owner) so that they can review the users and the role assignments.

From an audit perspective, check whether the control described above is in place, whether feedback is provided appropriately by reviewers, and whether feedback provided is implemented in a timely manner (e.g., by assessing whether users have been deleted as described in the previous section).

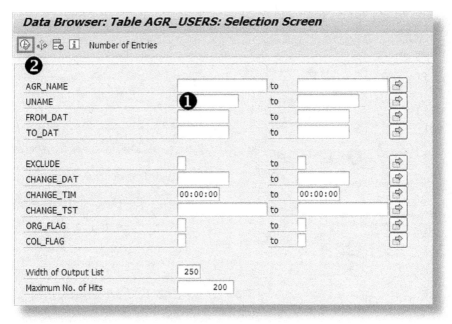

Figure 4.70: Table AGR_USERS: selection screen

No use of generic accounts/use of the correct user types

Generally, end users are not allowed to work with generic accounts in SAP systems. In order to check whether this requirement is fulfilled, obtain a list of all SAP accounts that are not locked at the time of the audit and whose validity date is in the future. In addition, only users of the type **dialog** and **service** are required, because only these user types grant a dialog logon (e.g., logon via the SAP GUI using a user ID and password). To generate such a list, open transaction SUIM and navigate through the menu: USER INFORMATION SYSTEM • USER • USERS BY COMPLEX SELECTION CRITERIA • USERS BY COMPLEX SELECTION CRITERIA.

In the selection criteria (Figure 4.71), first specify that only users of the type *A Dialog* and *S Service* are included in the report ❶. Secondly, select the ONLY USERS WITHOUT LOCKS option ❷. Finally, define the validity period by setting today's date in the VALID FROM field ❸ (this translates into a validity period from today (03/18/2018) to 12/31/9999. Initiate the selection by clicking EXECUTE ❹ or by pressing F8.

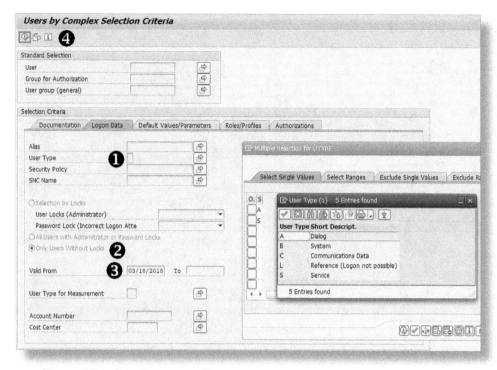

Figure 4.71: Creating a user list

As soon as you have generated the list, check whether it contains only personalized user IDs or whether it also contains generic accounts. Generic user IDs that are used by end users must be prevented. However, if you do find generic user IDs, used for example for interfaces or for batch jobs, the user type must be changed to either *System* or *Communications Data*.

No use of reference users

To check that no reference users are used, open table USR02 in transaction SE16 or SE16N. On the selection screen, in the USTYP field (user type) ❶, choose the value *L* (reference user). Initiate the selection by clicking EXECUTE ❷ or by pressing [F8], as depicted in Figure 4.72.

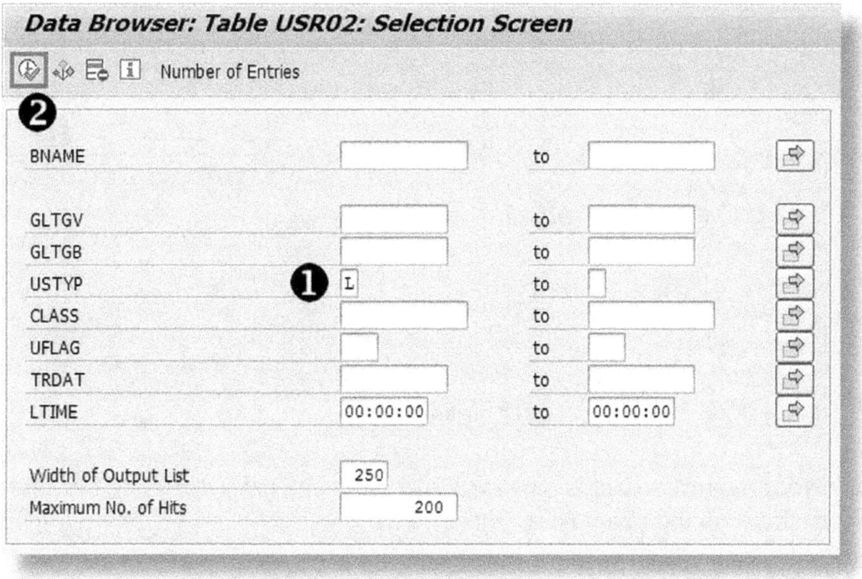

Data Browser: Table USR02: Selection Screen

⊕ ⬧ 🖃 ⓘ Number of Entries

❷

BNAME		to		⇨

GLTGV		to		⇨
GLTGB		to		⇨
USTYP	❶ L	to		⇨
CLASS		to		⇨
UFLAG		to		⇨
TRDAT		to		⇨
LTIME	00:00:00	to	00:00:00	⇨

Width of Output List	250
Maximum No. of Hits	200

Figure 4.72: Table USR02: selection screen

If no results are displayed, this means that no reference users are available in your SAP system and your testing would therefore end here. If results are displayed, as shown in Figure 4.73, your testing continues with an additional step.

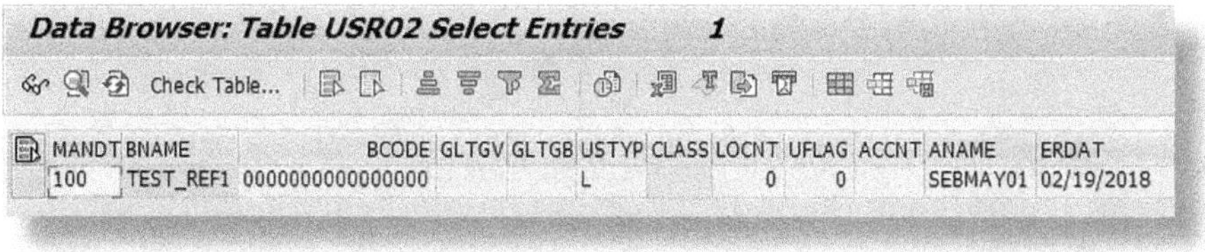

Data Browser: Table USR02 Select Entries   1

⊗ ⚟ ⟳ Check Table...   🖃 🖃 ⬆ ⬇ 🔽 Σ ⊕ 🗐 🔢 🗔 🗗 ⊞ ⊡ ⬚

MANDT	BNAME	BCODE	GLTGV	GLTGB	USTYP	CLASS	LOCNT	UFLAG	ACCNT	ANAME	ERDAT
100	TEST_REF1	0000000000000000			L		0	0		SEBMAY01	02/19/2018

Figure 4.73: Table USR02: results

The next step is to analyze whether the detected reference user has been assigned to another account. The result would be that the user would receive the same authorizations as the reference user. To check this, open table USREFUS in transaction SE16 or SE16N. Specify that the REFUSER field is not equal to *empty* ❶. Initiate the selection by clicking EXECUTE ❷ or by pressing F8, as depicted in Figure 4.74.

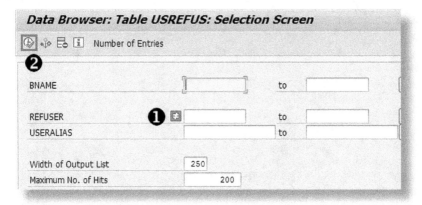

Figure 4.74: Table USREFUS: selection screen

If your reference user is assigned to an account, it will appear in this table, as shown in the example in Figure 4.75.

Figure 4.75: Table USREFUS: results

Treatment of reference users

If you detect a reference user that is not assigned to an account, you could request that the user is deleted immediately. If a reference user is assigned to individuals, ensure that appropriate authorizations are granted to them before deleting the reference user.

Built-in accounts

To assess whether SAP built-in accounts have been protected appropriately, execute program RSUSR003 in transaction SA38. Alternatively, you can start the program in transaction RSUSR003 or transaction S_ALR_87101194. As shown in Figure 4.76, this program provides an overview of whether built-in user IDs are locked and whether the standard passwords of those accounts have been changed. The user *DDIC* in client 100 ❶ has been locked (column: Lock) by a user administrator (column: Reason for User Lock), which means no one can currently log on to this account. Furthermore, the standard password has been changed (column: Password Status, value: *Exists, Password not trivial.*). The value *Does not exist.* in the Password Status column ❷ means that the standard user is generally not available within the specific SAP client. Furthermore, the value *Password SUPPORT well known.* ❸ indicates that the standard password of a built-in account has not been changed. Finally, the value *Does not exist. Logon possible with p/w PASS. See Note 2383* ❹ means that on the one hand, the user *SAP** has been deleted, and on the other hand, that you can still log on to the client using the user ID *SAP** and the password *PASS* as the password parameter login/no_automatic_user_ sapstar is set to *0*.

Deleting SAP*

 Always exercise caution when deleting the user SAP*. If the parameter LOGIN/NO_AUTOMATIC_USER_SAPSTAR is set to *0* (intentionally or accidentally), everyone could log on to the SAP system using the user ID SAP* and the password PASS, even though the ID has been deleted (please refer to SAP Note 2383). If the user has not been deleted but merely locked, and the standard password is changed, no one can log on to the user SAP* even if the parameter LOGIN/NO_ AUTOMATIC_USER_SAPSTAR is set to *0*. Deleting the user SAP* is only recommended if the parameter LOGIN/NO_AUTOMATIC_USER_ SAPSTAR is set to the value *1*, which generally disables the use of the user SAP*. If this has been done in your SAP system, in the event of an emergency (e.g., if all users in an SAP system are locked), the profile parameter LOGIN/NO_AUTOMATIC_USER_SAPSTAR can be changed to *0* (enabling logon to the SAP system through SAP*) by changing the file storing the profile parameters at application server level (please refer to SAP Note 68048).

If the parameter is set to *1*, regardless of whether SAP* is available or has been deleted, no one can log on to this account. In this case, you would find the value *Does not exist. Logon not possible. See Note 2383*. Please refer to Section 4.9 for information on how to check password parameters.

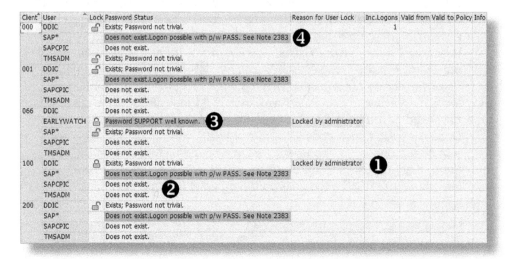

Client	User	Lock	Password Status	Reason for User Lock	Inc.Logons	Valid from	Valid to	Policy Info
000	DDIC	🔓	Exists; Password not trivial.					
	SAP*		Does not exist.Logon possible with p/w PASS. See Note 2383 ④		1			
	SAPCPIC		Does not exist.					
	TMSADM	🔓	Exists; Password not trivial.					
001	DDIC	🔓	Exists; Password not trivial.					
	SAP*		Does not exist.Logon possible with p/w PASS. See Note 2383					
	SAPCPIC		Does not exist.					
	TMSADM		Does not exist.					
066	DDIC		Does not exist.					
	EARLYWATCH	🔒	Password SUPPORT well known. ③	Locked by administrator				
	SAP*	🔓	Exists; Password not trivial.					
	SAPCPIC		Does not exist.					
	TMSADM		Does not exist.					
100	DDIC	🔒	Exists; Password not trivial.	Locked by administrator ①				
	SAP*		Does not exist.Logon possible with p/w PASS. See Note 2383					
	SAPCPIC		Does not exist. ②					
	TMSADM		Does not exist.					
200	DDIC	🔓	Exists; Password not trivial.					
	SAP*		Does not exist.Logon possible with p/w PASS. See Note 2383					
	SAPCPIC		Does not exist.					
	TMSADM		Does not exist.					

Figure 4.76: SAP built-in user IDs: overview (program RSUSR003)

As a next step, check whether built-in user IDs are set up as user type *DIALOG* or *SERVICE*. If they are not, this may prevent a user from being able to log on with a user name and password. To check the user type for standard accounts, either double-click the user name within report RSUSR003 or open the corresponding user in transaction SU01D. Here, on the LOGON DATA tab ①, you can find the user type (Figure 4.77).

Finally, check whether any roles ② or profiles ③ are assigned to the corresponding user ID (also shown in Figure 4.77). In the present example, the profiles *SAP_ALL* and *S_A.SYSTEM* are assigned to the user *DDIC*. Both profiles provide extensive access rights and should be removed as long as the built-in user ID is not being actively used. In the case of user DDIC, such profiles should only be added if a patch requiring the use of the account needs to be implemented.

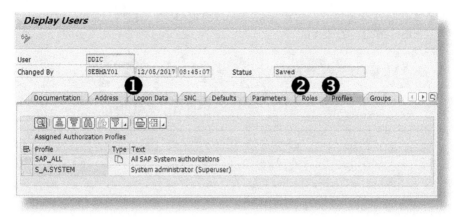

Figure 4.77: SAP built-in user IDs: review of user type, assigned profiles and roles

4.6.3 Critical access rights

The access rights listed in this section are considered as critical in the area of user access management. Therefore, check that the following transactions and associated authorization objects are granted only to appropriate users by using the report **Users by Complex Selection Criteria** in transaction SUIM (for further information, please refer to Section 3.2).

▶ **Maintain users/user master records**

Authorization object	Field	Field value
S_TCODE	TCD	SU01, SU01_NAV, SU10, SUID01, or SUID10
S_USER_GRP	ACVT	01 (create), 02 (change), or 06 (delete)

▶ **Assign roles to users (if parameter CHECK_S_USER_SAS = NO in table PRGN_CUST)**

Authorization object	Field	Field value
S_TCODE	TCD	SU01, SU01_NAV, SU10, SUID01, or SUID10
S_USER_GRP	ACTVT	02
S_USER_AGR	ACTVT	22
S_USER_PRO	ACTVT	22

▶ **Assign roles to users (if CHECK_S_USER_SAS = YES in table PRGN_CUST)**

Authorization object	Field	Field value
S_TCODE	TCD	SU01, SU01_NAV, SU10, SUID01, or SUID10
S_USER_GRP	ACTVT	02
S_USER_SAS	ACTVT	22

▶ **Assign roles to users through transaction PFCG (if CHECK_S_USER_SAS = NO in table PRGN_CUST)**

Authorization object	Field	Field value
S_TCODE	TCD	PFCG
S_USER_AGR	ACTVT	03
S_USER_GRP	ACTVT	22
S_USER_PRO	ACTVT	22

▶ **Assign roles to users through transaction PFCG (if CHECK_S_USER_SAS = YES in table PRGN_CUST)**

Authorization object	Field	Field value
S_TCODE	TCD	PFCG
S_USER_AGR	ACTVT	03
S_USER_GRP	ACTVT	22
S_USER_SAS	ACTVT	22

▶ Create users and assign roles through transaction **PFCG_EASY/ PFCG_EASY_NEW**

Authorization object	Field	Field value
S_TCODE	TCD	PFCG_EASY or PFCG_EASY_NEW
S_USER_GRP	ACTVT	01, 22
S_USER_AGR	ACTVT	01, 02, 64
S_USER_PRO	ACTVT	01
	PROFILE	* or T*
S_USER_VAL	OBJECT	*
	AUTH_FIELD	*
	AUTH_VALUE	*
S_USER_TCD	TCD	*

▶ Assign roles through transaction **PFCG_EASY/PFCG_EASY_NEW**

Authorization object	Field	Field value
S_TCODE	TCD	PFCG_EASY or PFCG_EASY_NEW
S_USER_GRP	ACTVT	22
S_USER_AGR	ACTVT	01, 02, 64
S_USER_PRO	ACTVT	01
	PROFILE	* or T*
S_USER_VAL	OBJECT	*
	AUTH_FIELD	*
	AUTH_VALUE	*
S_USER_TCD	TCD	*

▶ Unlock user IDs/password maintenance (assign new password to user)

Authorization object	Field	Field value
S_TCODE	TCD	SU01, SU01_NAV, SU10, SUID01, or SUID10
S_USER_GRP	ACTVT	05

▶ **Deletion of user SAP***

Authorization object	Field	Field value
S_TCODE	TCD	SU01, SU01_NAV, SU10, SUID01, or SUID10
S_USER_GRP	ACVT	06
	CLASS	User group to which SAP* is assigned (by default SUPER)

▶ **Unlock user SAP*/other built-in user IDs**

Authorization object	Field	Field value
S_TCODE	TCD	SU01, SU01_NAV, SU10, SUID01, or SUID10
S_USER_GRP	ACVT	05
	CLASS	User group to which SAP*/built-in user IDs are assigned (by default SUPER)

4.7 Review of privileged access rights

4.7.1 Background to the control and associated risk

Due to the potentially far-reaching consequences of privileged access rights, we have created this separate section in addition to the details of critical access rights found at the end of every section in this chapter.

Definition of privileged access rights

 The term *privileged access rights* describes the broader access to information technologies given to an individual compared to the access required by **ordinary** users. As a rule, privileged authorizations are only assigned to roles, groups, or persons who are predominantly entrusted with the administration of information technology.

SAP provides a number of standard authorizations in various forms in their systems. The SAP built-in accounts, which require particular protection, have already been discussed in Section 4.6.

In addition to the SAP built-in accounts, there are further privileged access rights to be aware of:

▶ **SAP default profiles**
As the name implies, SAP default profiles are profiles that are available by default in each SAP system for different purposes. Table 4.3 provides an overview of the most important SAP default profiles, together with an explanation of their purpose.

SAP default profile	Purpose
SAP_ALL	This profile includes all permissions for the SAP system—e.g., basis, customization, development, and almost all module-specific permissions.
SAP_NEW	SAP_NEW is a profile that consists of all individual profiles that contain authorizations which are added through an SAP release (as of 2.1C).
S_A.SYSTEM	This profile contains all basis permissions.
S_A.DEVELOP	This profile contains all permissions for developing in SAP systems.
S_A.ADMIN	This profile contains specific basis permissions—e.g., maintaining client-independent tables, maintaining and executing external commands, as well as batch administration.

Table 4.3: SAP default profiles

▶ **SAP default roles**
Similar to SAP default profiles, SAP default roles are roles that are available by default in each SAP system. There are regularly a large number of SAP default roles after the installation of a new SAP system; they differ in particular in their purpose and their criticality. For example, there are default roles that contain display-only access in certain modules and there are some that have far-reaching permissions, such as basic administration or accounting. SAP default roles can be identified by the fact that their name usually begins with the prefix SAP_.

▶ **Extremely critical transactions and authorization objects**
Extensive critical access rights are transactions and authorization objects that allow users to extensively circumvent or suspend controls described in these sections and which might be regarded as violating law. As an example of extensive critical access rights, the debug and replace access right is worthy of mention here. Debug and replace can be used for the following purposes: to intervene in business processes (for instance, replacement of default values, e.g., bank details of a payee, with other values, e.g., own account data); to change data (retrospective change of entries in the accounting ledger, violation of the erasure prohibition, which is for instance stated in §239 HGB (German Commercial Code) [an entry or a record in the accounting ledger must not be altered in such a way that the original content is no longer identifiable]); or to cover tracks (adjustments of change logs and change documents).

All of the aforementioned and described privileged access rights authorize individuals to perform either extremely far-reaching activities in SAP systems or, if they are not set up according to the requirements of your company, may contain more authorizations than an individual needs to fulfill their job. This constitutes a violation of the principle of least privilege. In addition, these authorizations can be used to circumvent other control mechanisms—for example, allowing development directly in the production system (change management, development management)—or allowing logs to be altered (Security Audit Log, table logging).

Associated risk: Privileged access rights

 If there is no assurance that privileged access rights in an SAP system are restricted to a minimum, taking account of the principle of least privilege, and there is no appropriate monitoring of the use of these access rights, business-critical data may be compromised, manipulated, or deleted without this being detected.

In order to ensure that the risk described above does not come into effect, privileged access rights must be checked regularly as well as during an audit.

4.7.2   Test steps in the SAP system

SAP default profiles

To check whether SAP default profiles are used in your SAP system, open transaction SUIM and navigate through the menu: USER INFORMATION SYSTEM • USER • USERS BY COMPLEX SELECTION CRITERIA • USERS BY COMPLEX SELECTION CRITERIA. On the selection screen, open the ROLES/PROFILES tab and in the PROFILE NAME field ❶, enter SAP default profiles as listed and described in Section 4.7.1. In the example shown, the aim is to figure out who the profile *SAP_ALL* is assigned to (Figure 4.78). Initiate your selection by clicking EXECUTE ❷ or by pressing ⌨ F8 .

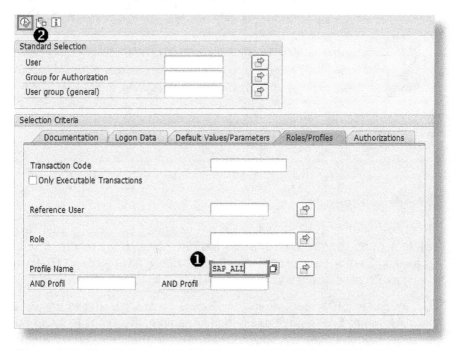

Figure 4.78: User Information System: checking SAP default profiles

Figure 4.79 shows all users to whom a defined (SAP default) profile is assigned. If you searched for a name pattern instead of a specific profile, select a specific user or specific users and click IN ACCORDANCE WITH SELECTION to see which profile has been assigned to a specific user (an example is shown in the next section—"SAP default roles").

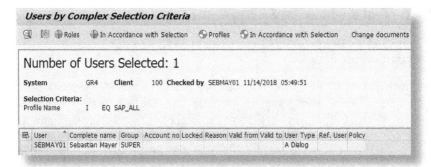

Figure 4.79: User Information System: checking SAP default profiles—results

Alternative determination method

 Instead of using transaction SUIM, you can also open table UST04 in transaction SE16 or SE16N. On the selection screen, in the PROFILE field, enter *SAP_ALL*, for example, and execute. The results table shows you which selected profiles (profiles that meet your selection pattern) are assigned to which users. However, you are not given any additional information such as the full name of the user or role type.

SAP default roles

To check whether SAP default roles are assigned to users in your SAP system, open transaction SUIM and navigate through the menu: USER INFORMATION SYSTEM • USER • USERS BY COMPLEX SELECTION CRITERIA • USERS BY COMPLEX SELECTION CRITERIA.

On the selection screen, open the ROLES/PROFILES tab and in the ROLE field ❶, enter SAP default roles. In the example, the aim is to figure out who SAP default roles are generally assigned to (Figure 4.80). Therefore, you must search for assigned *SAP** roles. Initiate your selection by clicking EXECUTE ❷ or by pressing ⌐F8⌐.

Figure 4.81 shows all users to whom a defined (SAP default) role is assigned. If you searched for a name pattern instead of a specific profile, select a specific user or specific users ❶ and click IN ACCORDANCE WITH

SELECTION ❷ to see which profile has been assigned to a specific user (Figure 4.81).

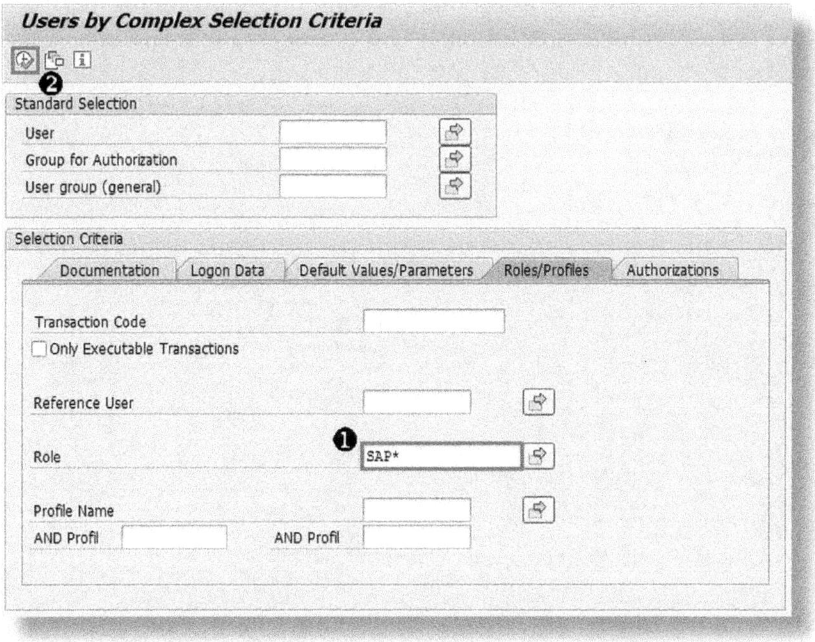

Figure 4.80: User Information System: checking SAP default roles

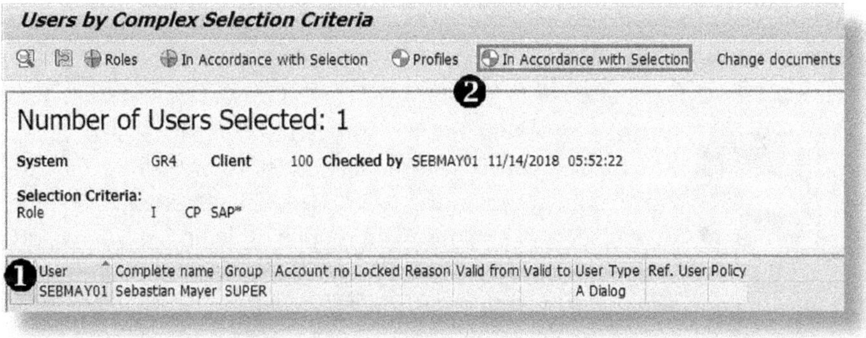

Figure 4.81: User Information System: checking SAP default roles—results

All users (column: USER NAME), their full name (column: FULL NAME), and the assigned roles that match your search (column: ROLE) are displayed, as you can see in Figure 4.82. Furthermore, you can see whether the role is a single role or a composite role (column: TYPE), whether the role is assigned directly or indirectly (column: ASSIGNMENT TYPE), the date from and until which the role assignment is valid (columns: START DATE and END DATE), and the short description of the assigned role (column: SHORT ROLE DESCRIPTION).

Users by Complex Selection Criteria

Relevant roles: 1 of 1 users have assignments.

System GR4 Client 100 User SEBMAY01 (11/14/2018 05:54:15)

User Name	Full Name	Role	Type	Assignment Type	Start date	End date	Short Role Description
SEBMAY01	Sebastian Mayer	SAP_GRAC_ACC_			08/31/2015	12/31/9999	Role for Access Request Approver
		SAP_GRAC_ACC_			08/31/2015	12/31/9999	Role for Access Request Administrator
		SAP_GRAC_ACC_			08/31/2015	12/31/9999	Role for End user
		SAP_GRAC_ALL			08/31/2015	12/31/9999	Super Admin for AC
		SAP_GRAC_BASE			08/31/2015	12/31/9999	Base Role for all Access Control Users
		SAP_GRAC_CO_			08/31/2015	12/31/9999	Create AC MIT control, approve, assign, Alerts and perform Risk Analysis
		SAP_GRAC_CO_			08/31/2015	12/31/9999	Ability to assign MIT control to a Risk and perform Risk Analysis
		SAP_GRAC_CO_			08/31/2015	12/31/9999	Create AC MIT control.
		SAP_GRAC_DIS_			08/31/2015	12/31/9999	Display Access To All AC Objects.
		SAP_GRAC_END			08/31/2015	12/31/9999	End User as a GRC Guest User
		SAP_GRAC_NW_			08/31/2015	12/31/9999	View Access Control Information Architecture.
		SAP_GRAC_REP_			08/31/2015	12/31/9999	Ability to run all AC reports.
		SAP_GRAC_RIS_			08/31/2015	12/31/9999	Ability to Perform Risk Analysis
		SAP_GRAC_RUL_			08/31/2015	12/31/9999	Ability to define Access Rules
		SAP_GRAC_SET_			08/31/2015	12/31/9999	Ability to setup Access Control
		SAP_GRAC_SUP_			08/31/2015	12/31/9999	Super User Administrator Role
		SAP_GRAC_SUP_			08/31/2015	12/31/9999	Super User Controller Role
		SAP_GRAC_SUP_			08/31/2015	12/31/9999	Super User Owner Role
		SAP_GRAC_SUP_			08/31/2015	12/31/9999	Super User Firefighter
		SAP_GRC_FN_A_			08/31/2015	12/31/9999	GRC - Power User
		SAP_GRC_FN_B_			08/31/2015	12/31/9999	GRC - Base role to run GRC applications
		SAP_GRC_FN_B_			08/31/2015	12/31/9999	GRC - Business User
		SAP_GRC_FN_D_			08/31/2015	12/31/9999	GRC - Display
		SAP_GRC_MSM_			08/31/2015	12/31/9999	MSMP Overall Administrator

Figure 4.82: User Information System: checking SAP default roles—role details

Alternative determination method

Instead of using transaction SUIM, you can also open table AGR_USERS in transaction SE16 or SE16N. On the selection screen, in the AGR_NAME field, enter *SAP**, for example, and execute. The results table shows you which selected roles (roles that meet your selection pattern) are assigned to which users. However, you are not given any additional information such as the full name of the user or role type.

Extremely critical transactions and authorization objects

In principle, each corresponding section in this chapter provides an overview of critical authorizations for each control. However, there are some permissions that are not directly related to controls but which are highly critical because they are very far-reaching and may even constitute a violation of the law. We will now introduce these extremely critical transactions and the risks associated with these permissions. First, however, we will briefly show you how to check whether the authorizations have actually been granted to a user in your SAP system.

To analyze whether extremely critical transactions and authorization objects are assigned to users in your SAP system, open transaction SUIM and navigate through the menu: User Information System • User • Users by Complex Selection Criteria • Users by Complex Selection Criteria.

On the selection screen, open the Authorizations tab. Here, you can select specific authorization objects and check whether they are assigned to users. In the example shown in Figure 4.83, the aim is to find out who has the authorizations to create or update roles in transaction *PFCG* ❶, which requires the following authorizations ❷:

▶ S_TCODE
  ▶ Field TCD = PFCG
▶ S_USER_AGR
  ▶ Field ACTVT = 01 or 02
  ▶ Field ACT_GROUP = empty (equals any potential value)

Initiate your selection by clicking Execute ❸ or by pressing ⌐F8⌐. If you want to exclude users that are locked or not valid, or you want to execute specific user types in your selection, please refer to Section 3.2 where we introduced transaction SUIM.

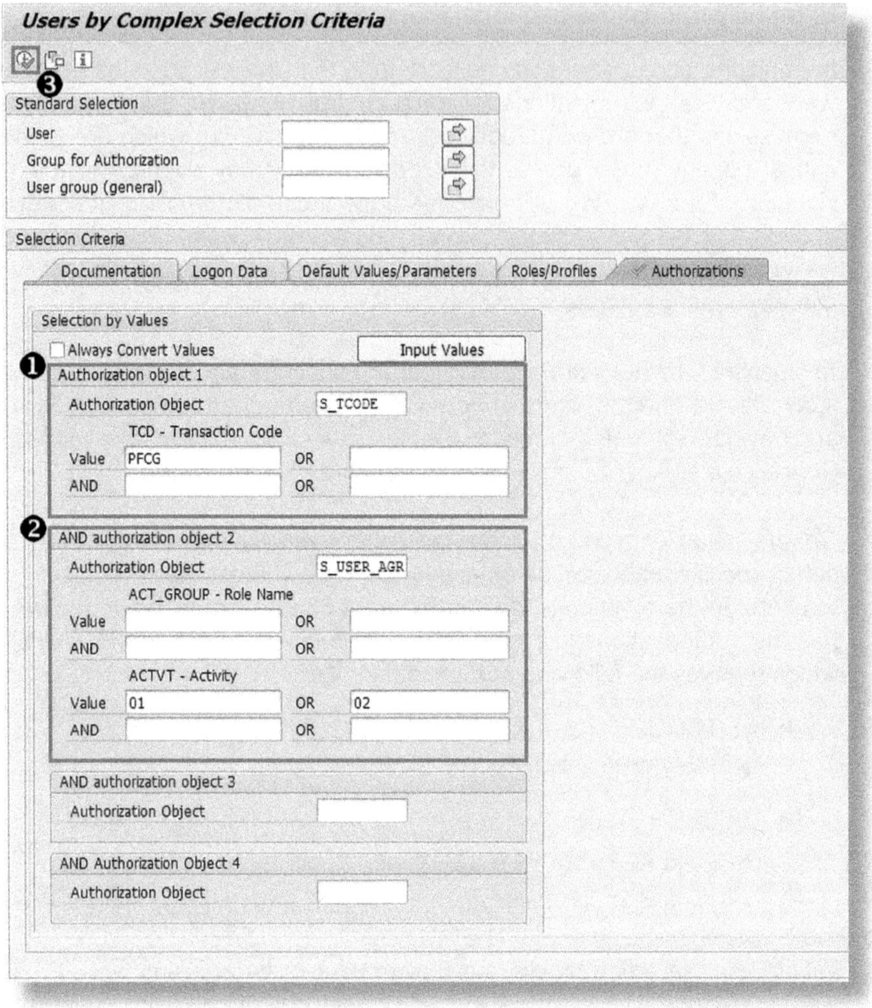

Figure 4.83: User Information System: extremely critical transactions and authorization objects

Overview of extremely critical transactions and authorization objects

The following list provides an overview of the extremely critical transactions and/or authorizations (critical permissions that have already been or will be explained within a specific control are not included in this overview) that should either not be assigned at all or should be assigned only very restrictively in an SAP system. We list *Description*, *Risk* and *Authorization values*.

▶ **Debug & replace**

Provides the possibility to tamper with business processing, business data, and logs (violation of the erasure prohibition, which is for instance stated in §239 HGB (German Commercial Code) (an entry or a record in the accounting ledger must not be altered in such a way that the original content is no longer identifiable))

S_DEVELOP (authorization object)

ACTVT = 02 (field value)

OBJTYPE = DEBUG (field value)

▶ **Execution of all function modules**

Allows execution of critical function modules that, in some cases, have inadequate authorization checks.

S_DEVELOP (authorization object)

ACTVT = 16 (field value)

OBJTYPE = FUGR (field value)

OBJNAME = '*'

▶ **Change of system profile parameters**

May allow system controls to be bypassed.

S_RZL_ADM (authorization object)

ACTVT = 02 (field value)

▶ **Deletion of change documents**

Change documents must be considered as accounting documents and must therefore be kept in accordance with the legal requirements (in Germany, for example, for 10 years according to §257 HGB (German Commercial Code)).

S_SCD0 (authorization object)

ACTVT = 06 (field values)

or

S_SCD0_OBJ (authorization object)

ACTVT = 06 (field values)

▶ Deletion of table logs

Table logs must be considered as accounting documents and must therefore be kept in accordance with the legal requirements (in Germany, for example, for 10 years according to §257 HGB (German Commercial Code)).

S_TABU_DIS (authorization object)

ACTVT = 02 (field values)

DICBERCLS = &NC& or SA (depends on which authorization group table DBTABLOG is assigned to).

or

S_TABU_NAM (authorization object)

ACTVT = 02 (field values)

TABLE = DBTABLOG

▶ Deletion of versions

Change documents must be considered as accounting documents and must therefore be kept in accordance with the legal requirements (in Germany, for example, for 10 years according to §257 HGB (German Commercial Code)).

S_CTS_ADMI (authorization object)

CTS_ADMFCT = TABL

or

S_CTS_SADM (authorization object)

CTS_ADMFCT = TABL

▶ **Implement source code per RFC and execution in main memory**

Provides the possibility to tamper with business processing, business data, and logs (violation of the erasure prohibition, which is for instance stated in §239 HGB (German Commercial Code) (an entry or a record in the accounting ledger must not be altered in such a way that the original content is no longer identifiable)).

S_RFCRAIAR (authorization object)

ACTVT = 16 (field values)

and

S_RFC (authorization object)

ACTVT = 16 (field values)

RFC_TYPE = FUGR (field values)

RFC_NAME = SUTL (field values)

or

S_RFCRAIAR (authorization object)

ACTVT = 16 (field values)

and

S_RFC = 16 (authorization object)

ACTVT (field values)

RFC_TYPE = FUNC (field values)

RFC_NAME = RFC_ABAP_INSTALL_ AND_RUN (field values)

▶ **Execution of all programs**

Allows execution of critical programs that, in some cases, have inadequate authorization checks.

S_PROGRAM (authorization object)

P_ACTION = SUBMIT or BTCSUBMIT (field values)

P_GROUP = '*' (field values)

▶ **Change any client-dependent table**

Allows, in the case of a client not being protected against changes, direct access to and change of data.

S_TABU_DIS (authorization object)

ACTVT = 02 (field values)

DICBERCLS = '*' (field values)

or

S_TABU_NAM (authorization object)

ACTVT = 02 (field values)

TABLE = '*' (field values)

▶ **Change any client-independent table**

Allows, in the case of a client not being protected against changes, direct access to and change of data.

S_TABU_DIS (authorization object)

ACTVT = 02 (field values)

DICBERCLS = '*' (field values)

and

S_TABU_CLI (authorization object)

CLIIDMAINT = X (field values)

or

S_TABU_NAM (authorization object)

ACTVT = 02 (field values)

TABLE = '*' (field values)

and

S_TABU_CLI (authorization object)

CLIIDMAINT = X (field values)

► **Implement developments**

Allows, in the case that a client is not protected against changes, implementation of customer developments in production clients.

S_DEVELOP (authorization object)

ACTVT = 01, 02, 06 (field values)

Process of reviewing privileged access rights

Check whether there is a process to regularly (e.g., annually) review privileged access rights and whether this process is documented. The decision (e.g., by a line manager or by a data owner) must be documented and the corresponding files containing the decisions must be retained to enable third parties (such as auditors) to trace back decisions and activities subsequently performed. Furthermore, for a representative sample, check whether the decision to revoke a user's privileged access rights has actually been implemented within the SAP system.

4.7.3 Critical access rights

The access rights listed in this section are considered as critical in the area of privileged access rights. Therefore, check whether the following transactions and associated authorization objects are granted only to appropriate users by using the report **Users by Complex Selection Criteria** in transaction SUIM (for further information, please refer to Section 3.2).

▶ **Assign (critical) profiles to users (if parameter CHECK_S_USER_SAS = NO in table PRGN_CUST)**

Authorization object	Field	Field value
S_TCODE	TCD	SU01, SU01_NAV, SU10, SUID01, or SUID10
S_USER_GRP	ACTVT	02
S_USER_PRO	ACTVT	22

▶ **Assign (critical) profiles to users (if parameter CHECK_S_USER_SAS = YES in table PRGN_CUST)**

Authorization object	Field	Field value
S_TCODE	TCD	SU01, SU01_NAV, SU10, SUID01, or SUID10
S_USER_GRP	ACTVT	02
S_USER_SAS	ACTVT	22

4.8 Emergency access management

4.8.1 Background to the control and associated risk

In special circumstances, especially in emergencies, it may be necessary to provide far-reaching authorizations in an SAP productive system to an end user, and possibly even enable them to bypass existing processes and controls, such as those defined within change management.

Emergency situation

 Assume you are the IT manager of a medium-sized manufacturing company whose machines are operated 24 hours a day, 7 days a week, without any breaks. Imagine it's the weekend and, due to a bug in the SAP system, commodity production cannot continue. Your standard change management process typically requires you to implement an error correction in a development system first, and then test it in a quality assurance system, with a review by a change advisory board, and then get it to production within the next release cycle, which takes place at the end of the week. In this case, your machines would be disrupted for days, which could result in considerable financial damage. You would need to react quickly and get the machines working again promptly.

However, as emergency users usually have extremely far-reaching permissions, it is important to ensure a minimum level of security and control in such situations—this is the main task of *emergency access management*. To meet this requirement, emergency access management must ensure that activities performed with an emergency user are logged every time and that activities can be traced back to an individual. In addition, you must also ensure that access to emergency users is granted only to authorized end users and only in appropriate emergency cases. However, according to the need-to-know principle (see Section 4.6), emergency access management must also ensure that adequate emergency users are available and accessible in an emergency.

The following is an overview of controls to consider as part of emergency access management.

▶ **Emergency access approval process**
Use of the emergency user must be allowed only after authorization by appropriate management. Authorization must be obtained in written form and must be archived for auditing purposes.

Associated risk: Emergency access approval process

 If appropriate segregation of duties through independent approvals prior to access to emergency users being granted is not ensured, these users may be accessed without authorization or without a valid business reason. Given that these users have extensive access to the SAP system, business-critical data may then be manipulated, compromised, or deleted. Moreover, lack of segregation of duties prevents actions performed with emergency accounts being tracked back to specific persons. Lower levels of traceability increase the risk of these user accounts being used for unauthorized actions.

▶ **Protection of emergency users**
Access to emergency users must be protected with a complex password that is safely locked away (e.g., in a safe or locker). Every time an emergency user is used, the password must be changed afterwards (e.g., by putting the password in an envelope and sealing the envelope so that use of the password is clearly identifiable). The emergency user must be protected against denial of service attacks (e.g., through special password requirements) to ensure its availability in the event of a disaster/emergency.

Associated risk: Protection of emergency users

 Without appropriate security controls around emergency users, these users may not be appropriately protected against unauthorized access. In the event of any such unauthorized access, business-critical data may be manipulated, compromised, or deleted given that these users have extensive access to the SAP system.

▶ **Emergency user authorizations**

It must also be ensured that permissions for emergency users (albeit with extensive authorizations) are assigned only according to the need-to-know and least-privilege principles (e.g., the profiles SAP_ALL and SAP_NEW should not be assigned to each and every emergency user).

Associated risk: Emergency user authorizations

 If there is no assurance that critical access rights in SAP systems are restricted to a minimum, taking into account the principle of least privilege, and there is no appropriate monitoring of the use of these access rights, business-critical data may be compromised, manipulated, or deleted without this being detected.

▶ **Logging and review of emergency user activities**

All activities performed with the emergency user must be logged by the system at a detailed level (transaction/value) and subsequently analyzed to ensure that no unauthorized actions have been performed. The result of the review must be documented in written form and must be archived for audit purposes.

Associated risk: Logging and review of emergency user activities

 If transactions performed by highly privileged users/emergency users (firefighters) are not reviewed, inappropriate activities performed by these users may not be identified and followed up on in a timely manner. This may negatively impact the availability, confidentiality, or integrity of business-critical data.

The aforementioned controls should be formally documented in an emergency access management procedure which generally describes the use of emergency users and the emergency user process, including an explanation of how the controls outlined above and related activities have been implemented.

Tool support for emergency access management

There are a variety of tools that can help you implement your emergency access management process, such as SAP Access Control with the component Emergency Access Management (EAM). However, in this book, the focus is on default tools that are available in every SAP system.

4.8.2   Test steps in the SAP system

Emergency access approval process

As described above, any use of an emergency user must be approved in advance. The approval must be obtained in written form and must be archived. To check whether this requirement has been followed, first analyze when a specific emergency user was last used. For emergency user assignments, the appropriate approvals must be assessed for completeness and appropriateness.

To find out which emergency users have been used, open table USR02 in transaction SE16 or SE16N. In the BNAME field (user), specify the emergency user names in scope. In the example shown, this is the user *EU_ BASIS1* ❶, which is an emergency user used by the SAP basis team. In the TRDAT (last logon date) and LTIME (last logon time) fields ❷, choose *greater than or equal to* the date and time of the beginning of your audit period. Initiate the selection by clicking EXECUTE ❸ or by pressing [F8], as depicted in Figure 4.84.

Excluding users

At this point, we strongly recommend that you do not exclude users (for example locked or invalid users) from this selection. There could be a deliberate protection mechanism to lock emergency users when they are not being used. If these users were excluded from this analysis, you would not get full and complete results.

Figure 4.84: Table USR02: selection screen

The results show the last logon date and time (columns: TRDAT and LTI-ME) of the selected emergency users. In the example presented, the last logon to EU_BASIS1 occurred on May 1, 2018 (Figure 4.85). To conclude this test step, check whether there is a written approval for this emergency user usage and whether the approval was granted prior to use.

Figure 4.85: Table USR02: results

Protection of emergency users

This test step consists of several sub-steps. The first step is to check whether emergency users are protected by means of a strong authentication mechanism. Often, the mechanism chosen is the input of a user ID along with a password. Make sure that the password of the emergency user is long enough (at least 12 characters are recommended) and as complex as possible (uppercase, lowercase, number, and special characters). It must be ensured that only passwords that meet the aforementioned criteria can be used for the emergency user (for example, by setting special password parameters and password policies for emergency users). The current password of an emergency user must also be kept in a safe place that only authorized persons can access in the event of an emergency. This can either be a physical safe in which the password is stored in printed form, or an application that handles the secure management of passwords.

The aforementioned sub-steps must be performed outside the SAP system.

Furthermore, the password of the emergency user must be changed after each use, so that clear assignment of the use of an emergency user to an individual is ensured. If the current password of an emergency user is known to several people, this clear assignment can no longer be guaranteed. In order to check whether the password has been changed after the use of emergency users, compare the last logon information obtained in the previous test step (emergency access approval process) with the actual changes of passwords of emergency users. To do this, open transaction SUIM and navigate through the menu: USER INFORMATION SYSTEM • CHANGE DOCUMENTS • FOR USERS. In the USER field ❶, enter the names of the emergency users that have logged on and activate the PASSWORD checkbox ❷ (Figure 4.86). In addition, determine the relevant period to limit the search entries (FROM DATE/FROM TIME/TO DATE/TO TIME fields) ❸. In the example given, the last logon took place on May 1, 2018, which is why the selection period should be set from April 25, 2018 to May 5, 2018.

Figure 4.87 shows three different log entries regarding the change of the password for user *EU_BASIS1*. The first entry (time = 03:14:39) ❶ was created when the user was created. Here, the user was given an initial password (a password that can be used only once and must be changed immediately). The second entry (time = 03:15:29) ❷ shows the change of the initial password by the end user who initially logged on with the user EU_BASIS1 (old value = *Initial*; new value = *Production*). The third entry (time = 05:56:41) ❸ shows that after completion of the emergency user application (the logon took place, as previously shown, at 03:15:29—see

Figure 4.85), the password has been changed back to an initial password (old value = *Production*; new value = *Initial*). This password must now be kept in a safe place until the next use.

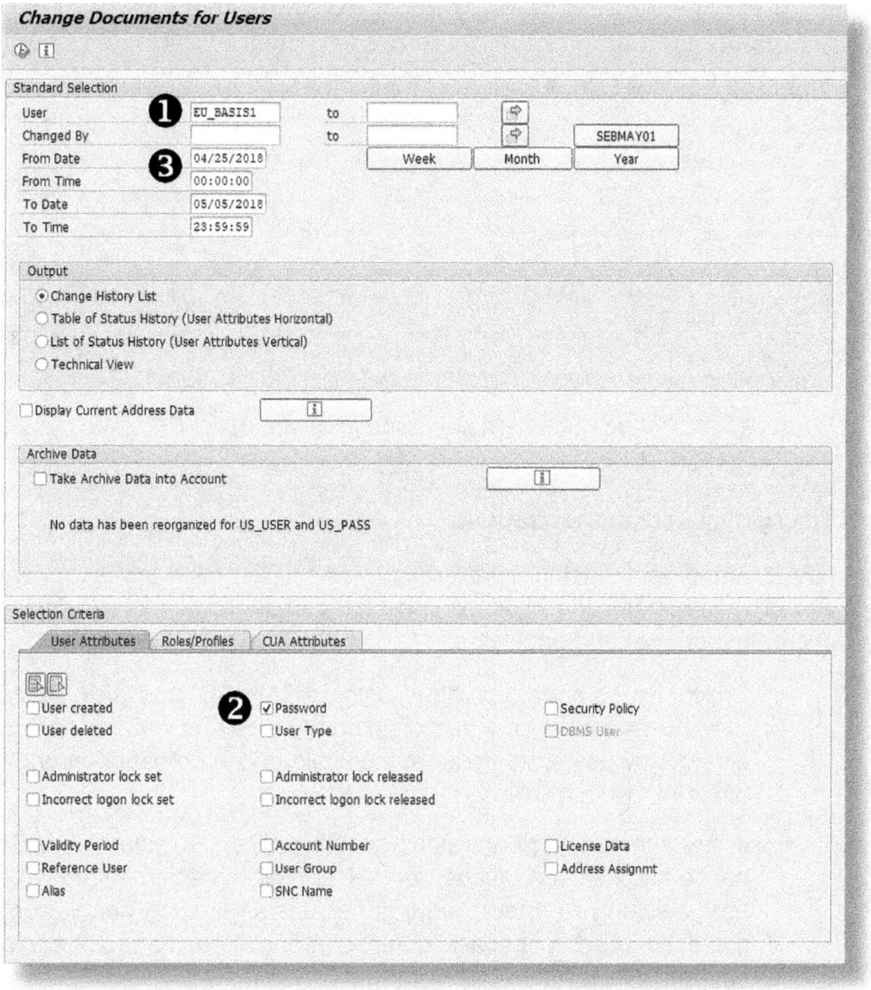

Figure 4.86: Change documents for users: selection screen

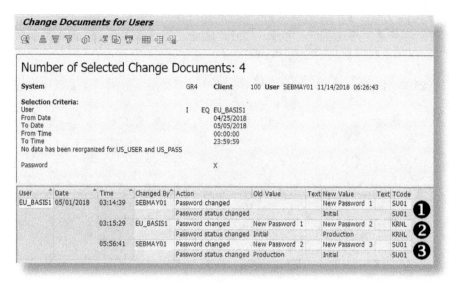

Figure 4.87: Change documents for users: results

Emergency user authorizations

This test step again includes several sub-steps. The following is an overview of requirements that must be considered in the context of the design of emergency user authorizations:

▶ Critical SAP standard profiles (such as SAP_ALL and SAP_NEW) may be assigned only in exceptional cases and only to special emergency users, as these authorizations can be used, amongst other things, to modify logs.

▶ In the same way, permissions such as debug & replace, maintenance and deletion of logs, as well as user management, may be assigned only to special emergency users, as such permissions could be used to bypass controls around the management of emergency users.

▶ In principle, different emergency users should be created for IT (e.g., SAP basis) and for the business (e.g., Finance or HR) so that only appropriate data can be accessed.

To verify whether these principles have been followed, use transaction SUIM, which we introduced in Section 3.2. Please also refer to Section

4.7 for more detailed information regarding the review of privileged access rights.

Logging and review of emergency user activities

> **Before using an emergency user**
>
> Before an individual uses an emergency user, it must be ensured that, in addition to obtaining approval, the individual also documents the reason for using the emergency user in advance and keeps track of which activities they intend to perform with this user. It is also advisable to refer to tickets (e.g., incidents) at this point, which must be handled and resolved as part of the emergency user use. The reasons for using an emergency user can be recorded either manually or with tool support.

Once the access to the emergency user is no longer required, the reviewer must check (for example, by comparison using logs) whether the activities actually performed with the emergency user correspond to what was stated in the original justification.

First, you must check whether all emergency users have been included in the Security Audit Log.

We have already described the general setup of the Security Audit Log as well as the activation in Section 4.4. However, to find out whether specific filters have been set up for emergency users, open transaction SM19 (Figure 4.88). Check in one of the existing filters ❶ whether there is an entry for your emergency user(s) ❷. In the present example, a prefix is used, which means that all emergency users begin with the string *EU_*. Therefore, you do not have to define a filter for each individual user—you can select all users that start with *EU_**. Next, check whether the filter is active ❸ and whether all audit classes ❹ and all events ❺ were included. Finally, check whether the profile containing the filter currently displayed also corresponds to the active profile ❻. If you do not find specific filters for emergency users in your SAP system, check whether there is an alternative filter that includes all users (user ID = *) and for which the remaining criteria also apply. This would be just as adequate.

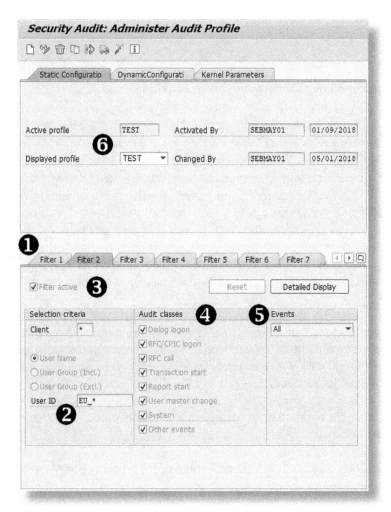

Figure 4.88: Security Audit Log: emergency users—filters

If an emergency user has been accessed, it is the reviewer's responsibility to review the logs of the corresponding emergency user and match them with the justification originally given by the user. Transaction SM20 should be used to do this. This transaction allows access to the results of the Security Audit Log. In the selection criteria, specify the appropriate client as well as the emergency user for which you want to retrieve logs ❶, as shown in Figure 4.89. Make sure that the evaluation of the logs takes into account the audit classes ❷ and events ❸ that are relevant to you. Finally, click REREAD AUDIT LOG ❹ to initiate the creation of the logs according to your selection.

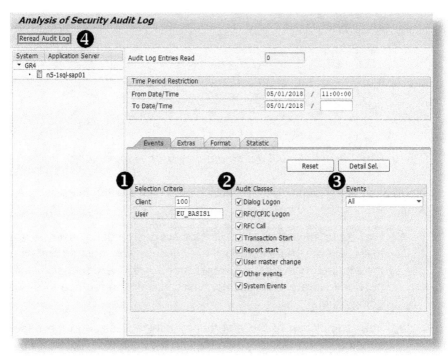

Figure 4.89: Security Audit Log: emergency users—log selection

The result is a display of all relevant log entries for the selected time period (Figure 4.90).

Figure 4.90: Security Audit Log: emergency users—log results

From an audit perspective, you now have to answer the following questions:

▶ Was there advance justification for every emergency user access to explain why the emergency user access was required and what the planned activities to be performed with the emergency user provided were (in the optimal case, including reference to an ongoing ticket)?

▶ After completion of the emergency user access, was the necessary log checked and compared with the initial justification for use of the emergency user?

▶ Was this analysis, including the log files and the respective results, stored centrally so that the assessment is also available at a later point in time?

Emergency access management procedure

The goal of the review of the emergency access management procedure is to find out whether the emergency users, their authorizations, and the responsibilities within the approval and review of emergency accesses are documented adequately. Therefore, the auditee must hand over the emergency access management procedure and you must check whether the following points are taken into account in the procedure and are sufficiently documented:

▶ List of all existing emergency users in the relevant SAP system

▶ Purpose of the emergency users

▶ Assigned access rights

▶ User group/job function authorized to use the role

▶ Emergency user owner (i.e., the person that has to approve the use of an emergency user)

▶ Emergency user reviewer (i.e., the person that has to review the activities performed with an emergency user)

▶ Segregation of duties and privileged access rights (e.g., which authorizations should not be assigned together in one emergency user as the combination of authorizations leads to a segregation of duties conflict; also, which privileged access rights should generally be avoided in emergency users or should be assigned only to very specific emergency users)

4.8.3 Critical access rights

The access rights listed in this section are considered as critical in the area of emergency access management. Therefore, check whether the following transactions and associated authorization objects are granted only to appropriate users by using the report **Users by Complex Selection Criteria** in transaction SUIM (for further information, please refer to Section 3.2).

▶ **Unlock emergency user IDs/password maintenance (assign new password to user)**

Authorization object	Field	Field value
S_TCODE	TCD	SU01_NAV, SU10, SUID01, or SUID10
S_USER_GRP	ACVT	05
	CLASS	User group to which emergency users are assigned

▶ **Assign emergency user roles to end users
(if CHECK_S_USER_SAS = NO in table PRGN_CUST)**

Authorization object	Field	Field value
S_TCODE	TCD	SU01, SU01_NAV, SU10, SUID01, or SUID10
S_USER_GRP	ACTVT	02
S_USER_AGR	ACTVT	22
	ACT_GROUP	Naming convention for emergency user roles (e.g., Z_FF*)
S_USER_PRO	ACTVT	22

▶ **Assign emergency user roles to end users
(if CHECK_S_USER_SAS = YES in table PRGN_CUST)**

Authorization object	Field	Field value
S_TCODE	TCD	SU01, SU01_NAV, SU10, SUID01, or SUID10
S_USER_GRP	ACTVT	02
S_USER_AGR	ACTVT	22
	ACT_GROUP	Naming convention for emergency user roles (e.g., Z_FF*)
S_USER_SAS	ACTVT	22

▶ **Assign roles to users through transaction PFCG
(if CHECK_S_USER_SAS = NO in table PRGN_CUST)**

Authorization object	Field	Field value
S_TCODE	TCD	PFCG
S_USER_AGR	ACTVT	03
	ACT_GROUP	Naming convention for emergency user roles (e.g., Z_FF*)
S_USER_GRP	ACTVT	22
S_USER_PRO	ACTVT	22

▶ **Assign roles to users through transaction PFCG
(if CHECK_S_USER_SAS = YES in table PRGN_CUST)**

Authorization object	Field	Field value
S_TCODE	TCD	PFCG
S_USER_AGR	ACTVT	03
	ACT_GROUP	Naming convention for emergency user roles (e.g., Z_FF*)
S_USER_GRP	ACTVT	22
S_USER_SAS	ACTVT	22

4.9 Password security and authentication

4.9.1 Background to the control and associated risk

One way to log on to an SAP system is by using a user ID and password. Passwords are secret, memorized by only one individual, and are considered an authentication mechanism to grant access to authorized persons and to prevent access for unauthorized persons. The authenticity of an identity, however, is only retained if the password remains secret—that is, unknown to third parties. To ensure the best possible secrecy of passwords, various good practice recommendations have been published outlining the minimum standards for secure passwords.

One of the most common good practice recommendations can be found in the Digital Identity Guidelines released by the National Institute of Standards and Technology (NIST), U.S. Department of Commerce. These guidelines outline, for example, that one of the primary factors in characterizing password strength is password length; strong passwords should contain at least eight characters (NIST Special Publication 800-63B, Chapter 5.1.1.1).

Discussion on good practice recommendations for passwords

 At present, there are controversial discussions on using good practice recommendations to define minimum requirements for secure passwords. For example, a past suggestion was that passwords should be changed every 90 days. However, leading experts, including Bill Burr, one of the authors of the aforementioned NIST secure password requirements, agree that this does not increase the security of passwords. Rather, these experts suggest ensuring that no compromised passwords are used. As leading auditing firms still use old password requirements for their examinations, this chapter also discusses parameters that are currently under discussion.

To meet password requirements, password parameters can be defined in the SAP system. Non-compliance with the setup of password parameters is accompanied by the following risk.

Associated risk: Password parameters

 If system password configuration is inadequate, users are not enforced to use passwords in line with internally defined password requirements. As a result, passwords may be too weak and unauthorized personnel may gain access to the system, for instance through brute force attacks.

4.9.2   Test steps in the SAP system

Password parameters

Password parameters are part of the general SAP system settings. Table 4.5 provides an overview of relevant password parameters to be considered within an SAP audit, along with a corresponding description and minimum requirements based on good practice recommendations.

SAP password parameter	Description	Recommendation
login/min_password_lng	Minimum number of characters to be used in a password (i.e., password length)	8
login/min_password_letters	Minimum number of letters to be used in a password	1
login/min_password_uppercase	Minimum number of uppercase letters to be used in a password	1
login/min_password_lowercase	Minimum number of lowercase letters to be used in a password	1
login/min_password_digits	Minimum number of numbers to be used in a password	1
login/min_password_specials	Minimum number of special characters to be used in a password	1
login/password_compliance_to_current_policy	Check whether the password currently set is compliant with the password settings and requires a password change if this is not the case	1 (activated)
login/password_expiration_time	Length of time a password is valid and after which a password must be changed	90
login/password_history_size	Number of expired passwords the system remembers and that cannot be used as a new password	5
login/min_password_diff	Number of characters a new password must contain different to the previous password	2

SAP password parameter	Description	Recommendation
login/fails_to_user_lock	Number of failed login attempts before user is locked	5
login/fails_to_session_end_	Number of failed login attempts before GUI session is ended	3
login/password_change_waittime	Length of time until a password can be changed again	1 [day]
login/password_max_idle_productive	Maximum length of time a password remains active even though the user has not logged in to the SAP system	30 [days]
login/password_max_new_valid	Length of time an initial password for a new user remains valid	10 [days]
login/password_max_idle_initial	Length of time a reset password for an existing user remains valid	10 [days]
login/password_downwards_compatibility	Define whether passwords of older kernel versions are still compatible with the current kernel. In this case, passwords are saved in a special format (not case-sensitive, only a maximum of eight characters saved (additional characters are truncated)).	0 (not compatible, as password formats of older kernel versions are considered as weak; prevents common password hacks though use of strong encryption mechanisms)
login/disable_multi_gui_login	Define whether multiple dialog logins are allowed (exceptions for specific users can be defined through the parameter login/multi_login_users)	1 (not allowed)

Table 4.5: Overview of the SAP password parameters

To determine whether password parameters have been implemented appropriately in the SAP system and to assess whether the control is effective, open transaction SA38 and execute program RSPARAM. This program shows all available system parameters. However, this option does not allow you to select specific parameters in advance. Alternatively, you can execute program RSPFPAR in transaction SA38. In comparison to program RSPARAM, this program allows you to select specific parameters, as depicted in Figure 4.91.

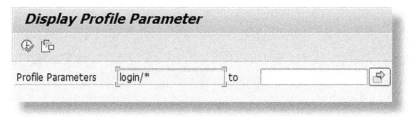

Figure 4.91: Executing program RSPFPAR—parameter: login/*

Executing either program RSPARAM or RSPFPAR displays an overview of the (selected) parameters (Figure 4.92). The overview is comprised of five columns. The first column ❶ contains the parameter name; the second column, USER VALUE ❷, indicates whether a user value has been defined for a particular parameter; and column three ❸ contains the SAP system default value. In column four ❹, the system default values are shown in an unsubstituted form—that is, variables/placeholders such as the symbols # and $ are not translated. Finally, the last column ❺, COMMENT, provides a brief explanation of the purpose and basic function of a specific parameter.

If no user value is specified in the second column ❻, the system uses the system default value. If a user value has been defined ❼, the system always prefers this value regardless of whether the user value is smaller than or greater than the system default value.

Display Profile Parameter

Parameter Name ❶	User Value ❷	System Default Value ❸	System Default Value(Unsubstituted Form) ❹	Comment ❺
login/min_password_digits ❻		0	0	min. number of digits in passwords
login/min_password_letters	1	0	0	min. number of letters in passwords
login/min_password_lng ❼	3	6	6	Minimum Password Length
login/min_password_lowercase	1	0	0	minimum number of lower-case characters in passwords
login/min_password_specials	1	0	0	min. number of special characters in passwords
login/min_password_uppercase		0	0	minimum number of upper-case characters in passwords
login/multi_login_users				list of exceptional users: multiple logon allowed
login/no_automatic_user_sapstar	0	1	1	Control of the automatic login user SAP*
login/password_change_for_SSO		1	1	Handling of password change enforcements in Single Sign-On situations
login/password_change_waittime		1	1	Password change possible after # days (since last change)
login/password_charset		1	1	character set used for passwords
login/password_compliance_to_current_policy		0	0	current password needs to comply with current password policy
login/password_downwards_compatibility		1	1	password downwards compatibility (8 / 40 characters, case-sensitivity)
login/password_expiration_time		0	0	Dates until password must be changed
login/password_hash_algorithm		encoding=RFC2307, al	encoding=RFC2307, algorithm=iSSHA-1, ite	encoding and hash algorithm used for new passwords
login/password_history_size		5	5	Number of records to be stored in the password history
login/password_logon_usergroup				users of this group can still logon with passwords
login/password_max_idle_initial		0	0	maximum #days a password (set by the admin) can be unused (idle)
login/password_max_idle_productive		0	0	maximum #days a password (set by the user) can be unused (idle)
login/quiet_mode		1	1	no rabax during user login
login/server_logon_restriction		0	0	Server Logon Restriction

Figure 4.92: Password parameter settings

To prove the design effectiveness of the **password parameters** control, compare the settings implemented within your SAP system to your company-specific requirements or good practice recommendations.

Security policies

Password parameters can be overridden at the user level by means of security policies. If a security policy has been assigned to a user, password parameters that were defined centrally are no longer valid; instead, the parameters defined in the security policy apply. Therefore, as part of the testing of the effectiveness of password controls, you must check whether security policies have been assigned to users and, if this is the case, whether there is a sufficient justification and approval.

To do this, open table USR02 in transaction SE16 or SE16N. Filter for values that are not equal to empty in the SECURITY_POLICY field ❶. Initiate the selection by clicking EXECUTE ❷ or by pressing F8 (Figure 4.93).

In this example, there is only one user (*TEST_SECPOL*) to which a security policy (*Z_ESPRESSO*) has been assigned (Figure 4.94).

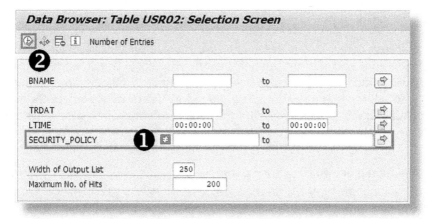

Figure 4.93: Table USR02: selection screen

Data Browser: Table USR02 Select Entries   1

🔲	MANDT	BNAME	SECURITY_POLICY
	100	TEST_SECPOL	Z_ESPRESSO

Figure 4.94: Table USR02: results

In table SEC_POLICY_RT, you can determine which parameters and which settings are contained in the security policy. In the case of the security policy *Z_ESPRESSO*, the number of failed logon attempts (*MAX_FAILED_PASSWORD_LOGON_ATTEMPTS*) after which the user is blocked was increased to *90* days (Figure 4.95).

Data Browser: Table SEC_POLICY_RT Select Entries   1

🔲	CLIENT	NAME	ATTRIB_KEY	ATTRIB_VALUE
	100	Z_ESPRESSO	MAX_FAILED_PASSWORD_LOGON_ATTEMPTS	90

Figure 4.95: Table SEC_POLICY_RT: results

4.9.3 Critical access rights

The access rights listed in this section are considered as critical in the area of password security and authentication. Therefore, check whether the following transactions and associated authorization objects are granted only to appropriate users by using the report **Users by Complex Selection Criteria** in transaction SUIM (for further information, please refer to Section 3.2).

▶ **Maintain (password) system parameters**

Authorization object	Field	Field value
S_TCODE	TCD	RZ10
S_RZL_ADM	ACTVT	01

▶ **Maintain security policies**

Authorization object	Field	Field value
S_TCODE	TCD	SECPOL
S_SECPOL	ACTVT	01 (create), 02 (change), 06 (delete)

▶ **Assign security policies to users**

Authorization object	Field	Field value
S_TCODE	TCD	SU01, SU01_NAV
S_SECPOL	ACTVT	22
S_USER_GRP	ACTVT	02

▶ **Unlock user IDs/password maintenance (assign new password to user)**

Authorization object	Field	Field value
S_TCODE	TCD	SU01_NAV, SU10, SUID01 or SUID10
S_USER_GRP	ACVT	05

4.10 Batch processing

4.10.1 Background to the control and associated risk

Batch processing allows data processing to be scheduled and executed in SAP systems in the background. In this case, background processing means that a job that performs some background data processing—that is, without further end user interaction—is scheduled in the SAP system. A scenario for using a batch job, for example, is the creation of a report that takes a long time due to the large volume of data to be processed. The advantage from an end user perspective is that the user can continue to perform other activities in the SAP system and is not blocked by the data processing being executed in the background. In addition, background processing allows resource-intensive computing activities to be scheduled in an SAP system at a time when no or at least few end users are using the system, thus making the best use of the system's performance capabilities.

However, batch processing not only enables processes to be moved from dialog to background processing; it also allows the processing of batch (input) sessions. These sessions are input files with data to be imported and processed in an SAP system. Batch input sessions are used, for example, when transferring data from a legacy system, or when an interface to an upstream system cannot be established due to technical limitations but the SAP system still requires the data for further processing.

Both forms of batch processing allow the automated and consistent background processing of (a huge volume of) data. Therefore, it is a fundamental part of SAP audits to understand whether the batch processing is adequately set up and protected by suitable processes and controls. This includes the following focus areas:

▶ **Documentation of batch jobs/batch processing**
   All batch jobs/batch processing must be documented. This documentation must include, amongst other things, information about the job/processing owner, the purpose of the job/processing, and steps to be initiated in case of failure.

> ### Associated risk: Documentation of batch jobs/batch processing
>
> If there is no transparent batch documentation that outlines batch process steps and corresponding responsibilities, key controls, and expected documentation for each key control, key activities may not be unequivocally understood by key stakeholders. This may result in process steps and key controls not being followed on a continuous and standardized basis.

▶ **Batch job user IDs**
Recurring system batch jobs must be exclusively scheduled and executed under technical user IDs explicitly set up for the purpose.

> ### Associated risk: Batch job user IDs
>
> If technical user IDs are not used for batch job processing, the availability of batch job processing may be negatively impacted. This is due to non-technical user IDs, such as common user accounts, not being flagged transparently for batch job processing, with the result that these users may be deactivated following user termination or unauthorized logon attempts. If user IDs in place for batch job processing are deactivated, the batch job cannot be executed.

▶ **Batch job monitoring**
Mechanisms must be implemented to detect errors in the processing of batch jobs at an early stage. In the case of errors, appropriate countermeasures must be taken.

> ### Associated risk: Batch job monitoring
>
> If batch jobs are not monitored appropriately, errors may not be identified and resolved in a timely manner, thus negatively impacting business operations relying on this data.

▶ **Protection of batch input files**
The integrity and confidentiality of batch input files must be ensured by appropriate safeguards.

Associated risk: Protection of batch input files
Batch input files are typically located outside the SAP system. As a result, technical controls implemented in the SAP system do not apply. If batch input files are not protected adequately, data may be manipulated prior to being loaded to the SAP system by personnel who would not have the ability to change the data within the SAP system itself.

4.10.2 Test steps in the SAP system

Documentation of batch jobs/batch processing

The first step in assessing whether scheduled batch jobs are adequately documented is to get an overview of which jobs are currently available in your SAP system. Open transaction SM37 or SM37DISP (alternatively, you can use table TBTCP via transaction SE16 or SE16N; we will introduce the method in the next test step). On the selection screen, first, as shown in Figure 4.96, define that all jobs for all users are included in the analysis (enter * in each of the fields JOB NAME and USER NAME) ❶. Then, select the JOB STATUS options SCHED., RELEASED, READY, ACTIVE, and FINISHED ❷. Finally, select a representative period for the analysis, for example, a period of two weeks ❸. Initiate the selection by clicking EXECUTE ❹ or by pressing F8 .

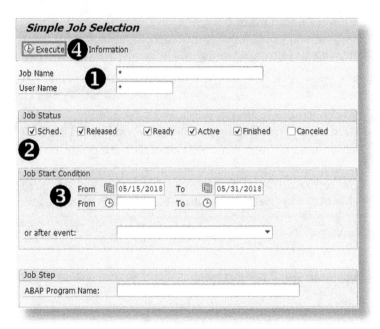

Figure 4.96: Transaction SM37/SM37DISP: selection screen

The result is a list of all jobs scheduled, released, ready, active, or finished in the specified period. In the case of recurring jobs, the jobs are listed multiple times. Request the corresponding documentation for a represent- ative sample of batch jobs and check whether the documentation contains the following:

► Name of the job

► Job owner/person responsible

► Purpose of the job

► Order (if a job builds on the results of another job)

► Failure/back-out procedure if the job ends with errors

Batch job user IDs

There are two main things that need to be considered when scheduling jobs. Unique end user background processing that is part of a business process, for example, should be scheduled only under the user ID of the person who actually needs the batch job.

Batch jobs and authorizations

 When batch jobs are executed, the authorizations of the user under which the job is scheduled are checked. If a user used to run a batch job does not have the authorizations required by the underlying program, the execution of the batch job will end in failure.

If an end user is able to schedule jobs under an external user ID with far-reaching authorizations, they might be able to extend their current permissions. This means that an end user could execute a program for which he would not usually be authorized by executing the program in the background through a batch job under an external user ID with sufficient permissions. The ability to schedule batch jobs under external user IDs can be restricted using permissions (for further details, please refer to Section 4.10.3).

However, in the case of recurring system jobs (for instance, sending messages from the SAP system), these jobs should always be scheduled under specific technical users created explicitly for batch jobs. Technical users, unlike end users, are subject to different requirements in terms of, for example, authentication and authorization. If an end user who has scheduled a job under his own user ID leaves the company and their user is consequently terminated in the system, the job would no longer be executed successfully because a valid and sufficiently authorized user is a prerequisite for execution. This would also be the case if a user is locked due to incorrect password entries. Furthermore, using dedicated technical accounts to run batch jobs also avoids the need to assign extensive permissions required by programs executed through a batch job to end users. However, only batch job administrators should be able to schedule jobs under external user IDs.

Therefore, in this step, check whether (recurring) batch jobs have been scheduled exclusively under appropriate user IDs. To do this, open table TBTCP in transaction SE16 or SE16H. As shown in Figure 4.97, you must first define an analysis period ❶. Initiate the selection by clicking Exe-cute ❷ or by pressing ⎡F8⎤.

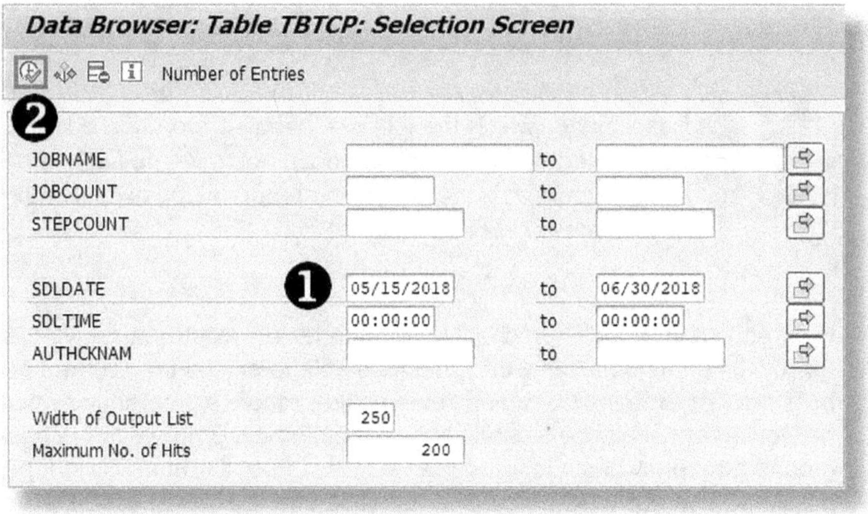

Data Browser: Table TBTCP: Selection Screen

⊕ ⊲ᵖ ⊟ ⅈ Number of Entries

❷

JOBNAME		to	
JOBCOUNT		to	
STEPCOUNT		to	
SDLDATE **❶**	05/15/2018	to	06/30/2018
SDLTIME	00:00:00	to	00:00:00
AUTHCKNAM		to	

Width of Output List	250
Maximum No. of Hits	200

Figure 4.97: Table TBTCP: selection screen

Figure 4.98 shows the results of the evaluation. In the example outlined, there are two different batch jobs. Column SDLUNAME ❶ shows which user set up the batch job. The AUTHCKNAM column ❷ shows the user ID used to schedule the job. The job *Z_ESPRESSO_TEST_1* was scheduled under the user ID of the person who also set up the job, whereas the job *Z_ESPRESSO_TEST_2* was scheduled under a technical user ID *WF-BATCH*. Since this example refers to recurring system processing, the recommendation is to perform the scheduling under a technical account that is explicitly intended for batch jobs.

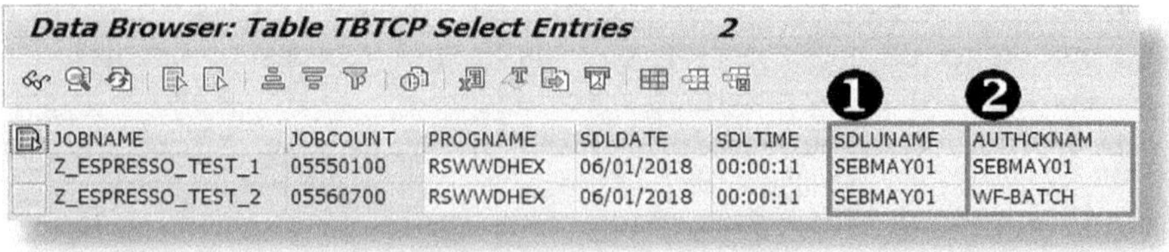

Data Browser: Table TBTCP Select Entries   2

JOBNAME	JOBCOUNT	PROGNAME	SDLDATE	SDLTIME	SDLUNAME ❶	AUTHCKNAM ❷
Z_ESPRESSO_TEST_1	05550100	RSWWDHEX	06/01/2018	00:00:11	SEBMAY01	SEBMAY01
Z_ESPRESSO_TEST_2	05560700	RSWWDHEX	06/01/2018	00:00:11	SEBMAY01	WF-BATCH

Figure 4.98: Table TBTCP: results

Batch job monitoring

There are several reasons why batch jobs could end up with errors. You have already seen an example in the previous test step: the user under which a job was scheduled is locked, has been deleted, or no longer has sufficient permissions. Since the correct execution of batch jobs is often essential to correct system function as well as the maintenance of business processes, it must be ensured that errors in the processing of batch jobs are detected at an early stage and countermeasures are taken in the event of errors.

First, you need to develop an understanding of the process of monitoring batch jobs and how errors are handled. This can basically be done in two ways:

▶ **Automated**: batch jobs are monitored by automated tools—in the event of an error, either corresponding notifications are sent to persons responsible or a ticket/incident is opened in the IT service management tool.

▶ **Manually**: the status of batch jobs is monitored manually by a corresponding person/team; batch jobs are checked regularly (the recommendation is at least once every day) and analyzed for errors; in the case of errors, countermeasures and corrections are initiated manually (e.g., by manually opening a ticket/incident).

In both cases, it is important to follow the back-out procedures that have been documented in the batch job documentation.

The next step is to check whether the process defined is effective operationally. Therefore, as a first step, take a representative sample of failed batch jobs. Open transaction SM37 or SM37DISP. On the selection screen, define that all jobs for all users are included in the analysis (enter * in each of the fields JOB NAME and USER NAME) ❶, as shown in Figure 4.99. Then, select the JOB STATUS option CANCELED ❷. Finally, select a representative period for the analysis, for example, a period of two weeks ❸. Initiate the selection by clicking EXECUTE ❹ or by pressing [F8].

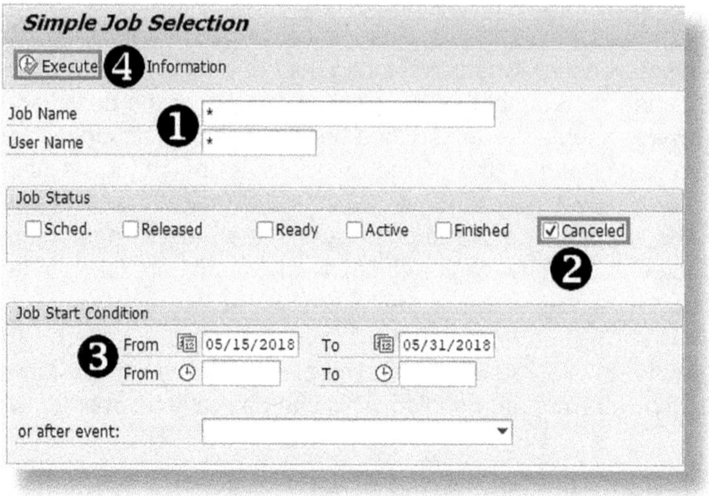

Figure 4.99: Transaction SM37/SM37DISP: selection screen

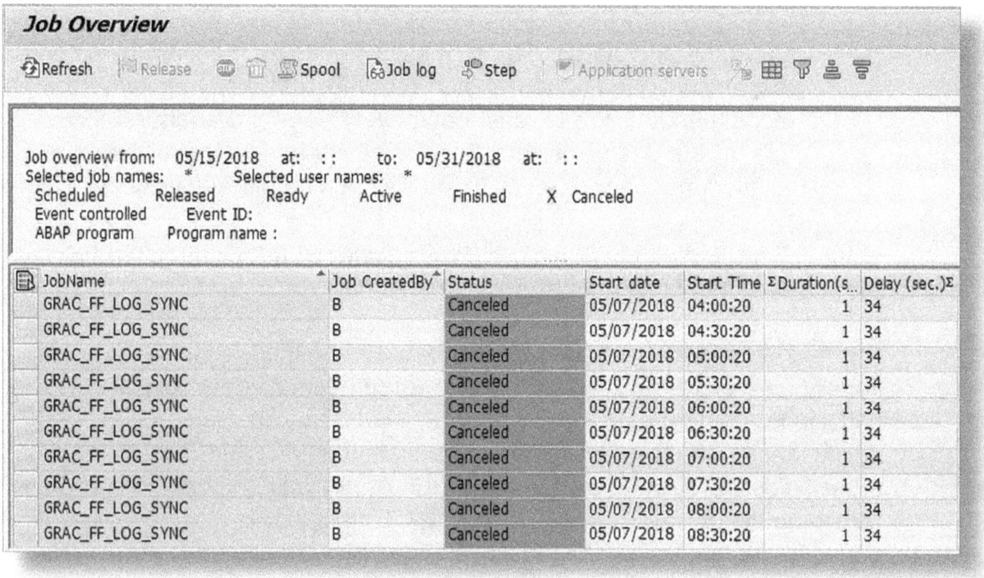

Figure 4.100: Transaction SM37/SM37DISP: results

The result is an overview of the erroneous jobs that occurred in the selected period (Figure 4.100). Here you have to filter out the jobs that belong to the category of recurring system jobs (like the synchronization of logs in this example).

For a representative sample of failed recurring system batch jobs, check whether they have been handled according to the batch job back-out processes defined by your organization and whether corrective actions have been taken according to the back-out procedures defined in the batch job documentation.

Protection of batch input files

In this test step, the focus is on the processing and protection of batch input files. The use of batch input is usually very individual, which is why we will introduce basic control mechanisms and test steps. To secure the batch input processing, the following questions should be considered:

▶ How are files exchanged between two systems?

▶ Are files transferred exclusively in encrypted form?

▶ Is the integrity of files checked (for example, by comparing hash values found before shipping and after receipt)?

▶ If the files are cached (for example, on a shared network drive), do only authorized persons have access to the file?

▶ Is data validated and reconciled?

Evaluate whether the answers to these questions are generally sufficient to ensure the integrity and confidentiality of batch input files and the information they contain. If they are, check the controls for design and operating effectiveness through, for instance, inquiry, observation, re-performance, or examination of evidence.

4.10.3 Critical access rights

The access rights listed in this section are considered as critical in the area of batch processing. Therefore, check whether the following transactions and associated authorization objects are granted only to appropriate users by using the report **Users by Complex Selection Criteria** in transaction SUIM (for further information, please refer to Section 3.2).

▶ **Schedule batch jobs under own user ID**

Authorization object	Field	Field value
S_TCODE	TCD	SM36
S_BTCH_ADM	BTCADMIN	Y

or

Authorization object	Field	Field value
S_TCODE	TCD	SM36
S_BTCH_JOB	JOBACTION	PLAN, MODI, RELE

▶ **Schedule batch jobs under any external user ID**

Authorization object	Field	Field value
S_TCODE	TCD	SM36
S_BTCH_ADM	BTCADMIN	Y
S_BTCH_NAM	BTCUNAME	*

or

Authorization object	Field	Field value
S_TCODE	TCD	SM36
S_BTCH_JOB	JOBACTION	PLAN, RELE
S_BTCH_NAM	BTCUNAME	*

▶ **Maintain batch jobs**

Authorization object	Field	Field value
S_TCODE	TCD	SM37
S_BTCH_ADM	BTCADMIN	Y

or

Authorization object	Field	Field value
S_TCODE	TCD	SM37
S_BTCH_JOB	JOBACTION	MODI, RELE

▶ Delete batch jobs

Authorization object	Field	Field value
S_TCODE	TCD	SM37
S_BTCH_ADM	BTCADMIN	Y

or

Authorization object	Field	Field value
S_TCODE	TCD	SM37
S_BTCH_JOB	JOBACTION	DELE

▶ Maintenance of batch input files

Authorization object	Field	Field value
S_TCODE	TCD	SM35
S_BDC_MONI	BDCAKTI	AONL (run batch input file), DELE (delete batch input file), REOG (reorganize batch input files), LOCK (lock/unlock batch input files)

▶ Maintenance of input and output queues

Authorization object	Field	Field value
S_TCODE	TCD	SM38
S_QIQ_MONI	QOIAKTI	QANL (create queue), QAEN (change queue), QDEL (delete queue), QSTA (start queue)

4.11 RFC interfaces

4.11.1 Background to the control and associated risk

There are many ways to set up interfaces in SAP systems internally—that is, between different clients of the same system or between different SAP/non-SAP systems. We have already described one of the technologies—batch processing—in Section 4.10. However, the most central of interface technologies, and therefore often included in the scope of audits, is *Remote Function Calls (RFC)*. RFC interfaces are used to execute function modules (ABAP as well as non-ABAP) in external systems or in other clients of the same system. RFC interfaces are used, for instance, to transfer transports, with the result that changes are automatically transmitted from one system to the next.

RFC connections are divided into two main categories:

▶ Classic RFC connections

▶ Trusted RFC connections

Classic RFC connections

We create this type of RFC connection in transaction SM59, as shown in Figure 4.101 (this step is also necessary when creating a trusted RFC connection). In this transaction, we must first specify the target system by defining a target host.

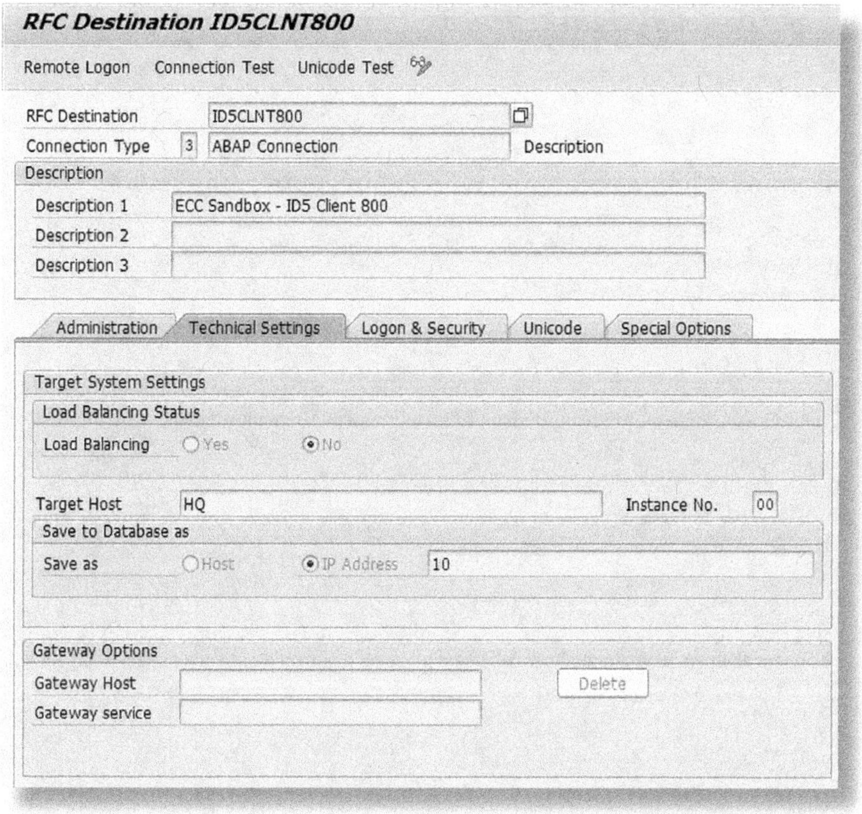

RFC Destination ID5CLNT800

Remote Logon   Connection Test   Unicode Test 🔍

RFC Destination	ID5CLNT800		
Connection Type	3	ABAP Connection	Description

Description

Description 1	ECC Sandbox - ID5 Client 800
Description 2	
Description 3	

Administration / Technical Settings / Logon & Security / Unicode / Special Options

Target System Settings

Load Balancing Status

Load Balancing   ○ Yes   ⦿ No

Target Host	HQ		Instance No.	00

Save to Database as

Save as   ○ Host   ⦿ IP Address   10

Gateway Options

Gateway Host		Delete
Gateway service		

Figure 4.101: Transaction SM59: setting up classic RFC connections— step 1

Next (as depicted in Figure 4.102), we have to specify the target client (CLIENT), the user (USER), and, if applicable (optional), the password of the user (PASSWORD and/or PW STATUS) for connections to an SAP system. The AUTHORIZATION FOR DESTINATION field can contain any value that is queried during the execution of an RFC interface via the authorization object S_ICF, field ICF_VALUE, and thus provides additional protection for the interface against unauthorized access.

241

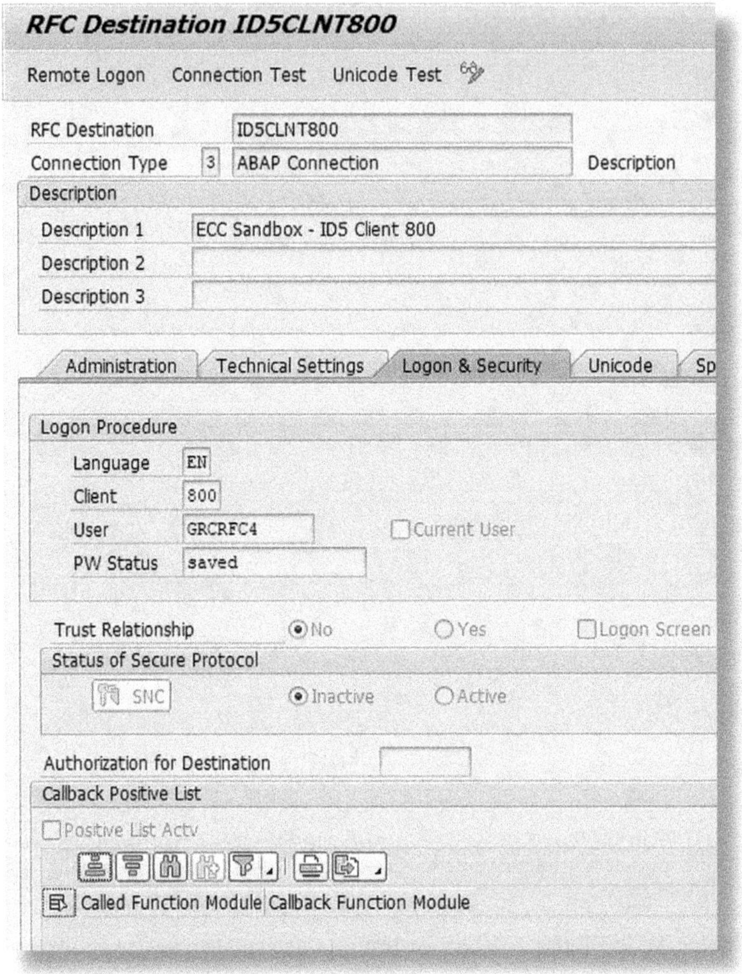

RFC Destination ID5CLNT800

Remote Logon   Connection Test   Unicode Test

RFC Destination	ID5CLNT800
Connection Type	3 ABAP Connection

Description

Description 1	ECC Sandbox - ID5 Client 800
Description 2	
Description 3	

Administration   Technical Settings   Logon & Security   Unicode   Sp

Logon Procedure

Language	EN
Client	800
User	GRCRFC4
PW Status	saved

☐ Current User

Trust Relationship   ⦿ No   ○ Yes   ☐ Logon Screen

Status of Secure Protocol

SNC   ⦿ Inactive   ○ Active

Authorization for Destination

Callback Positive List

☐ Positive List Actv

☐ Called Function Module Callback Function Module

Figure 4.102: Transaction SM59: setting up classic RFC connections—step 2

Once we have set up an RFC connection, we can test it by clicking CONNECTION TEST and via the menu: UTILITIES • TEST • AUTHORIZATION TEST.

In the area of classical RFC connections in particular, the user type of the user used in the RFC connection must be taken into account. If passwords are saved for RFC users, a distinction must be made between DIALOG or SERVICE and SYSTEM or COMMUNICATION users.

Associated risk: RFC user type and password

 If RFC interfaces are not protected, users may be able to authenticate to the target system through the interface user credentials without knowing the password and thus work in the target system with these accounts and their authorizations. In this case, actions performed cannot be traced back to one specific individual. Lower levels of traceability increase the risk of these user accounts being used for unauthorized and fraudulent actions. Moreover, additional manual controls are required to ensure access to generic accounts remains appropriate, resulting in increased management effort and higher susceptibility to errors.

The following example illustrates the effects of this risk. Figure 4.103 shows the setup of two RFC interfaces (in both cases from an SAP GRC to an SAP ERP system). In the first case, a user of type DIALOG is being used in the RFC connection. In the second case, a user of the type SYSTEM is used.

RFC Destination ID5CLNT800-2

Remote Logon	Connection Test	Unicode Test

RFC Destination	ID5CLNT800-2	
Connection Type	3 ABAP Connection	Description
Description		

Description 1	Test Connection Espresso Tutorials
Description 2	
Description 3	

| Administration | Technical Settings | Logon & Security | Unicode | Sp |

Logon Procedure

Language	EN
Client	800
User	SEBMAY01	☐ Current User
PW Status	saved
Password	⁎⁎⁎⁎⁎⁎⁎⁎⁎⁎⁎⁎

← Dialog User

| Trust Relationship | ⦿ No | ○ Yes | ☐ Logon Screen |

Status of Secure Protocol

| 🔒 SNC | ⦿ Inactive | ○ Active |

Authorization for Destination

Callback Positive List

☐ Positive List Actv

☐ Called Function Module | Callback Function Module

RFC Destination ID5CLNT800

Remote Logon	Connection Test	Unicode Test

RFC Destination	ID5CLNT800	
Connection Type	3 ABAP Connection	Description
Description		

Description 1	ECC Sandbox - ID5 Client 800
Description 2	
Description 3	

| Administration | Technical Settings | Logon & Security | Unicode | Sp |

Logon Procedure

Language	EN
Client	800
User	GRCRFC4	☐ Current User
PW Status	saved

← System User

| Trust Relationship | ⦿ No | ○ Yes | ☐ Logon Screen |

Status of Secure Protocol

| 🔒 SNC | ⦿ Inactive | ○ Active |

Authorization for Destination

Callback Positive List

☐ Positive List Actv

☐ Called Function Module | Callback Function Module

Figure 4.103: Transaction SM59: setting up classic RFC connections— dialog vs. system user

In both cases, a connection test and an authorization test were performed successfully to ensure that the connection is working. If a remote logon is performed for a system user (by clicking REMOTE LOGON), no actions are performed by the system. The end user remains in the transaction SM59 RFC configuration overview. This leads to the conclusion that, if this kind of connection is used within an SAP functionality, end users would have to authenticate again with their own user ID and password before the connection is established. Thus, an active and sufficiently authorized user is needed in the target system.

If, on the other hand, a remote logon is performed for a dialog user, a connection to the target system is established automatically. No further authentication is required for this. In the target system, end users then act under the user ID of the user stored in the RFC connection and with the authorizations granted to this user (see Figure 4.104).

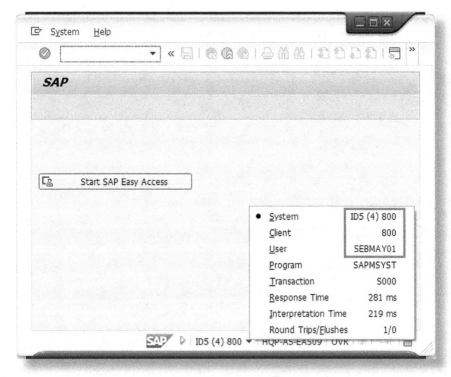

Figure 4.104: Transaction SM59: setting up classic RFC connections—remote connection

Password storage up to SAP NetWeaver Release 6.40

 Up to SAP NetWeaver Release 6.40, passwords of RFC users were stored in the field RFCOPTIONS within table RFCDES. This field contained concatenated information (for example, server name (H =), user (U =)), including the unencrypted password of the RFC user used (V =). In order to find out the passwords of RFC users, the search string *V=* had to be entered in the field RFCOPTIONS in table RFCDES using either transaction SE16 or SE16N. Up to SAP NetWeaver Release 6.40, protecting this table against unauthorized access is of great importance. As of Release 7.0, passwords of RFC users are only stored encrypted in table RSECTAB and can no longer be displayed with standard table display transactions. Table RFCDES, however, now contains, as a placeholder, the value v=%PWD.

Trusted RFC connections

Trusted RFC connections are used to give users access to external SAP systems without having to re-authenticate themselves again. This provides an alternative to the unsafe storage of dialog users presented in the previous section in a classic RFC connection. Trusted RFC connections are therefore an alternative to the insecure use of dialog users as part of a classic RFC connection (presented in the previous section) and can be used to avoid additional authentication.

In the case of trusted RFC connections, there is always one SAP system that is trusted by another SAP system—that is, is granted access to another SAP system (*trusted system*)—and an SAP system that trusts another SAP system—that is, grants access to another SAP system (*trusting system*). As Figure 4.107 shows, there are two different ways in which a trusted relationship between two SAP systems can be designed:

▶ **Scenario 1: Current User = Yes (option selected)**
If you have defined that the current user should be used for the trusted RFC connection, an automated check is performed when the RFC connection is opened to see whether the calling user also has an account in the target system. If this is the case, activities take place in the target system under the user ID of the accessing

user and only if the user has sufficient authorizations in the target system. As shown in Figure 4.105, the remote logon to the target system via an RFC connection is initiated in the system GR4 ❶ under the user ID SEBMAY01 ❷. Once the connection has been established, the user works on the target system ID5 ❸ still with the user ID SEBMAY01 ❹. If the accessing user does not have an account in the target system, the logon via the trusted RFC connection is rejected.

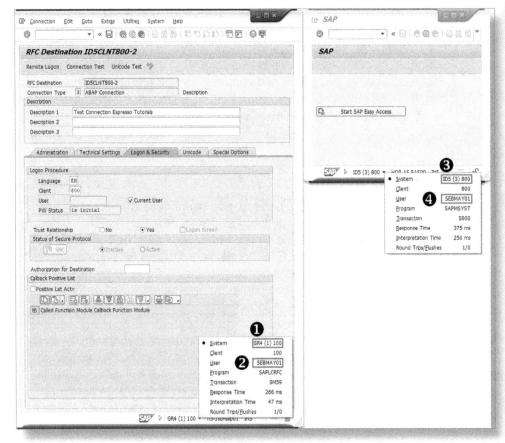

Figure 4.105: Trusted RFC connections: Current User = Yes

▶ **Scenario 2: Current User = No (option not selected)**
   If you have not defined that the current user should be used for the trusted RFC connection, when the RFC connection is opened, no check is performed to determine whether the calling user also has

an account in the target system. In this case, in the target system, the calling user accesses the user account stored in the RFC connection, performs activities under this user ID, and also uses the authorizations that the RFC user has in the target system for these activities. As shown in Figure 4.106, the remote logon to the target system via an RFC connection is initiated in the system GR4 ❶ under the user ID SEBMAY01 ❷. Once the connection has been established, the user now works on the target system ID5 ❸ with the user ID SEBMAY04 ❹.

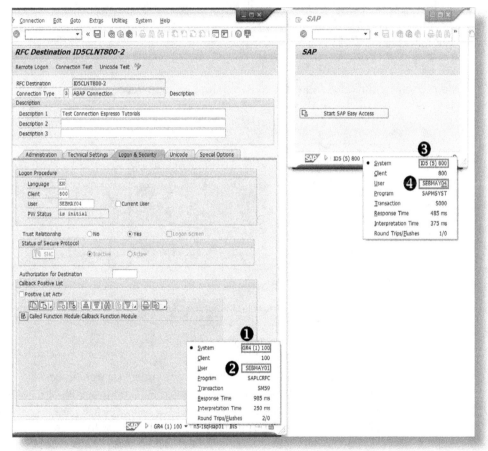

Figure 4.106: Trusted RFC connections: Current User = No

Associated risk: Current User setting

 If RFC interfaces are not protected, users may be able to authenticate to the target system through the interface user credentials without knowing the password and thus work with these accounts and their authorizations in the target system. In this case, actions performed cannot be traced back to one specific individual. Lower levels of traceability increase the risk of these user accounts being used for unauthorized and fraudulent actions. Moreover, additional manual controls are required to ensure that access to generic accounts remains appropriate, resulting in increased management effort and higher susceptibility to errors.

The recommendation is therefore to avoid trust relationships.

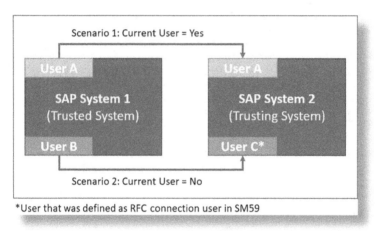

Figure 4.107: Trusted RFC connection scenarios

In order to implement a trusted RFC connection, you must first set the connection up in transaction SM59, analogous to classic RFC connections. In order to define an RFC interface as a trusted connection, set the parameter TRUST RELATIONSHIP to YES (Figure 4.108). Furthermore, within these settings, you can specify whether the current user will be used (parameter CURRENT USER).

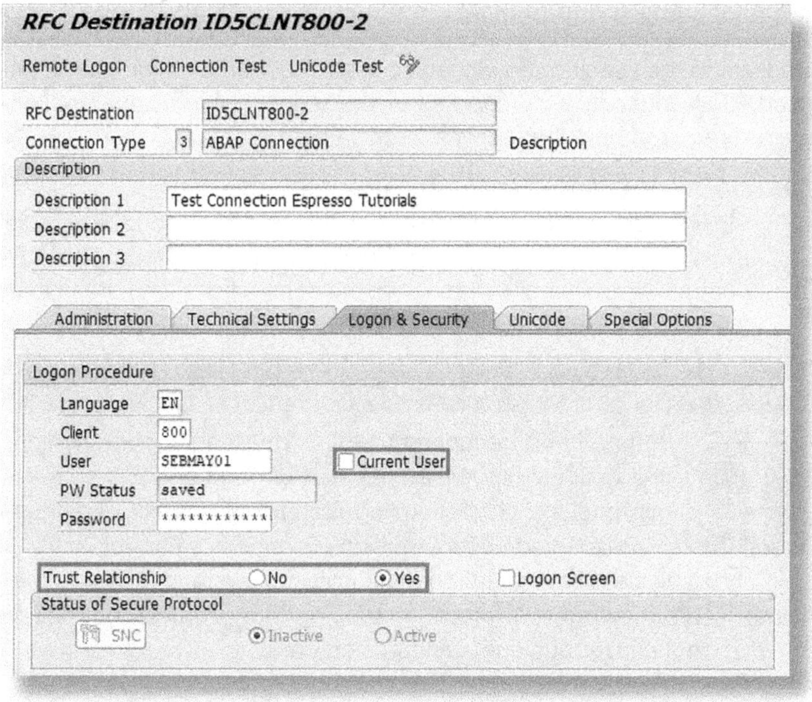

RFC Destination ID5CLNT800-2

Remote Logon   Connection Test   Unicode Test

RFC Destination	ID5CLNT800-2	
Connection Type	3 ABAP Connection	Description

Description

Description 1	Test Connection Espresso Tutorials
Description 2	
Description 3	

Administration / Technical Settings / Logon & Security / Unicode / Special Options

Logon Procedure

Language	EN
Client	800
User	SEBMAY01 ☐ Current User
PW Status	saved
Password	************

Trust Relationship   ○ No   ⦿ Yes   ☐ Logon Screen

Status of Secure Protocol

SNC   ⦿ Inactive   ○ Active

Figure 4.108: Transaction SM59: defining a trust relationship

As the next step, enter the trusted RFC connection in transaction SMT1. In this transaction, a distinction is made between a list of systems whose calls are trusted, and a list of systems that trust the current system (Figure 4.109).

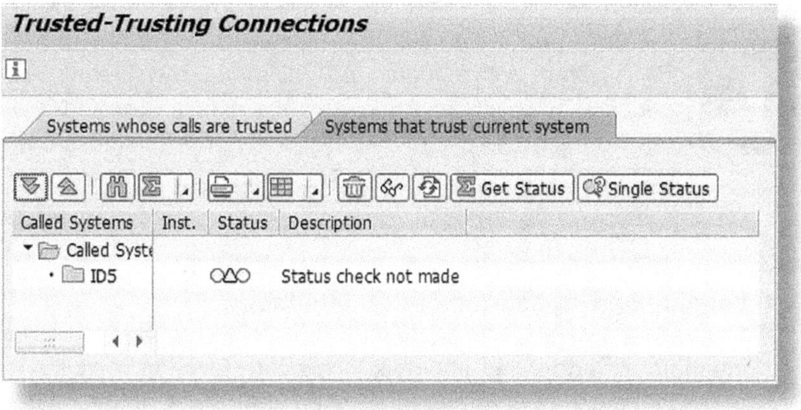

Trusted-Trusting Connections

ℹ

Systems whose calls are trusted / Systems that trust current system

[toolbar icons] Get Status Single Status

Called Systems	Inst.	Status	Description
▾ 🗀 Called Syst			
· 🗀 ID5		∞	Status check not made

◄ ►

Figure 4.109: Transaction SMT1: trusted/trusting connections

Additional general requirements in the context of RFC connections

In addition to the specific security and control requirements for classic and trusted RFC connections presented in the respective previous sections, there are requirements that apply in both cases:

▶ **Documentation of RFC interfaces**
All RFC connections must be documented. This documentation must include, amongst other things, information about the RFC connection owner, the purpose of the connections, and steps to be initiated in case of failures.

Associated risk: Documentation of RFC connections

 If there is no transparent RFC connection documentation that outlines processes handled through an RFC connection and the corresponding responsibilities, key controls, and expected documentation for each key control, key activities may not be unequivocally understood by key stakeholders. This may result in process steps and key controls not being followed on a continuous and standardized basis.

▶ **Authorizations of RFC users**
It must also be ensured that permissions for RFC users are assigned only according to the need-to-know and least-privilege principles (e.g., the profiles SAP_ALL and SAP_NEW should not be assigned to each and every emergency user).

Associated risk: Authorizations of RFC users

 If there is no assurance that critical access rights in the SAP system are restricted to a minimum, considering the principle of least privilege, and there is no appropriate monitoring of the use of these access rights, business-critical data may be compromised, manipulated, or deleted without being detected.

▶ **Logging and monitoring of RFC interfaces**
Mechanisms must be implemented to detect unauthorized logon attempts, unauthorized attempts to execute function modules, or errors in the use of RFC interfaces at an early stage. In the case of

errors or detection of unauthorized activities, appropriate counter-measures must be taken.

Associated risk: Logging and monitoring of RFC interfaces

 If RFC interfaces are not logged and monitored appropri-ately, unauthorized activities may not be identified and fol-lowed-up on in a timely manner. Moreover, analysis and forensic activities cannot be performed following an inci-dent if audit log files do not exist. Furthermore, RFC inter-face errors may not be identified and resolved in a timely manner, thus negatively impacting business operations relying on this data.

4.11.2 Test steps in the SAP system

Documentation of RFC interfaces

Check whether implemented RFC connections are adequately document-ed. To do this, open table RFCDES in transaction SE16 or SE16N. Do not enter any selection limitations on the screen that appears (as shown in Figure 4.110). Initiate the selection by clicking EXECUTE or by pressing F8.

Data Browser: Table RFCDES: Selection Screen

⊕ ⊶ ▤ ⓘ Number of Entries

RFCDEST		to	⇨
RFCTYPE	☐	to ☐	⇨
RFCOPTIONS		to	⇨
RFCOPTIONT		to	⇨
RFCOPTIONU		to	⇨
RFCOPTIONV		to	⇨

Width of Output List	250
Maximum No. of Hits	200

Figure 4.110: Table RFCDES: selection screen

The result is a list of all RFC connections. Request the corresponding documentation for a representative sample of RFC connections and check whether the documentation contains at least the following:

▶ Name of the connection

▶ Connection owner/person responsible

▶ Purpose of the connection

▶ Failure/back-out procedure if the connection does not work properly

RFC user type and passwords

As a next step, check whether there are classic RFC connections for which a password has been saved and whether these users are of user type DIALOG or SERVICE. Open table RFCDES in transaction SE16 or SE16N. In the RFCOPTIONS field, add the selection *v=%_PWD*. Initiate the selection by clicking EXECUTE, as outlined in Figure 4.111, or by pressing F8.

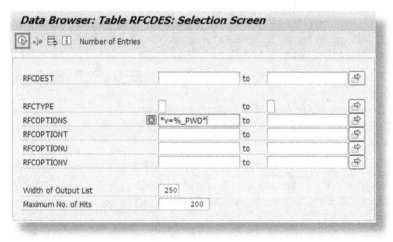

Figure 4.111: Table RFCDES: selection screen

The result is a display of all RFC connections for which a password has been saved (Figure 4.112).

RFCDEST		RFCTYPE	RFCOPTIONS
ID5CLNT100	3	H=h	,S=00,M=100,U=GRCUSER,Y=2,h=2,z=-2 v=%_PWD W=Y,
ID5CLNT400	3	H=H	,S=00,M=400,U=GRCRFC2,L=E,Y=2,h=2,z=-2 v=%_PWD W=Y,B=N,C=N,
ID5CLNT400_GRAC	L	H=H	,S=00,M=400,U=SEBMAY01,L=E,Y=2,h=2 v=%_PWD W=Y,B=N,C=N,E=
ID5CLNT800	3	H=1	,S=00,M=800,U=GRCRFC4,L=E,Y=2,h=2,z=-2 v=%_PWD W=Y,B=N,C=N,E=
ID5CLNT800-2	3	H=1	,S=00,M=800,U=SEBMAY01,L=E,Y=2,h=2,z=-2 v=%_PWD W=Y,B=N,C=N,
ID5HR800	3	H=H	,S=00,M=800,U=GRCRFC2,Y=2,h=2,z=-2 v=%_PWD W=Y,B=N,C=N,E=N,

Data Browser: Table RFCDES Select Entries 6

Figure 4.112: Table RFCDES: results

In the target system, check whether the user stored in the RFC connection setup (in the calling system) is of user type either DIALOG or SERVICE.

Trusted RFC connection

In this step, you want to check whether there are trusted RFC connections that do not use the option CURRENT USER = *Yes*. Again, open table RFCDES in transaction SE16 or SE16N. In the RFCOPTIONS field, enter the search string *Q=Y*u=N* and initiate the selection by clicking EXECUTE or by pressing [F8] (Figure 4.113).

Data Browser: Table RFCDES: Selection Screen

Number of Entries

RFCDEST			
RFCTYPE		to	
RFCOPTIONS	*Q=Y*u=N*	to	
RFCOPTIONT		to	
RFCOPTIONU		to	
RFCOPTIONV		to	

Width of Output List	250
Maximum No. of Hits	200

Figure 4.113: Table RFCDES: selection screen

The result is a display of all RFC interfaces that have been set up as a trusted connection but do not use the option CURRENT USER (Figure 4.114). In addition, the stored user can be seen (*U =*).

Figure 4.114: Table RFCDES: results

Authorizations of RFC users

Finally, you should check whether appropriate authorizations are used for RFC users. To do this, once again open table RFCDES in transaction SE16 or SE16N. In the RFCOPTIONS field, enter the search string *U=* and initiate the selection by clicking EXECUTE or by pressing F8 (Figure 4.115)

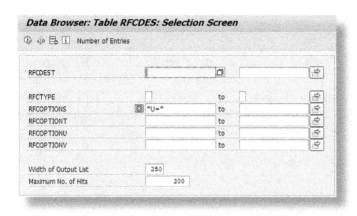

Figure 4.115: Table RFCDES: selection screen

The result is a display of all RFC interfaces where user IDs have been entered in the RFC settings (transaction SM59) (Figure 4.116).

In the target system, check whether the users are set up with appropriate access rights.

Data Browser: Table RFCDES Select Entries		23

RFCDEST	RFCTYPE	RFCOPTIONS
FIORI	3	H=fiorilogon.compute-1.amazonaws.com,S=00,M=100 U=GRC_RFC Y=2,h=2...
GR2CLNT001-2	3	H=10.255.32.78,M=001 U=SEBMAY01 Y=2,h=2,z=-2,W=Y,B=N,C=N,E=N,...
GR4000CLNT	3	H=10.255.32.96,S=00,M=000 U=SAP* Y=2,h=2,z=-2,v=%_PWD,W=Y,B=...
HANA_DB_DEMO	L	U=ADMIN_GRC Y=2,h=2,v=%_PWD,W=Y,B=N,C=N,E=N,T=N,K=Y,s=N,u=...
ID5CLNT100	3	H=hqp-as-eas09.na.msds.rhi.com,S=00,M=100 U=GRCUSER Y=2,h=2,z=-2,v...
ID5CLNT400	3	H=HQP-AS-EAS09,S=00,M=400 U=GRCRFC2 L=E,Y=2,h=2,z=-2,v=%_PWD,...

Figure 4.116: Table RFCDES: results

Logging and monitoring of RFC interfaces

RFC interfaces are logged using the Security Audit Log. As introduced in Section 4.4, check whether the Security Audit Log has been activated and whether the following events have been included in the logging for the relevant clients and the relevant users:

▶ **AUL** (Failed RFC Call &C (Function Group = &A))

▶ **AU5** (RFC/CPIC logon successful (type=&A, method=&C))

▶ **AU6** (RFC/CPIC logon failed, reason=&B, type=&A, method=&C)

▶ **AUK** (Successful RFC Call &C (Function Group = &A))

▶ **CUZ** (Generic table access by RFC to &A with activity &B)

▶ **DUJ** (RFC callback rejected (destination &A, called &B, callback &C))

▶ **DUI** (RFC callback executed (destination &A, called &B, callback &C))

▶ **DUK** (RFC callback in simulation mode (destination &A, called &B, callback &C))

▶ **FU1** (RFC function &B with dynamic destination &C was called in program &A)

4.11.3 Critical access rights

The access rights listed in this section are considered as critical in the area of RFC interfaces. Therefore, check that the following transactions and associated authorization objects are granted only to appropriate users by using the report **Users by Complex Selection Criteria** in transaction SUIM (for further information, please refer to Section 3.2).

▶ **Maintenance of RFC connections (from release 7.0)**

Authorization object	Field	Field value
S_TCODE	TCD	SM59
S_RFC_ADM	ACTVT	01 (create), or 02 (change), or 06 (delete)

▶ **Use of all RFC connections**

Authorization object	Field	Field value
S_ICF	ICF_FIELD	DEST
	ICF_VALUE	*

▶ **Execution of all function modules**

Authorization object	Field	Field value
S_TCODE	TCD	SE37 or SE80
S_DEVELOP	ACTVT	16
	OBJTYPE	FUGR
	OBJNAME	*
	DEVCLASS	*
	P_GROUP	*

▶ **Execution of all function modules through external programs**

Authorization object	Field	Field value
S_RFC	ACTVT	16
	RFC_TYPE	FUGR (function module group), FUNC (function module)
	RFC_SYSID	*

▶ **Maintenance of trusted/trusting systems**

Authorization object	Field	Field value
S_TCODE	TCD	SMT1 or SMT2
S_RFC_TT	ACTVT	01 (create), or 02 (change), or 06 (delete)

▶ **Use of Current User option in target system**

Authorization object	Field	Field value
S_RFCACL	ACTVT	16
	RFC_EQUSER	Y

4.12 Database and server security

4.12.1 Background to the control and associated risk

As already described in detail in Section 2.2, a typical SAP architecture consists of three different layers (see Figure 4.117).

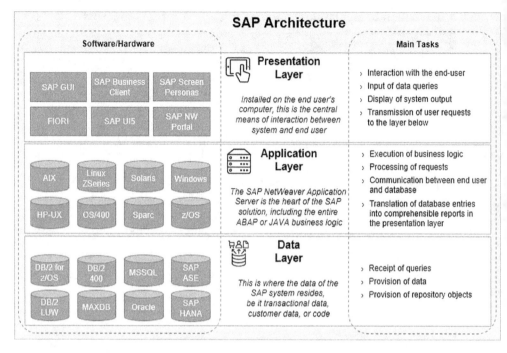

Figure 4.117: Rough SAP three-tier client-server architecture

Within the scope of this book, the focus is on SAP NetWeaver Application Server and the ABAP logic it contains. In order to perform a holistic audit of SAP systems, however, it is also important and necessary to check the database layer and other components of the application layer, amongst other things. In particular, servers and their operating systems (application layer) as well as the database used by the SAP application (data layer) must be included in an audit, since these components provide immediate access to data and thus directly influence the availability and integrity of business-critical data processed in SAP systems.

Associated risk: Server/operating system & database security

Business-critical data of SAP systems can be accessed through all three architecture layers: the application layer, the server layer, and the database layer. If there is no assurance that appropriate security controls are implemented on all layers to prevent unauthorized access, business-critical data may be manipulated, deleted, or compromised through any of these layers.

In Section 4.12.2, we will introduce three example test steps in the areas of operating systems and databases. This excursus is intended to raise awareness of the far-reaching planning and wide-ranging scope of a holistic SAP audit. Because it is widespread and up to date, Linux (distribution Red Hat) was chosen as an operating system for the example, with SAP HANA as the database.

> ## Example test steps for operating systems and databases
>
> As already mentioned, the test steps presented below are only initial examples. Accordingly, the test steps make absolutely no claim to completeness. Full consideration of the topic of auditing different databases or operating system technologies would require a separate book for each available software solution.

In principle, all controls/control areas described and presented in the previous sections should also be checked accordingly within operating systems or in databases (i.e., as change management controls are required at application level, for example, there should also be controls at operating system and database level). The following test steps contain instructions on how to perform the corresponding test steps in either Linux Red Hat or in SAP HANA. In addition, for each test step, there is a reference to the relevant previous section and, if particularly worth considering, an explanation of the corresponding risk or the consequence if a setting considered was not implemented as recommended.

4.12.2 Test steps in the SAP system

Operating system security—example test steps for Linux Red Hat

▶ **Password parameters**

First of all, let us look at password settings in the area of operating system security.

Reference to SAP application layer

This test step relates to the control area introduced and described in Section 4.9.

In Linux Red Hat, the relevant parameters for configuring passwords are stored in two files:

▶ /etc/login.defs

▶ /etc/security/pwquality.conf

Figure 4.118 shows an example of the file /etc/login.defs. In this file, amongst other things, the parameters defining the length of time a password is valid and after which it has to be changed (parameter PASS_MAX_DAYS), the length of time until a password can be changed again (parameter PASS_MIN_DAYS), the minimum password length (parameter PASS_MIN_LEN), and the number of days before a password expires that a warning is given (parameter PASS_WARN_AGE) can be maintained.

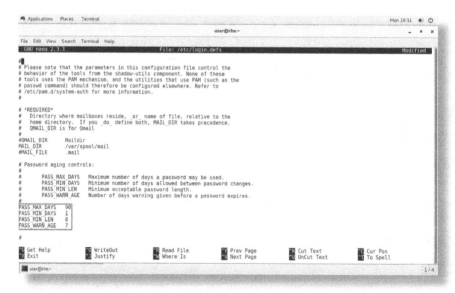

Figure 4.118: Linux Red Hat—password settings 1 (/etc/login.defs)

Figure 4.119 shows an example of the file /etc/security/pwquality. conf. The complexity requirements can be specified in this file. This is done via the parameters LCREDIT (lowercase letter), UCREDIT (uppercase letter), DCREDIT (numeric digit), and OCREDIT (special case letter).

Password configuration credits

 The parameter MINLEN (minimum credits/password length) has a special feature that must be taken into account: the parameter is used to determine the minimum length of passwords but can be overridden using complexity parameters. For the first use of a complexity character (digits (DCREDIT), lowercase letters (LCREDIT), uppercase letters (UCREDIT), or special characters (OCREDIT)), the corresponding amount specified in the parameter is added to the minimum length. A password with MINLEN = 8 means that you have to reach in total eight credits. For each digit used, the length is incremented by one if, for example, DCREDIT = 1. Therefore, even if only lowercase characters are used, seven characters are enough to reach a MINLEN of 8 (seven credits for each character used plus one additional credit for using lowercase characters, which is a total of eight credits). If an uppercase letter is used as well, another credit is added and the minimum length can already be reached by using only six characters. To prevent this, the values in the credit parameters (DCREDIT, LCREDIT, UCREDIT, and OCREDIT) must be negative. If the value in the corresponding credit parameters is negative, you do not get an additional credit for the first time the specific character is used, but the minimum use of a specific character is enforced. UCREDIT = -1 therefore means that at least one uppercase letter must be used. The use of an uppercase letter, however, would not add a credit for achieving the defined number in the parameter MINLEN.

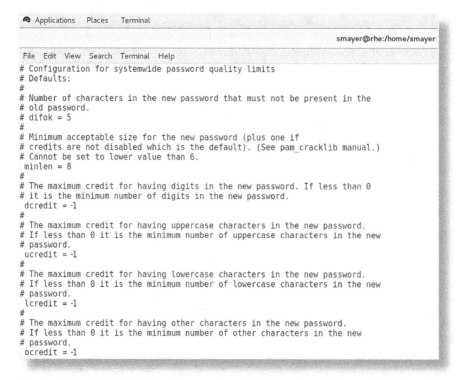

```
 Applications   Places   Terminal

                                          smayer@rhe:/home/smayer

File  Edit  View  Search  Terminal  Help
# Configuration for systemwide password quality limits
# Defaults:
#
# Number of characters in the new password that must not be present in the
# old password.
# difok = 5
#
# Minimum acceptable size for the new password (plus one if
# credits are not disabled which is the default). (See pam_cracklib manual.)
# Cannot be set to lower value than 6.
 minlen = 8
#
# The maximum credit for having digits in the new password. If less than 0
# it is the minimum number of digits in the new password.
 dcredit = -1
#
# The maximum credit for having uppercase characters in the new password.
# If less than 0 it is the minimum number of uppercase characters in the new
# password.
 ucredit = -1
#
# The maximum credit for having lowercase characters in the new password.
# If less than 0 it is the minimum number of lowercase characters in the new
# password.
 lcredit = -1
#
# The maximum credit for having other characters in the new password.
# If less than 0 it is the minimum number of other characters in the new
# password.
 ocredit = -1
```

Figure 4.119: Linux Red Hat—password settings 2 (/etc/security/pwquality.conf)

To prove the design effectiveness of this control, compare the settings implemented in your operating system to your company-specific requirements or good practice recommendations.

Multi-factor authentication

 In addition to authenticating users with passwords, Linux provides other authentication mechanisms that can be used to implement multi-factor authentication. For example, one common method is to use a key (private/public key file) in addition to entering passwords.

► **Root/sudo access**

User *root* is a superuser in Linux with very extensive administrator privileges (comparable to SAP* at SAP application level). This user is initially created when a Linux system is set up. The user root has practically all functionalities in Linux, it owns nearly all files in the system, and it is the only account that can process system files. Since the user root is a very powerful user, direct user logons to this account should be prevented.

Sudo is not a user comparable to root but is a command that is used to execute processes with the privileges of the user root without knowing its password. Figure 4.120 shows an example of the use of the command sudo. The user ECB first tried to access the file /etc/shadow without using sudo. However, as the user is not authorized to perform this action, an error message is shown (/ETC/SHADOW: PERMISSION DENIED). If the same user initiates the file call using the sudo command, access is not denied but the user is prompted to authenticate using his password.

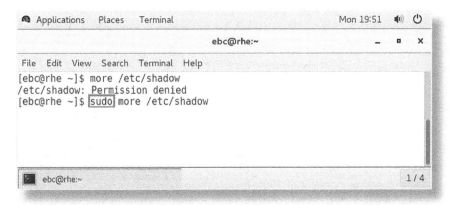

Figure 4.120: Linux Red Hat—sudo access 1

Avoid being locked out of the system

First, set up at least one other user who has **sudo** permissions to ensure you do not lock yourself out of the system. Make sure that the user name is not trivial and thus easy for attackers to guess (such as the username **Admin**).

After successful authentication, ECB is now granted access to the /etc/shadow file as the call was executed with the far-reaching privileges of the user root (Figure 4.121).

Figure 4.121: Linux Red Hat—sudo access 2

Since sudo can be used to gain access to far-reaching permissions, during an audit it is important to check whether only authorized persons are able to execute this command.

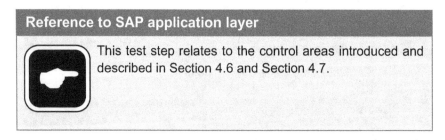

Reference to SAP application layer

This test step relates to the control areas introduced and described in Section 4.6 and Section 4.7.

We will now show you how to check whether direct user logins to the account root are prevented in your Linux Red Hat system. To do this, open the file /etc/passwd (Figure 4.122). If the entry for the user root has been changed from the extension /BIN/BASH to /SBIN/NOLOGIN, the direct user logins to the user root are prevented. If direct logins to the user root are not prevented, you must check whether a strong password is being used to secure this account and make sure that only appropriate personnel have access to this password.

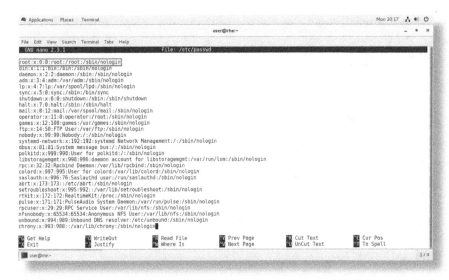

Figure 4.122: Linux Red Hat—locking the root account (/etc/passwd)

Next, check which users are authorized to use the sudo command. To do this, open the file `/etc/sudoers`. Figure 4.123 shows that there is one user group named WHEEL that gives users who are assigned to the group the right to execute the sudo command (ALL = (ALL) ALL).

Figure 4.123: Linux Red Hat sudo permissions (/etc/sudoers)

Through the file /etc/group, you can now test which users are assigned to the WHEEL group (Figure 4.124). In this example, only the user EBC is assigned to the user group WHEEL and is, therefore, granted sudo access rights through this group.

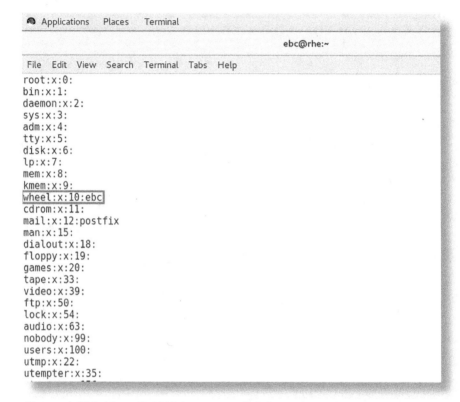

Figure 4.124: Linux Red Hat—groups (/etc/group)

Finally, check whether only appropriate users are authorized to execute the sudo command through the group WHEEL (or any other group with equivalent privileges).

► **SSH root login**

The central administration interface in Linux is called *Secure Shell* or *SSH*. SSH is a program that enables remote login to Linux systems and remote execution of commands. For Linux operating systems, the recommendation is to disable SSH root logins as attackers often try to gain access to

Linux systems through an SSH connection. Opening an SSH requires a valid user name and password combination. As the account root is available on all Linux systems, attackers often focus on this account to try to get access to root through brute force attacks.

Reference to SAP application layer

 This test step relates to the control areas introduced and described in Sections 4.6, 4.7, and 4.9.

We will now illustrate the consequences of an SSH root login not being disabled. The file /etc/ssh/sshd_config (Figure 4.125) shows that root SSH logins were not deactivated (# sign in front of the parameter PERMIT-ROOTLOGIN (moreover, the parameter itself would also be set to *Yes*)).

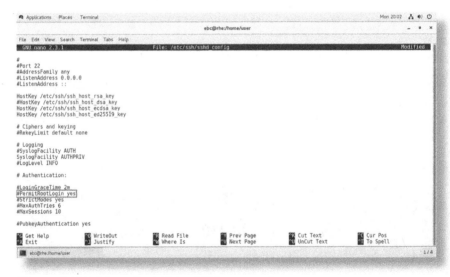

Figure 4.125: Linux Red Hat—SSH access 1

Using the SSH client PuTTY, you can access your Linux system remotely. By entering the IP address, you can initiate the setup of the remote SSH connection (Figure 4.126).

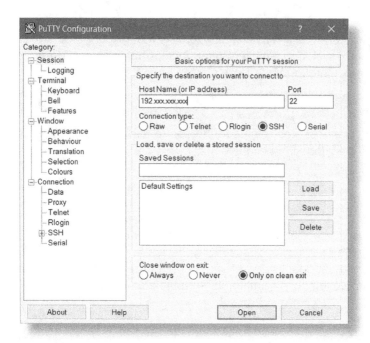

Figure 4.126: Linux Red Hat—SSH access 2

After you enter the IP address, the system asks you to enter the password of the account root (Figure 4.127). After authentication, you can work remotely on your Linux system with the extensive privileges of the user root ([ROOT@RHE~] #).

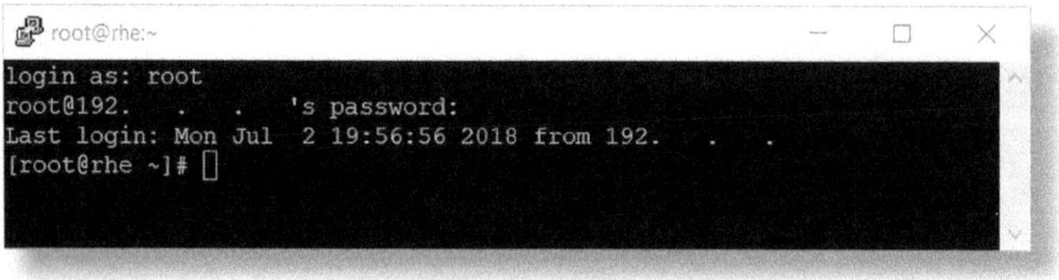

```
root@rhe:~                                                    —    □    ×
login as: root
root@192.   .    .    's password:
Last login: Mon Jul  2 19:56:56 2018 from 192.    .    .
[root@rhe ~]# []
```

Figure 4.127: Linux Red Hat—SSH access 3

To check whether SSH root logins are disabled, open the file /etc/ssh/sshd_config again (Figure 4.128). To disable SSH root logins, set the parameter PERMITROOTLOGIN to *No*.

Figure 4.128: Linux Red Hat—SSH access 4

If you now try to open an SSH connection via the account root, the access will be denied (Figure 4.129).

Figure 4.129: Linux Red Hat—SSH access 5

There are valid reasons to allow remote SSH connections to the Linux system. However, the recommendation is that this is not done through the user root but through specifically defined users (that attackers cannot guess easily). You also define such users via the file /etc/ssh/sshd_ config, using the parameter ALLOWUSERS. In this example, the user EBC was allowed to use remote SSH connections (Figure 4.130).

Figure 4.130: Linux Red Hat—SSH access 6

As a result of this setting, the user EBC can now use the functionalities of the SSH, as depicted in Figure 4.131 (in contrast to the unregistered user USER1, whose access attempt is rejected by the system).

Figure 4.131: Linux Red Hat—SSH access 7

Database security—example test steps for SAP HANA

▶ **Password parameter**

Analogous to the field of operating system security, the password settings also have to be checked in the area of databases.

270

Reference to SAP application layer

This test step relates to the control area introduced and described in Section 4.9.

The relevant parameters for configuring passwords can be found in the SAP HANA Administration Console under the path SECURITY • PASSWORD POLICY (Figure 4.132). In contrast to the SAP application and the Linux Red Hat operating system, the descriptions of the parameters in SAP HANA are self-explanatory.

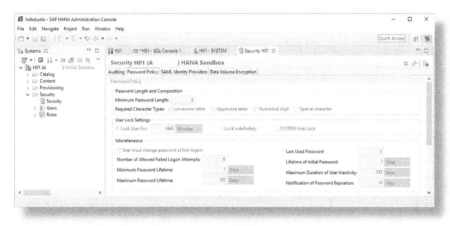

Figure 4.132: SAP HANA—password settings

To prove the design effectiveness of this control, compare the settings implemented in your database to your company-specific requirements or good practice recommendations.

▶ **Built-in account SYSTEM**

Similar to the SAP application, the SAP HANA database is also provided with built-in user IDs which have very extensive authorizations and which must therefore be protected accordingly against unauthorized access.

Reference to SAP application layer

This test step relates to the control area introduced and described in Section 4.6.

The most relevant user in this context is the user **SYSTEM**. This user should always be disabled except for approved and documented exceptions. To check whether this is the case, in the SAP HANA Administration Console, navigate through the path SECURITY • USERS • SYSTEM. The status of the user should always be *Deactivated*, as shown in Figure 4.133.

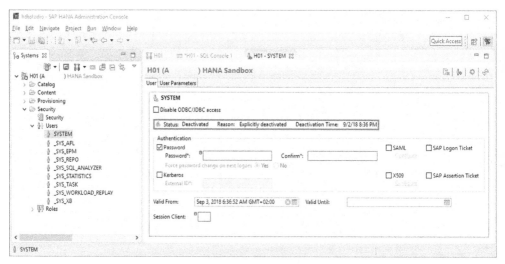

Figure 4.133: SAP HANA—deactivation of built-in user ID SYSTEM

▶ **Security Audit Log**

In SAP HANA databases, it must also be ensured that critical events are logged and, if necessary, mitigating measures are initiated.

In the SAP HANA Administration Console, open the path SECURITY • AUDITING. Activating the Security Audit Log consists of two main steps. First, the auditing status must be set to *Enabled* (Figure 4.134). In addition, audit policies must be defined. Using these audit policies, you can define which specific events are to be captured in the log individually in each situation.

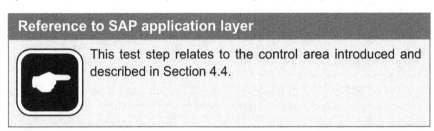

Reference to SAP application layer

This test step relates to the control area introduced and described in Section 4.4.

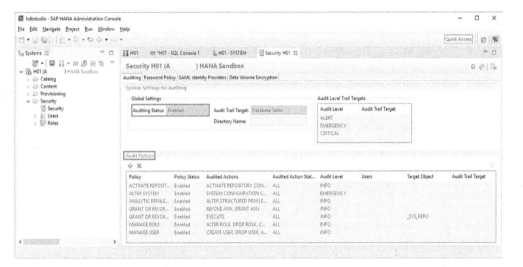

Figure 4.134: SAP HANA—Security Audit Log

From an audit perspective, at least the following events should be included in the log:

▶ System changes

▶ User changes (creation, update, deletion)

▶ Role changes (creation, update, deletion)

▶ Assignment of repository objects

▶ Assignment of privileges

▶ Activation of repository objects

▶ Superuser events (e.g., user SYSTEM or administrator access)

▶ Authentication (especially failed logon attempts)

▶ Unauthorized actions

4.12.3 Critical access rights

Analogous to the SAP application, it is also important to take critical author-izations regarding databases and operating systems into account and to evaluate their appropriateness. In the following, we introduce examples of critical authorizations at operating system (Linux Red Hat) and database level (SAP HANA).

▶ **Critical access rights—Linux Red Hat (example)**

As described in the previous section, the most critical access right for Linux is the possibility to perform activities with the **sudo** command. As a result, activities are initiated with the privileges of the superuser **root** without knowing the credentials of this user.

In addition, authorizations can be configured individually by file. You must therefore check which files in particular need protection and whether only authorized users have access to these files.

▶ **Critical access rights—SAP HANA database (example)**

Authorizations within the SAP HANA database are comparable to author-izations in the SAP application. In SAP HANA, authorizations can be as-signed to users by means of privileges (comparable to transactions and authorization objects in the SAP application), which can also be aggregat-ed in roles. The following are examples of critical SAP HANA privileges:

▶ Privilege to maintain HANA users: USER ADMIN

▶ Privilege to maintain HANA catalog roles: ROLE ADMIN

▶ Privilege to maintain audit log settings/audit policies: AUDIT ADMIN

▶ Privilege to clear the audit log: AUDIT OPERATOR

▶ Various different privileges to administrate the HANA system: ADAPTER ADMIN, AGENT ADMIN, BACKUP ADMIN, CERTIFI-CATE ADMIN, CREATE SCENARIO (and many, many more)

5 Conclusion and outlook

Well done, you have made it to the end of this guide! Hopefully this book will help you in the preparation and conduct of an SAP audit by:

- ▶ Giving you general input on internal audits and IS audits, typical laws, and standards

- ▶ Providing you with details of the specifics of SAP architecture

- ▶ Reminding you how to use SAP-specific tools to perform an audit

- ▶ Providing ideas about which risks or controls might be relevant to examine, whether they should be included in your audit plan, and how to conduct the detailed control steps

SAP is specific in its architecture, system settings, authorization concept, and much more. Hence, the selected controls covered throughout Chapter 4 are mainly subject to the audit universe clusters I **Governance**, III **System Setup**, and VII **Infrastructure**. Figure 5.1 shows the fields covered by the 12 controls discussed in Chapter 4.

What you have learned in this book is relevant to a vast number of different SAP systems. The control steps and risks apply to SAP ERP systems, CRM systems, SRM systems, and others alike. However, some general IT developments and specific SAP developments already influence or will influence the SAP audit universe and the way you think and perform IS audits.

These developments include:

- ▶ SAP S/4 HANA

- ▶ Robotic process automation (RPA)

- ▶ Artificial intelligence (AI)

SAP has developed a business suite of applications that run on new database technology and a modern user interface, SAP Fiori.

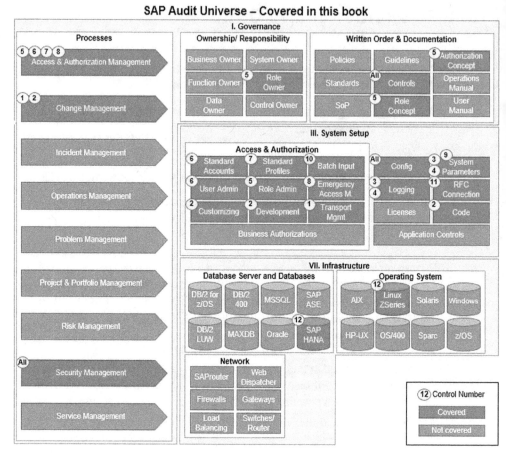

Figure 5.1: Controls in the SAP audit universe covered in this book

The SAP HANA platform is the underlying database that uses in-memory technology to execute OLAP as well as OLTP transactions in the memory, and thus performs processes faster than traditional database systems. While reports used to take hours to run, they may now run in seconds.

The SAP S/4 HANA applications are new solutions that natively incorporate the HANA platform and the latest UI technology Fiori.

The use of SAP HANA brings a fundamental architectural change into the SAP landscape: the integration of the application layer and database layer. This integration impacts the security of the database. The most obvious impact is of course that this concept does not comply with the golden rule of single-purpose servers because the application and database server run on the same machine. The design of the solution impacts further security disciplines, such as:

► Access and authorization management: while in a traditional setup, the database might be reserved for database admins only, in the new setup, end users and developers also have access. How are their SQL privileges controlled and managed? Do they comply with SoD requirements and the principle of least privilege?

► Network and communication: is client-server and system-internal communication protected? Are SQL, RFC, HTTP connections encrypted?

► Encryption: is data at rest, including data backups, encrypted?

An auditor must be aware of these differences to the traditional setup and adjust the audit plan accordingly.

RPA is the use of a software robot to process business and IT processes, transactions, workflows, etc. The robots act like real persons across applications and systems. They are virtual employees that work 24 hours per day based on rules. In general, RPA is useful whenever processes are logical, standardized, repeatable, digital, work with structured inputs, and have a low number of exceptions. RPA can be integrated into existing IT architectures without complex new interfaces, and a variety of companies around the world are already using it. Of course, there are a lot of processes within SAP systems that are indeed repetitive, occur on a larger scale, and are standardized.

Scenarios such as posting incoming payments, entering incoming invoices, creating sales orders, and many more are already automated today via RPA in SAP landscapes around the world.

However, this is only the first step. RPA will take more steps towards cognitive systems that will learn from the data they process and use what they have learned in future situations. Robots with full AI may further replicate human capabilities, which has multiple impacts for an IS audit. How do you assess the effectiveness of robots and how they process data to draw the right conclusions? How can you evaluate whether a robot is applying its learning in future situations correctly? No matter the case, robotics technologies will expand the SAP audit universe with further software components. A company must also configure, secure, and apply these components correctly.

The impact on auditing is even higher with AI, which is a technology that mimics or applies ordinary human skills. AI can learn and apply; it can solve complex problems; it may be cognitive; it may sense and comprehend. AI is already used extensively within the world of IT. For example, cloud providers are managing resources more efficiently or Salesforce's Einstein AI is delivering predictions and recommendations (*https://www. salesforce.com/products/einstein/overview/*). Tools that detect network behavior anomalies can learn autonomously what is normal behavior in your network and raise alerts automatically as soon as something strange happens. How can an IS auditor assess an AI? How can the IS auditor evaluate whether the mechanisms used to learn and apply are correct? How can you audit the decision-making process once AI makes decisions?

The world of IT is changing, and so is the world of internal audit. All the technologies mentioned above might make it more difficult to audit an SAP system, ask the right questions, and derive the correct conclusion. But in every risk lies an opportunity. SAP's fraud management solution is installed on HANA and performs calculations at a fast pace to prevent financial harm through fraudsters. Machine learning and AI can help auditors to flip through enormous amounts of data for hints and evidence, and RPA may be used for automated continuous auditing and thus, finally significantly increase the monitoring capabilities of companies and auditors. This will allow auditors to increase transparency, allow earlier risk detection, and reduce control inefficiencies in your SAP environment.

6 Abbreviations and glossary

6.1 Abbreviations

Abbreviation	Description
AI	Artificial intelligence
CAAT	Computer assisted auditing techniques
COSO	Committee of Sponsoring Organizations of the Treadway Commission
CUA	Central user administration
Dev	Development
DSAR	Data subject access request
ERP	Enterprise resource planning
GDPR	General Data Protection Regulation
HANA	High-performance analytic appliance
HTTP	Hypertext Transfer Protocol
HTTPs	Hypertext Transfer Protocol Secure
ICS	Internal control system
IdM	Identity management
IIA	Institute of Internal Auditors
IPPF	International Professional Practices Framework
IS	Information systems
ISACA	Information Systems Audit and Control Association
ISO	International Organization for Standardization
ITAF	Information Technology Assurance Framework
ITGC	IT general controls
NIST	National Institute of Standards
OS	Operating system
PAM	Privileged account management
QA	Quality assurance
RDP	Remote Desktop Protocol
RPA	Robotics process automation
SLA	Service level agreement
SNC	Secure Network Communications

Abbreviation	Description
SolMan	Solution Manager
SoP	Standard operating procedure
SOX	Sarbanes-Oxley Act
SSH	Secure Shell
SSL	Secure Sockets Layer
TCP/IP	Transmission Control Protocol/Internet Protocol

6.2 Glossary

Term	Description
Internal audit	Internal auditing is an independent, objective assurance and consulting activity designed to add value and improve an organization's operations. It helps an organization accomplish its objectives by bringing a systematic, disciplined approach to evaluate and improve the effectiveness of risk management, control, and governance processes. (*https://www.iia.org.au/ about-iia-australia/WhatIsInternalAudit/DefinitionOfIA. aspx*)
Internal control system	Set of organizational, processual, and technical measures to ensure the effectiveness of business processes, information integrity, and compliance with rules.
Risk appetite	The level of risks a company is willing to attain and take.
Risk assessment	Determination of a qualitative or quantitative level of risk.
Risk capacity	The level of risks a company can withstand or absorb without substantial harm.
Risk register	Record of all known risks, including a detailed description, assessment results, owner, and actions taken.
Risk treatment	The way a company handles risks; the measures include risk acceptance, transfer, sharing, mitigation, and avoidance.

You have finished the book.

A About the authors

Sebastian Mayer is an associate director within the IT Internal Audit solution at Protiviti Germany with several years of experience in SAP consulting, IT audit, IT internal control systems, and information security. He has been employed at Protiviti since 2014 after gaining experience as an SAP consultant at T-Systems and CGI.

Sebastian has completed a multi-year tenure in the field of SAP GRC consulting and implementation of SAP Access Control and SAP authorization concepts. Furthermore, he has supported projects at different national and international customers in the areas of information security, IT internal audit, IT SOX, and security risk assessments. His professional experience is supplemented by a master's degree in controlling and consulting (M.Sc.) and in business law (LL.M.). He also holds the CISA and CRISC certification and is a certified Application Associate for SAP GRC Access Control as well as for SAP ERP Management Accounting.

Sebastian was born and raised in Mannheim and thus within the immediate vicinity of the SAP headquarters. Even today, he is loyal to his hometown and, together with his fiancée Kristin, enjoys the beauties of the Electoral Palatinate (Kurpfalz) region of Germany. He dedicates this book to Kristin, who is always 100% behind him and supports him unbelievably in all activities, and to Andrej Greindl, who, as a colleague, has always provided good advice and valuable feedback, and over the years has also become a close, trusted friend.

Martin Metz is a senior manager at Accenture who helps customers to increase their security posture.

Martin has a master's degree in controlling and consulting (M.Sc.) and completed coursework in the US, South Korea, Japan and Germany. Martin later became an IS auditor with assignments across Europe and the US. As security ran like a golden thread through his work life, he finally switched roles from IS audit to pure security consulting.

Martin's expertise includes the implementation of SAP Access Control and Risk Management, further access and authorization management systems, and privileged account management solutions. He has experience in managing large-scale security projects and programs with a broad range of additional security topics. Because of his years in the field of audit, he knows both sides of the coin: that of the auditor as well as that of the integrator. Martin is CISA, CISM, CRISC, CGEIT, PMP certified and holds multiple SAP consultant certificates.

His experience covers companies from various verticals, especially from the financial and healthcare sectors.

Martin is extraordinarily thankful to his wife, Nataliya, and his daughter, Victoria, who always supported him actively while he was writing this book.

B Index

C Disclaimer

This publication contains references to the products of SAP SE.

SAP, R/3, SAP NetWeaver, Duet, PartnerEdge, ByDesign, SAP Business-Objects Explorer, StreamWork, and other SAP products and services mentioned herein as well as their respective logos are trademarks or registered trademarks of SAP SE in Germany and other countries.

Business Objects and the Business Objects logo, BusinessObjects, Crystal Reports, Crystal Decisions, Web Intelligence, Xcelsius, and other Business Objects products and services mentioned herein as well as their respective logos are trademarks or registered trademarks of Business Objects Software Ltd. Business Objects is an SAP company.

Sybase and Adaptive Server, iAnywhere, Sybase 365, SQL Anywhere, and other Sybase products and services mentioned herein as well as their respective logos are trademarks or registered trademarks of Sybase, Inc. Sybase is an SAP company.

SAP SE is neither the author nor the publisher of this publication and is not responsible for its content. SAP Group shall not be liable for errors or omissions with respect to the materials. The only warranties for SAP Group products and services are those that are set forth in the express warranty statements accompanying such products and services, if any. Nothing herein should be construed as constituting an additional warranty.

More Espresso Tutorials Books

Tracy Juran

Beginner's Guide to SAP® Security and Authorizations

▶ Basic architecture of SAP Security and Authorizations
▶ GRC Access Control introduction
▶ User profile creation and role assignments
▶ Common security and authorization pain point troubleshooting

http://5013.espresso-tutorials.com

Maxim Chuprunov:

Leveraging SAP® GRC in the Fight Against Corruption and Fraud

▶ Overview of classic SAP ABAP interface techniques
▶ Design and implement an anti-corruption initiative
▶ Automated drivers and added value GRC
▶ Detection scenarios using SAP Fraud Management and SAP HANA

http://5216.espresso-tutorials.com

Bert Vanstechelman, Chris Walravens, Christophe Decamps:

Securing SAP® S/4HANA

▶ Effectively secure SAP S/4HANA, Fiori, and Gateway
▶ Privileges and roles, authentication, encryption, and monitoring
▶ Mobile access and SSO considerations
▶ Cross-system authorization concepts and implementation

http://5258.espresso-tutorials.com

www.ingramcontent.com/pod-product-compliance
Lightning Source LLC
LaVergne TN
LVHW022303060326
832902LV00020B/3244